BORN FAR FROM FREEDOM

ii

Born Far From Freedom

African Americans Born in Virginia Who Fought for
Freedom and the Union in the Civil War

Copyright 2026 by John L. Wood II
All Rights Reserved

ISBN: 979-8-9950452-0-5

Aight Ten Books

Cover Photo: Jackson Ridgeway was 15 years old in September 1863 when he enlisted in Company F of the 2nd Kansas Colored Infantry at Leavenworth, Kansas. His unit was later redesignated as the 83rd U.S. Colored Infantry Regiment. Private Ridgeway was discharged at Camden, Arkansas in October 1865. After the war, Ridgeway changed his name to J.W. Pollard. This photograph was taken May 30, 1906 after he participated in a G.A.R. parade in Illinois. Jackson Ridgeway was born in Fauquier County, Virginia. – *Photo: Library of Congress*

"Once let the black man put upon his person the brass letters 'US,' let him get an eagle on his button and a musket on his shoulder and bullets in his pocket and there is no power on earth that can deny that he earned the right to citizenship in the United States." – Frederick Douglass

TABLE OF CONTENTS

BORN FAR FROM FREEDOM

African Americans Born in Virginia Who Fought for
Freedom and the Union in the Civil War

By John Wood

x

Preface: History We Should Know

Early in 2024 my wife Dixie and I had to move into an apartment temporarily while emergency repairs were being made to our Rocky Mount, Virginia home. We lived in the apartment for a little over four months.

We met our landlord, Glenna Moore. As people do in small towns, we exchanged information about where we grew up, and who our families were. Glenna's maiden name was Hawkins. She had been raised in Rocky Mount and married a career Army officer, Larry Moore. Glenna and Larry were both retired educators. As it happened, Glenna's father, Mr. Sam Hawkins, was one of the school administrators when I attended Franklin County High School back in the seventies. Small world.

Glenna and Larry are nice people, personable, easy to talk to. They own the Angle House, a historic 19th century home in town and had remodeled it to create three furnished apartments. They specialize in short term rentals. Usually, they rent to travelling nurses, who stay for a few weeks or months at a time. We were very comfortable there.

We became friends with the Moores right away. As we got better acquainted, we found we shared a deep interest in the history of Rocky Mount and Franklin County. In college, Glenna had written her thesis about free African Americans living in Franklin County before the abolition of slavery. Recently, she had learned that seventy men born here had joined United States Colored Troop regiments during the Civil War. There were plans for a monument to be erected in the town of Rocky Mount, commemorating the Union soldiers. A local group called "Raising the Shade" was gathering information on them, as one of the conditions of the Mellon   Foundation   and   Monuments   Across

Appalachian Virginia grant that helped fund the statue. Would I be interested in helping with the research?

Well, yes, absolutely. Familiar with Civil War history, I knew a little about the U.S. Colored Troops that fought in the war. I had no idea that any of them had been born in Franklin County. Glenna asked if I might be willing to look up information on a soldier. She offered to lend me a book. I said I would be glad to research one, and give her a writeup on anything I found.

The book Glenna loaned to me was "*We Honor Those Who Served*" published by the Shenandoah Valley Black Heritage Project.[1] Dr. Mollie Godfrey of James Madison University initiated the research as a class project for some of her English students in 2015, and continued the work through 2017 with a group of students and interns from Blue Ridge Community College and Harrisonburg High School. The students focused on documenting information about soldiers and sailors from thirteen Virginia counties and one West Virginia county in the Shenandoah Valley. At the same time, researchers in the Shenandoah Valley Black Heritage Project were gathering genealogical information about any descendants they could identify.

I researched what I could find on Private Paul Robinson, who enlisted at age twenty-six in Company A of the 5th U.S. Colored Infantry regiment in 1863 in Ohio. Robinson fought at the siege of Petersburg, and was "absent wounded since Sept. 29, 1864." *What happened on September 29, 1864?* He was entitled to a bounty and back pay of $6.00 per month. *What was that about? Why was he owed back pay?*

Curious, I looked up two other men born in Franklin County who had served in the 5th U.S.C.I. regiment with Private Robinson. Herod Beverly and Samuel Beverly had enlisted on different dates, also in Ohio. *How did they get to Ohio?* Both had notations on their records saying they were free in April of 1861. *Were they born free, or had they escaped from slavery?* Samuel Beverly's record had conflicting entries. One said he was "Missing in Action Sept. 29, 1864." *There is that date again.* Another note indicated he was killed in action. Still another entry said he had been a prisoner of war in Richmond, Virginia and Salisbury, North Carolina and died of his wounds. *What really happened to Samuel Beverly?* Their great grandfather, Sylvester Beverly, had been a free person of color living in Franklin County who had fought in the Revolutionary War. *The Revolutionary War? What's his story?*

Intrigued, I kept looking. For every answer I found, I seemed to find a half dozen questions. What engagements did the 5th U.S. Colored Infantry regiment fight in? Where was Samuel Beverly buried? How did Samuel and his brother Herod make it to Ohio?

Born far from freedom, in a state that imposed harsh restrictions on the movement of slaves and free persons of color, seventy men had come into this world in Franklin County, then had enlisted in the United States Army from all parts of the country. They fought in dozens of Civil War battles. Almost all were volunteers. They didn't have to, but *chose* to fight for freedom. They suffered intense hardships; many survived combat only to die of disease in regimental hospitals far from their homes and families. The more I learned about these men, the more I was profoundly affected. I wanted to learn more about them.

The repairs on our house were completed; Dixie and I moved back home. In the fall I retired from my job in Roanoke. Occasionally we saw Glenna and Larry at events around town. I continued to search for information about the soldiers.

Ultimately, with other Raising the Shade researchers, I contributed information on several of the seventy U.S.C.T. soldiers born in Franklin County. I found

4

details about the men, their units, the engagements in which they fought, and the times in which they lived. When the results of our research were exhibited in a Raising the Shade educational forum in May of 2025, I was excited to learn that funds for the commemorative statue had been approved. The monument was to be dedicated in Rocky Mount in just a few months.

Every day I worked on the research, I was inspired by the stories. These men dealt with so much hardship – compared with what they went through, my problems, and those of most of the people I know, are insignificant. Many of these soldiers acted with extraordinary courage. The first regiment to assault the Confederate lines at New Market Heights did not know what they were in for – but the second regiment to make the charge on September 29, 1864 had watched that morning as hundreds of their comrades were shot to pieces. They *knew* what they were getting into. Despite the overwhelming odds against survival, they stood up, climbed over the obstacles, walked into that wall of rifle and artillery fire, and overran the enemy lines. Minutes later many of them marched across the battlefield to the next hot fight, a mile away, at Fort Gilmer.[2]

I wondered about U.S.C.T. soldiers from other communities I was familiar with. My wife was born in Henry County, where we lived and worked for many years; I compiled a list of thirty-two U.S.C.T. soldiers from there. I added a list of thirteen soldiers in nearby Patrick County, for good measure, and found that one white man born in Patrick County joined the Union Army and had become an officer in a U.S.C.T. infantry regiment. The last capital of the Confederacy was in Danville, in Pittsylvania County, Virginia – I found nineteen African American soldiers and one sailor from there. I wanted to learn more about soldiers and sailors born in different parts of Virginia. I kept digging.

Dixie and I visited some of the sites where these men had fought. One was New Market Heights, near Richmond. We went to Deep Bottom, where the Union Army built a pontoon bridge across the James River that U.S.C.T. regiments crossed again and again as they fought in that area. We stood at the edge of the Crater, at the Petersburg battlefield, where U.S. Army miners exploded 8,000 pounds of gunpowder under the Confederate lines, and where so many U.S.C.T. soldiers lost their lives on July 30, 1864.

As I investigated, I was surprised at the amount of research that had been documented on the U.S. Colored Troops. Many good books, articles, and websites discuss various aspects of the Civil War that black soldiers experienced. There are several books on the 54th Massachusetts Colored Infantry that distinguished itself in the July 1863 attack on Fort Wagner in South Carolina. The movie "Glory" was a fictionalized account of the heroism of the men of the 54th. Great histories of the 6th, 7th, and 9th regiments, and many others, have been written as well.

It is not difficult to find soldiers' service records on *Ancestry.com*, a little harder to find them on *FamilySearch.com*. Great websites have been published with information about black troops from different parts of the country. National Park Service websites are great resources for information about soldiers, battlefields and the histories of Civil War regiments. American Battlefield Trust websites are very informative and helpful.

I was surprised by what I did not find. I found information on the histories of U.S.C.T. regiments recruited in Virginia, but did not find a detailed listing of African American soldiers born here, but who may have enlisted elsewhere. Most battle summaries are either so extensive they need to be interpreted by an academic, or

6

so superficial they fail to inform the casual reader about what happened. Similarly, regimental histories sometimes contain too much or too little information about the soldiers that served. Finally, I was unable to find detailed instructions on how to look up information on individuals and groups of men that served in the United States armed forces during the Civil War.

The people that enslaved these men and fought to keep them enslaved are long dead and encountered their ultimate destiny long ago. The brave men who fought for freedom and unity have long since gone to their reward. A century and a half later, we reflect on a heritage of guilt mixed with glory, and wonder what we can learn from that heritage. I believe we can learn a lot.

The history of the U.S. Colored soldiers is an important and uniquely American story. At a time when they had little prospect of gain and everything to lose, they risked their lives to fight for their freedom, the freedom of others, and the freedom we all now enjoy. Helping to restore the Union and end slavery was their first challenge. Many decades would pass before their descendants could truly reap the benefits of the victory they helped to win.

I wanted to help share their stories. I began assembling stories of soldiers and sailors, the units in which they served, the battles in which they fought.

A quick Internet search will reveal that 5,723 African American soldiers enlisted in Virginia to fight for the Union Army during the Civil War.[3] While that figure is probably accurate for the number of black soldiers in Union Army units *recruited within Virginia*, more than 15,000 black men *born in Virginia* enlisted in the Union Army,[4] and more than 2,400 served in the Union Navy.[5] Virginia had a higher population of slaves and free blacks than any other state.[6]

Free persons of color and escapees from Virginia had made their way to every non-slave state in the North. Slave traders exported human beings from Virginia to every other state in the South. When the U.S. Army started enlisting African American volunteers, most recruits enlisted from the states where they were living at the time. Many of these men had not spent their lives here, but Virginia was part of their heritage.

In recent years, many monuments to Confederate soldiers and leaders have been taken down, generating heated controversy all over the nation. I have mixed feelings about this. While I agree we do not need to glorify the actions of leaders who dedicated their lives to the perpetuation of slavery and the destruction of the Union, many Americans are descended from ordinary Confederate soldiers who had no real choice in whether or not to fight for the rebellion. Like soldiers in every war and on every side, most just wanted to survive with their comrades and make it home to their families. We need to remember them. We can learn a lot from their mistakes. They are part of our history.

I believe we need to put up more monuments. We need to tell the rest of the story. We need to unite in remembering and celebrating a group of Americans that helped win the fight for freedom, but who did not live to fully experience the freedom they had won. They helped to create a "more perfect Union" for all Americans. Their accomplishments are part of our history.

This book, then, is about history we should know: the history of the African American soldiers and sailors born in Virginia, who fought for freedom and the Union during the Civil War.

My objective is to introduce their stories, to describe events and battles that involved or affected them, and to provide context for the reader. I try to explain terms and related topics that may be unfamiliar. I hope what I've found can be enjoyed by people who don't ordinarily read history.

I have included instructions to make it easy for others to access the kind of information I've been able to find. I believe my research can be useful for scholars, genealogists, historical societies, or anyone interested in the important role these soldiers played in American history. In 1861, what is now West Virginia was part of Virginia. I have included West Virginia's soldiers in my research. They are an important part of this American story, too.

I would love to see more organizations – like **Raising the Shade** - research, celebrate, and educate more Americans about the contributions made by these forgotten soldiers and sailors.[7]

Several groups and communities around the country have done commendable work in recognizing this part of our nation's heritage. These initiatives have led to events and monuments recognizing these soldiers in the communities where they lived.

The **Slaves to Soldiers Project** does an outstanding job telling the stories of more than 600 African American men born in Williamson County, Tennessee who served in the Union Army during the Civil War.[8]

Black Virginians in Blue, a digital project by the University of Virginia, introduces the stories of over 250 black soldiers and sailors born in Albemarle County who served in the Union military.[9]

Based in the United Kingdom, the **Civil War Bluejackets Project** has published excellent research on African American sailors who served in the war. This initiative is being spearheaded by the University of Northumbria and the University of Sheffield.[10]

During the fall of 2025, Dr. Sarah Plummer's class on Appalachian Studies at Virginia Tech researched African American Civil War soldiers from Richmond, Norfolk, and Fauquier counties for a midterm project. I hope their efforts will be a model for future research.

Lastly, this book introduces the reader to the history of the United States Colored troops born in Virginia, but it is only an *introduction*. I discuss thirty engagements of more than 240 in which U.S.C.T. soldiers fought, and elaborate on the personal stories of a few dozen individual soldiers and sailors. Thousands more stories have yet to be discovered and shared.

If you pursue your own research about these men, I believe you will find the results and the process as fascinating and inspiring as I have. It is truly a privilege to share the stories of these brave Americans.

1. A PECULIAR AND POWERFUL INTEREST

Slavery is an unthinkable abomination from prehistory, like cannibalism or human sacrifice, that persisted long after the point at which humanity believed itself to have become 'civilized'. It has been practiced for at least 6000 years, in nearly every part of the globe.[1] Archaeological evidence of slavery appears almost as early as the first signs of agriculture, but involuntary servitude likely existed before humans cultivated crops or domesticated animals. Throughout history, captives taken in war, criminal offenders, debtors and the otherwise vulnerable have been forced to serve the powerful as slaves.

Slaves have often been treated as capital, valued as commodities as well as for the services they could perform. Some of the oldest recorded laws and business transactions involved the buying and selling of slaves.[2] People from all cultures have at times enslaved others, and all cultures have at times found themselves enslaved.

Captive labor has been used to extract vast sums of wealth from the earth, and formed the basis of great commercial enterprises. Enslaved people have provided the motive power to build great monuments, cities, and empires. For most of human history, the use of slave labor was considered normal.

Even today, forms of slavery persist. In 2026, it is estimated that millions of human beings, in every part of the world, still suffer under some form of slavery.[3]

In the early seventeenth century, South American colonists were sending shiploads of treasure back to their investors and to the king in Spain, while colonists at the single North American settlement struggled to survive day to day. When a Dutch ship landed at Jamestown and offered twenty African slaves for sale, some colonists believed they had found the key to making their investment profitable – an affordable, perpetual source of labor.[4] Slavery had been practiced throughout history; instituting it in the North American colonies seemed the practical thing to do.

Over the following decades, wealthy slaveholders in Virginia did what powerful investors tend to do: they accumulated more of this valuable, self-sustaining source of capital, and carefully secured the new source of wealth within a protective barrier of law.[5]

In 1675 a dispute between factions led by Virginia's governor, William Berkley, and his nephew, Nathaniel Bacon, turned into an insurrection against the colonial authorities that came to be known as Bacon's Rebellion. Bacon and his followers – including many who were former indentured servants – favored a policy of warfare and extermination against the natives living near the colonies. Berkley favored a policy of peace and commerce with the tribes. When Bacon suddenly died of disease in 1676, the rebellion was suppressed, and Governor Berkley had twenty-three of the surviving insurrectionist leaders executed.[6]

Because so many former indentured servants had supported Bacon, the practice of contracting labor by indenture gradually fell out of favor. Indentured servants could only be controlled during the terms of their contracts, usually four to seven years. More colonists sought to acquire slaves, reasoning that they could be more effectively controlled throughout their lives.

In 1680 Virginia's House of Burgesses passed an Insurrection Act, restricting the freedom of slaves to move about without a pass, and prohibiting them from bearing arms. In 1705 the colony passed a harsh set of laws known as the Virginia Slave Codes. Slavery was explicitly defined in law. It was ruled that becoming a Christian did not change the legal status of a slave. Slaveholders were given full control over the lives of their slaves, and full authority to punish them. Enslaved and free black people were to be segregated from white people. Marriage was forbidden between members of the different races. Enslaved status was to be matrilineal. If a mother was enslaved, her child would be born a slave.[7]

Many colonies in the North, where landholdings were smaller and the cultivation of labor-intensive cash crops uncommon, eventually outlawed slavery. In the South, where crops like tobacco, rice, sugar and cotton drove the economy, lawmakers sought to empower and enhance the property rights of slaveholders.

When the colonies fought for independence from Great Britian in the late 18th century, 5,000 African Americans joined the fight for freedom, including 500 Virginians.[8] Many were still enslaved.

However, after the rule of the English king was overthrown, the successful revolutionaries continued to support slavery and to restrict the liberties of free African Americans. The new Constitution of the United States recognized slavery, and required the authorities in "free" states to return fugitive slaves to their owners in "slave" states.

This disparity between what Americans practiced and what they professed to believe was a fundamental flaw in the new society. The passions slavery aroused over the coming decades were to have far reaching consequences.

Legislators in Virginia, the most populous state and the state with the most slaves, were particularly thorough in defining the restrictions that applied to slaves. Many laws were enacted because owners were afraid their slaves might escape or revolt. The idea of an uprising was terrifying to slaveholders. A successful slave revolution had occurred in Haiti between 1791 and 1804.[9] In Virginia, slave revolts were attempted near Richmond in 1800 and at Chatham Manor near Fredericksburg in 1805.[10]

Virginia passed a law that required any slave manumitted after May 1, 1806 to leave the state within a year.[11] Importation of slaves into the United States was banned by an act of Congress in 1807, but African captives continued to be smuggled into the southern states as late as 1860.[12]

The American Colonization Society was founded in 1816 by a group that opposed slavery, but that felt free persons of color could not be successfully integrated into white America. The Society planned to help black colonists settle overseas. Colonization was seen by some as a means of transitioning away from slavery, but opposed by others who felt it would extend and strengthen the institution by exporting the most competent and educated African Americans away from the United States. The colonization initiative resulted in the founding of Liberia on the west coast of Africa, but remained controversial throughout its existence.[13]

Black slaves had cut trees, drained swamps, plowed fields, planted crops, tended livestock, and constructed buildings and roads. Their descendants, free and enslaved, felt they were every bit as invested in building the nation as their aristocratic masters, if not more so.

In Southampton County in 1831, a violent rebellion led by an enslaved preacher named Nat Turner resulted in the deaths of as many as sixty five white persons. Turner and his followers were caught and killed, along with up to 200 innocent black people.[14] As a result, even more restrictive slave codes were passed in 1832. Black people were forbidden to learn to read, or to assemble in groups. They were only allowed to worship under the supervision of white ministers.

William Lloyd Garrison, a Massachusetts journalist, began publishing an abolitionist newspaper called 'The Liberator' in 1831, and in 1833 helped to found the American Anti-Slavery Society. Garrison and others lobbied in Congress for the abolition of slavery throughout the United States. Predictably, abolitionism was viewed by slaveholders as a threat to their prosperity.[15]

Frederick Douglass escaped from slavery in Maryland in 1838 and became a popular writer, speaker and leader of the abolitionist movement. Harriet Tubman escaped in 1849 and made more than a dozen trips back into Maryland to help family members and friends escape from slavery. Sojourner Truth, who had escaped from New York before slavery was abolished in that state, became another popular speaker and advocate for the abolition of slavery.[16]

Among opponents, scriptures were quoted to justify the abolition of slavery. Among supporters, conflicting scriptures were used to justify the institution and persuade slaves to remain obedient.[17] Slaveholders devised elaborate 'scientific' arguments to convince themselves their slaves were not people. Virginia was not the first government to use law, faith and culture to keep a part of the population in subjection, and was not the last, but the state was one of the most aggressive and effective at promoting slavery.

As the nation grew, leaders of slave states were anxious to protect what Abraham Lincoln called their *'peculiar and powerful interest'*.[18] As more free states were admitted to the Union, slave state politicians were convinced Congress would enact laws restricting and ultimately eliminating the system on which much Southern wealth was based. Southern politicians sought to extend the institution to new states as they were formed.

The nation faced an existential crisis when a series of laws was passed by Congress allowing future states to determine whether or not to allow the practice of slavery and strengthening requirements for free states to return escaped slaves to non-free states.[19] The Compromise of 1850 postponed the crisis for ten years but did not solve the problem. Tensions continued to mount.

Novelist Harriet Beecher Stowe published "Uncle Tom's Cabin" in 1851. Stowe's graphic portrayal of the suffering of slaves and decadence of slave ownership helped persuade more people who had been indifferent, to actively oppose slavery.[20]

Before 1861 the Southern economy was overwhelmingly dependent on slavery. Southerners invested in slaves, even more than they invested in land. A slave was viewed as a commodity, a form of capital:

"One day Grandpappy sassed Miss Polly White, and she told him that if he didn't behave his self that she would put him in her pocket. Grandpappy was a big man, and I asked him how Miss Polly could do that. He said she meant that she would sell him, then put the money in her pocket. He never did suss Miss Polly no more." – Sarah Debro, former slave interviewed in 1937 as part of the Federal Writers Project [21]

In the North, investors were more diversified. Northerners invested in canals, railroads, roads and ships. Northern capital funded the expansion of communications by telegraph, and the publication of newspapers, magazines and books. Northern banks financed and insured the nations commerce. Eighty four percent of the capital funding manufacturing in America was contributed by investors from the free states.[22]

Yet sixty percent of the wealthiest Americans lived in the South. For many of these, slaves constituted the bulk of their wealth. It is hard to overstate the dependence of the Southern economy on the institution of slavery. Even Southerners that questioned the morality of slavery could see no way out. Freeing slaves would result in financial ruin. Southerners feared what might happen when the population that had been exploited for so long became free. Many slaveholders honestly believed that emancipation would lead to social chaos, bankruptcy, the starvation of their families, and the collapse of civilization.

The North enjoyed several advantages. A strong agricultural base assured Union citizens and armies were well-fed. Investments in manufacturing assured the Union could stay powerfully armed and abundantly supplied. Investments in transportation and communication strengthened the ability of the North to defend its borders. Most of the fighting ultimately took place in the South.

The North could field more soldiers: In 1860, the population of just three Northern states (New York, Pennsylvania, and Ohio) exceeded the population of what would become the entire Confederacy.[23] Getting the men of the North to volunteer was expected to be a challenge. At the beginning of the war, there was no draft.

Inevitably passionate rhetoric used by both sides led to violence. By 1856 pro-slavery and anti-slavery guerillas were openly fighting each other in 'Bleeding Kansas', where as many as 200 people on both sides of the issue were killed in acts of political bloodshed.[24]

On May 22, 1856, a pro-slavery Democrat from South Carolina, Preston Brooks, beat an anti-slavery Republican from Massachusetts, Charles Sumner, with a metal-tipped wooden cane on the U.S. Senate floor.

Sumner was injured so badly he was unable to return to his senatorial duties for three years.[25]

Tensions between pro-slavery and anti-slavery factions were further exacerbated when the U.S. Supreme Court ruled in the case of *Dred Scott vs. Sandford (1857)* that slaves were not U.S. citizens, could not expect protection from the federal government or judicial system, and stated that Congress had no authority to ban slavery from Federal territories.[26]

In October 1859 abolitionist John Brown and twenty followers led a raid on the U.S. Arsenal at Harpers Ferry, Virginia, in an attempt to incite a slave revolt. Colonel Robert E. Lee and ninety U.S. Marines were dispatched from Washington to put down the insurrection. Sixteen people were killed, including ten of Brown's men. Brown was captured and executed.[27]

In the U.S. Presidential Election of 1860, slavery was the dominant issue. Four candidates represented contending factions in the great dispute. Stephen Douglas, a Northern Democratic Senator from Illinois, argued that the territories should decide on slavery for themselves as they were admitted to the Union as states. John Bell, representing the Constitutional Union Party, advocated further compromise regarding slavery to keep the Union together. John Breckenridge, a Southern Democrat, argued that slavery should be allowed and protected in the territories. Abraham Lincoln, nominee of the Republican Party which had been founded in 1854, opposed the expansion of slavery into the territories, but promised not to interfere with slavery where it existed in the South.[28]

Lincoln's overriding priority was keeping the Union together. He won a majority of electoral votes and secured the presidency, but won less than forty percent of the popular vote. Pro-slavery southerners refused to accept Lincoln as leader of the divided nation. Even before the new president could take office, seven southern states had seceded from the Union.

In his inaugural speech on March 4, 1861, Lincoln adopted a conciliatory tone and sought to reassure the South:

"I have no purpose, directly or indirectly, to interfere with the institution of slavery in the States where it exists. I believe I have no lawful right to do so, and I have no inclination to do so."

Lincoln promised to uphold the clause of the Constitution in effect at that time regarding the return of fugitive slaves. He appealed to the southern states to remain in the Union, confident in the continued enforcement of existing laws, and in the processes enshrined in the Constitution for resolution of disputes. The new president ended his speech with the following exhortation:

"I am loathe to close. We are not enemies, but friends. We must not be enemies. Though passion may have strained, it must not break our bonds of affection. The mystic chords of memory, stretching from every battlefield and patriot grave to every living heart and hearthstone all over this broad land, will yet swell the chorus of the Union when again touched, as surely they will be, by the better angels of our nature."[29]

The archaic practice of exploiting the labor of innocent captives persisted, the reality of their humanity obscured by greed and fear. A nation founded on the principles of liberty and justice, America had yet to come to terms with its ideals.

The Southern slaveholders were determined. There could be no negotiated peace. The nation was broken, and must be violently reborn before a 'more perfect Union' could be made.

Truth was confused by self-interest. Faith, science, culture and law had been perverted to sustain injustice. Political violence and terrorism had been normalized. An enraged minority of the population refused to accept government by a duly elected leader with whom they disagreed.

Ironically, in their zeal to defend the 'peculiar institution', Southern aristocrats set the forces in motion that led to its demise. Weeks after Lincoln's Inauguration, secessionist leaders in South Carolina demanded the surrender of the Federal garrison guarding Fort Sumter in Charleston harbor. The presence of United States troops in the fort posed no threat to the new Confederate government. U.S. policy towards the South was still conciliatory. In early 1861 Lincoln still sought to restore the Union through compromise, rather than aggression.

Spoiling for a fight, the new Rebel president, Jefferson Davis, with his cabinet decided to "strike a blow" by asserting control over the U.S. installation in Charleston Harbor. Confederate forces began shelling Fort Sumter at 4:30 AM on April 12, 1861. On the afternoon of April 14, Major Robert Anderson and his men, their ammunition and supplies nearly exhausted, evacuated the burning fort. Rebels remained in control of the stronghold until February 1865.[30]

On April 15, President Lincoln issued a proclamation calling for state militias to supply 75,000 volunteers to suppress the rebellion, and called Congress into an emergency session.[31] In response, four more Southern states left the Union, including Virginia. The Civil War eventually cost more than 620,000 lives, equivalent to two percent of the nation's population. A million more

Americans were wounded, made prisoners of war, or died from disease.[32]

Freedom came at a high price. Generations passed before the promise of liberty could truly apply to all Americans. The experiences of slavery and slaveholding left behind legacies of shame, fear and resentment that continue to undermine our society in the 21st century.

In the American Revolution, 500 Virginian slaves and free men of color helped win the fight for independence.[33] Eight decades later, an estimated 17,000 African Americans born in Virginia joined a new fight for freedom that was to take place on land[34] and on the sea.[35] Enlisting after they had obtained their own liberty, recognizing that rights come with responsibilities, they chose to fight for freedom for all Americans. For most, their hardships continued well after the war.

In 1856 South Carolina Senator Preston Brooks beat Massachusetts Senator Charles Sumner with a wooden cane on the U.S. Senate floor during an argument over slavery. – *Image: New York Public Library*

2. THE DIVIDED HOUSE

After the attack on Fort Sumter, few Americans realized how much their lives were to be disrupted over the next few years. Many Southerners were confident they could win the war in a matter of weeks and didn't believe Northern armies could successfully subdue the South. Many Northerners were equally confident of victory. A significant number of Northerners were indifferent and not particularly concerned that slave-owning Southerners no longer wanted to be part of the Union.

Many African Americans in the North were ambivalent. They recognized that a defeat of the South was in their best interest, as it might at least help limit the expansion of slavery. In 1861, however, Northern leaders were saying the war was about preserving the Union, not about slavery; many felt the fight was a "white man's war." African Americans were not allowed to fight. For most, the fight to end slavery did not materialize for another year and a half.[1]

Men serving in the armed forces, and men eligible to do so, had to pick a side. President Lincoln was calling for 75,000 volunteers. Southern leaders called up state militias.

Robert E. Lee had a distinguished military career prior to the Civil War. In 1861, he was 54 years old. On April 18, six days after the attack on Fort Sumter and one day after Virginia seceded from the Union, he was offered command of the United States Army. Lee declined the offer, unwilling to bear arms against his native state, and resigned his commission.[2] Two days later, he accepted a commission in the Virginia state militia and in August 1861 was made a full general in the Confederate Army.

22

Of all military professionals then in service, with his long service as a staff officer and commander, his combat experience in the Mexican war, and his experience as Superintendent of West Point, Robert E. Lee must have recognized the overwhelming advantages the Northern states had in weaponry, supply, infrastructure, manpower and manufacturing. Still, he walked away from a promising career and committed his life to the fight for secession and slavery, causes in which he did not fully believe. Had Lee remained loyal to the Union, the conflict might have been resolved more quickly, and fewer Virginian lives might have been lost. Lee died at age sixty three in Lexington, Virginia in 1870.

By contrast, George H. Thomas, born in Southampton County, Virginia in 1816, remained loyal to the Union.[3] The son of a wealthy planter, Thomas grew up on a plantation and owned slaves. During the Nat Turner Rebellion in 1832, Thomas had to hide with his family in the woods. He graduated from West Point and served with distinction in the Mexican War. Returning to the Academy he became a cavalry and artillery instructor. At the time he reported to the Superintendent of West Point, Lt. Colonel Robert E. Lee.

When war broke out, Thomas turned down a senior militia role offered to him by the governor of Virginia to remain in the Union Army. Back in Southampton County his family turned his picture towards the wall. His sisters never spoke to him again.

His former student, J.E.B. Stuart, wrote to his wife: *"Old George H. Thomas is in command of the cavalry of the enemy; I would like to hang, hang him as a traitor to his native state."*[4]

Though criticized by Grant in his memoirs for being sluggish, Thomas became one of the most effective U.S. Army commanders in the war, winning a series of strategic Union victories, most notably at the Battle of

Nashville, where he virtually destroyed Confederate General John Bell Hood's Army of the Tennessee.[5] William Tecumseh Sherman wrote of Thomas after the war:

> *"During the whole war his services were transcendent, winning the first substantial victory at Mill Springs in Kentucky, January 20th, 1862, participating in all the campaigns of the West in 1862-3-4, and finally, December 16th, 1864 annihilating the army of Hood, which in midwinter had advanced to Nashville to besiege him."*[6]

George Thomas died of a stroke in 1870. He was fifty-three years old.

J.E.B. Stuart's father-in-law, Philip St. George Cooke, was born in Leesburg, Virginia, but remained loyal to the Union.[7]

General Winfield Scott, hero of the War of 1812 and the Mexican American War, remained loyal to the Union. Commander of the United States Army from 1841 to 1861, Scott was born in Virginia in 1786, and lived until 1866.[8]

Born in Fairfax County, General John Davidson remained loyal. He fought in the South and in the West during the Civil War. After the war he commanded the 10th Infantry Regiment - the "Buffalo Soldiers" - in the Oklahoma Territory and earned the nickname "Black Jack".[9]

Not all men born in Virginia who remained loyal to the Union were so well known.

Like J.E.B. Stuart, Toliver P. Vest was born in Patrick County, Virginia. When he was 16 years old, his family moved to Decatur, Illinois, where he worked for a grocer and then as a carpenter. On September 15, 1861, he married Mary Louisa Devore. His service records show he served as a Sergeant in Company A of the 8th Illinois Infantry for three months during 1861, then enlisted in the 116th Illinois Volunteer Infantry as a Private on July 17, 1862. On May 9, 1863, Vest accepted a commission as First Lieutenant in the 2nd Regiment Mississippi Infantry, African Descent, which later became the 52nd United States Colored Infantry.

When he mustered into the unit at Chickasaw Bayou on July 27, 1863 Vest was twenty-nine years old and an imposing 6' 2" tall. A picture shows him in uniform, with his sword at his side, and a dashing mustache. On May 12, 1864, he was assigned to command Company K of the 52nd U.S.C.I. On September 30, 1864, he was assigned by order of Colonel G.M. Ziegler to build a barracks for the enlisted men of the regiment, making use of his carpentry and engineering skills. In June 1865, after the war ended, he was assigned to command Company C. He mustered out of the company at Vicksburg on March 4, 1866, allowing him to accept a promotion to Captain and command of Company F, then stationed at Meridian, Mississippi. He was discharged April 23, 1867.

Toliver Vest returned to Decatur, Illinois, where he became a Mason and a member of the Grand Army of the Republic, a service organization for Union veterans. Vest and his wife had three daughters and a son, and lived in a home on 1908 Edward Street. Outliving his wife, who passed away in 1890, Vest died of apoplexy on the night of May 11, 1902 in his home and was buried at the Greenwood Cemetery in Decatur.[10]

There is no record indicating that Vest ever returned to his birthplace in Patrick County.

The war was to last four long years, dividing families, churches, and communities for decades to come.

Commodities, Conscripts, Contrabands, Combatants

When the average household income for most Virginia families was less than $1000 per year, the price of a slave was about one and a half times that amount.[11]

The purchasing power of a dollar in 1860 was about thirty-five times what a dollar will buy in 2026.[12]

In 1860, a modest two-bedroom home could be built in Virginia for around $2,000.[13] At the same time, a healthy male slave, twenty to twenty-five years old, cost $1,500. If that male slave was a skilled tradesman, he might sell for $2,500 or more.[14]

Slaves were capital investments. They could be bought, sold, leased, gifted or bequeathed to heirs. Owners sought to profitably employ slaves to make a return on their investments, preferably by raising cash crops like tobacco or livestock on the owner's land. Owners could also profitably rent out slaves to perform work for others. Slaves could be rented to perform jobs at cheaper rates than those charged by white laborers. The practice of renting slaves out for hire helped owners to offset the cost of purchasing them. Undercutting the price of labor also had the effect of keeping the pay of white laborers low.

A factory worker might earn forty-four cents in a day. A farm hand could make eight cents an hour, an unskilled laborer ten cents. A skilled blacksmith could earn eighteen cents an hour.[15] A slave could be rented to perform the same services for lower rates than these and the slaveholder could pocket the profits.

Slaves for the most part were self-sustaining. They could be employed in raising and preparing food for themselves. Slave labor could be used to build slave shelters. They could work autonomously; it was usually not necessary to provide each slave with constant supervision.

Investing in slaves in the South was seen as a quick, certain way to profit and drove much of the agrarian Southern economy. In the meantime, Northern investors were investing in industry. Ninety percent of all goods manufactured in the U.S. in 1860 were produced in Northern factories.[16] Cotton, the nation's most valuable export, was raised by slave labor in the South, but most of it was woven into fabric in Northern mills. While Northern investors sank a significant portion of their capital into machinery and equipment, Southern investors sunk almost all their capital into more slaves and land.

In 1860 land prices varied widely in Virginia. An acre of land in Henrico County might sell for $38, while an acre in Franklin County cost $9. In remote Wise County, an acre of land sold for $3.[17] Although inexpensive, land appreciated in value over time. Slaves were expensive, and once they reached adulthood depreciated in value as they aged.

In the years leading up to the Civil War, Virginia owners had a surplus of slaves, so many profited by exporting their surplus to buyers in other slave states. As a result, slaves born in Virginia lived in every part of the South. The ominous threat of being "*sold down south*" and separated from their families was used to help maintain discipline among slaves.

As Virginia law required most free black persons to leave the state, Virginia-born African Americans could be found living in every part of the United States. Most free black people migrated to the North; some made their way to the frontier in the West.

In the North, free African Americans helped to drive the booming economy; in the West, black settlers helped tame the wilderness. In the South, slave labor continued to sustain a faltering economic system that became less tenable as the North became more and more industrialized.

When hostilities broke out, Southerners were quick to figure out how they could employ slaves to support the war effort.

Confederate officers who owned slaves in some cases took their personal valet or cook with them as they deployed. Charles Brown, a slave from Page County, Virginia, served as a cook for the officers of Company K of the 10th Virginia Cavalry.[18] Robert E. Lee hired two former slaves from Arlington to serve as cooks on his first campaign.[19]

Bruce James of Pittsylvania County took his slave Charles along to serve by cooking and grooming horses when he went to war. In 1864 when Bruce was wounded in action, Charles was sent home with him to care for him.[20]

George Lemons took his slave John along when he joined the Rebel cavalry. When John Lemons filed his Virginia pension application, he was living in western Franklin County. He stated he began his service at Richmond and spent five months working on the breastworks there. He went *"with my master to Ohio, Kentucky and Georgia and back to Staunton. My master got wounded and I brought him home about two months before the surrender."*[21]

Most often, slaves were conscripted by Rebel authorities. Black men served the Confederacy by digging fortifications, cooking, washing laundry, driving wagons, and nursing the sick in hospitals. The vast Confederate breastworks guarding Richmond and Petersburg were built by conscripted slave labor, as were the trenches around Atlanta, Georgia, Fort Wagner in South Carolina, and the extensive fortifications around Mobile, Alabama.

The Confederate government made a nominal effort to compensate owners for the service of their conscripted slaves, at the rate of $16 for each thirty days of work.

Late in 1862 the Confederate government sent a requisition to Franklin County for 300 slaves "for public defense". Most were to be used in construction of the vast breastworks surrounding Richmond and Petersburg. In early 1863 the county court appointed committees of prominent citizens to compile lists of owners, the slaves to be sent to Richmond, and a valuation for each slave, in Confederate dollars. On the first list of eighty-seven names, compiled in January 1863, the average value listed for each enslaved man was $1,615. The average valuation of thirty enslaved men submitted on a list made in October 1863 was $2,566.[22] Of course, in 1863 a Confederate dollar was only worth six cents in gold. By late 1864 a Confederate "greyback" was only worth three cents.

On both sides, African Americans were required to support the war effort with picks and shovels. Conscripts were exposed to the same dangers as those experienced by soldiers. Poor diet, filthy water, accidents, exertion and inclement weather contributed to frequent sickness and death. In some battle zones they labored under enemy rifle and artillery fire.

Throughout 1861 and into 1862 the Confederate Army surprised Union commanders with an ability to inflict unexpectedly high numbers of casualties and win battles.

The First Battle of Bull Run in July of 1861 was a disaster for the Union. When a Rebel spy living in Washington, D.C, Rose Greenhow, was able to pass Union General Irvin McDowell's battle plan to General P.G.T. Beauregard in a coded message, the result was a costly Union defeat.[24] The Federals incurred significant losses in August in Wilsons Creek, Missouri[25] and at Ball's Bluff near Leesburg, Virginia[26] in October 1861.

On May 24, 1861, three African American fugitives crossed the harbor at Hampton Roads on a boat, making their way from Norfolk to Fort Monroe, then occupied by the Federals. Frank Baker, Shepard Mallory and James Townsend had been working as conscripted slave laborers, digging earthworks for a Rebel artillery battery at Sewell's Point. An agent was dispatched to request that they be returned to their owners. Major General Benjamin Butler, the Union commander, refused to send the men back.[27]

Once in a while, a commonsense decision can have revolutionary repercussions. In 1857 the Supreme Court had ruled, in the case of Dred Scott v. Sandford, that the U.S. government had to assist in returning fugitive slaves to their owners. However, Butler knew that if he returned these men they would be put back to work building Confederate fortifications. Butler reasoned that as the owners were in a state of rebellion, they no longer qualified for the protections of their 'property' guaranteed under the Fugitive Slave Laws. Butler refused to send them back, "confiscated" them from their Rebel owners, and declared that they were "contraband of war."

Butler's ruling was supported by the War Department and Congress. On August 16, President Lincoln signed the Confiscation Act of 1861 into law, authorizing military commanders to confiscate all property used to support the rebellion, including slaves. The law also stated that any slaveholder who had taken up arms against the United States forfeited ownership of his slaves. Of course, the law could only be enforced in areas the Union Army controlled, and fell short of clearly defining the legal status of the "contrabands" as free, but it was a start.

As the war continued, entire slave families fled from their masters into Union-held territory. By 1863, 10,000 former slaves had made their way to Washington. Contraband camps were set up to house the refugees. As the war progressed, more and more Federal Army commanders realized the contrabands could contribute to the Union war effort and put them to work building fortifications in battle areas. In Louisiana and Mississippi contrabands were put to work on plantations raising cotton and food crops.[28] The workers were paid a nominal wage. At first contraband workers building defensive fortifications around Washington were paid forty cents a day, but in November, 1863 it was determined that $1.00 per day was a more appropriate wage and their pay was increased accordingly.[29]

When the war began, self-liberated slaves flocked to Union Army camps, where they were identified as "Contrabands".
– *Photo: Historic Fort Pickering, Memphis*

Some Union officers, sympathetic to slavery, were inclined to send escaped Southern slaves back to their masters. In March 1862 legislation was passed forbidding this practice.[30]

Virginia suffered a hard year in 1862, as the armies fought in a series of brutal engagements around the state – at Drewry's Bluff on the James River, Front Royal, Winchester, and Seven Pines. In August, when the Second Battle of Bull Run resulted in over 14,000 Federal casualties, it looked to many like the Union might never be restored.

The border states of the North also experienced a hard year in 1862. In October, Confederate cavalry General J.E.B. Stuart led a raid on Chambersburg, Pennsylvania, capturing and paroling 280 wounded Federal soldiers, making hostages of thirty government officials, and confiscating 1,200 horses. Stuart successfully evaded the Union Army, embarrassing the Federal government and boosting Rebel morale while incurring few casualties. The incursion into Northern territory proved that no one was truly safe.[31]

The Southern economy was disrupted by slaves in combat areas who had fled from their plantations to Union lines. Requisition of slaves by the Confederate government for work on Rebel defenses imposed further hardships on the owners of the conscripted slaves. In welcoming contrabands, the Union Army was depriving the Confederacy of a key strategic resource. By putting the escaped slaves to work on Union fortifications, commanders were using that strategic resource to undermine the Confederate rebellion.

In July 1862, Congress passed two critical pieces of legislation pertaining to the status of enslaved Southerners and free African Americans.

The Confiscation Act of 1862 prescribed harsh penalties for leaders of the Southern rebellion, including criminal punishment and confiscation of their property, including their slaves. The status of slaves confiscated from the rebellious Southerners was legally defined – they would be forever free. Furthermore, the President was authorized to employ the freed slaves in any capacity he deemed suitable to support the war effort.

The Militia Act of 1862, along with other provisions designed to strengthen the military and boost recruitment, authorized African Americans to serve in the armed forces of the United States. Former slaves who enlisted in the military were to be freed along with most members of their families.

President Abraham Lincoln signed both acts into law on July 17, 1862. African American men who until this point during the war had been treated as commodities, as conscripts and as contrabands, could now become combatants. [32]

Almost before the ink was dry on these Acts, recruitment of African Americans for service in the Union Army was under way. The United States needed more manpower. Union commanders started cautiously recruiting and training African American soldiers.

In August 1862 the 1st South Carolina Volunteers, a regiment made up of former slaves, was organized under the command of General Rufus Saxon.[33] Senator James Lane, a militant abolitionist from Kansas, organized the 1st Kansas Colored Infantry.[34] In September, Major General Benjamin Butler, commanding Union forces in the Army of the Gulf at New Orleans, authorized the organization of the 1st and 2nd Regiments of Louisiana Native Guards.[35] African American soldiers now made up part of the United States Army.

3. FIGHTING FOR FREEDOM

Early on, African American servicemen were involved in the fighting. Because the Navy was partially integrated, African American sailors were serving at sea well before the beginning of the war. William Chalk, a 26-year-old from Norfolk, enlisted on June 1, 1859 and was given the rating of Landsman. Chalk mustered aboard the *USS Preble* on February 29, 1860.[1]

Greet Jonston, age twenty-two and living as a slave in Tennessee, was born in Buckingham County, Virginia. On August 23, 1862, Jonston joined Battery E of the 4th U.S. Colored Heavy Artillery Regiment, and became one of the first African Americans born in Virginia to enlist in the United States Army.[2]

Saint Helena Island – October 26, 1862

On October 26, 1862, men from the 1st South Carolina repelled an attempted landing on St. Helena Island by two boats filled with Confederate soldiers in the first recorded instance of an organized group of African American troops fighting in a defensive action during the Civil War. One Union soldier was killed and six more wounded in this engagement.[3]

Susie King Taylor, who had secretly learned to read as a slave in Georgia, escaped during the summer of 1862 and made her way to St. Simons Island. Fourteen years old when she arrived, the teenager opened a school at St. Simons for the children of the camp. She worked as a laundress and nurse for the regiment when they moved to Beaufort and eventually married a soldier, Sergeant Edward King. In 1902 she published a memoir of her time with the Union troops, recording the following account of an expedition to Jacksonville, Florida:

"March 10, 1863, we were ordered to Jacksonville, Florida. Leaving Camp Saxton between four and five o'clock, we arrived at Jacksonville about eight o'clock next morning, accompanied by three or four gunboats. When the rebels saw these boats, they ran out of the city, leaving the women behind, and we found out afterwards that they thought we had a much larger fleet than we really had. Our regiment was kept out of sight until we made fast at the wharf where it landed, and while the gunboats were shelling up the river and as far inland as possible, the regiment landed and marched up the street, where they spied the rebels who had fled from the city. They were hiding behind a house about a mile or so away, their faces blackened to disguise themselves as negroes, and our boys, as they advanced toward them, halted a second, saying, "They are black men! Let them come to us, or we will make them know who we are." With this, the firing was opened and several of our men were wounded and killed. The rebels had a number wounded and killed. It was through this way the discovery was made that they were white men. Our men drove them some distance in retreat and then threw out their pickets."[4]

The South Carolina troops returned to Camp Saxon in early April. King met another famous nurse at the hospital in Beaufort, South Carolina:

"When at Camp Shaw, I visited the hospital in Beaufort, where I met Clara Barton. There were a number of sick and wounded soldiers there, and I went often to see the comrades. Miss Barton was always very cordial toward me, and I honored her for her devotion and care of those men."[30]

Susie King Taylor remained with the regiment until they mustered out after the war ended. After the war, she operated a school for African American children in Savannah. Late in 1866 she became a widow when her husband, Edward King, was killed in a work accident. She worked as a domestic servant for several years, eventually moving to Boston, marrying a man named Russell Taylor in 1879 and leaving her job. She helped to

Susie King Taylor taught herself to read and escaped from slavery before becoming known as the first African American U.S. Army Nurse. – *Photo: Library of Congress*

found Corp 67 of the Women's Relief Corps, a group that raised money to support African American veterans of the Civil War. Susie King Taylor died on October 6, 1912 when she was 64 years old; she is buried at Mount Hope Cemetery in Roslindale, Massachusetts.[6]

The 1st South Carolina Infantry was involved in more raids in Florida, Georgia, and South Carolina, capturing supplies and liberating enslaved people. The 1st South Carolina recruited freed slaves into the Union Army. On February 8, 1864, the unit was redesignated as the 33rd United States Colored Infantry Regiment. The men of the 33rd played a significant role in the Battle of Honey Hill in November 1864, afterwards serving on guard and picket duty until the war ended. They were mustered out of service at Fort Wagner in February 1866.

Island Mound - October 27-29, 1862

By the time the Confederates opened fire on Fort Sumter at the beginning of the Civil War, pro-slavery and anti-slavery factions in Kansas and Missouri had been shooting at each other for almost a decade. In 1854 Congress had passed the Kansas-Nebraska Act, which allowed citizens of territories to vote on whether or not to allow slavery as the territories became states. This resulted in violence as pro-slavery forces organized in Missouri marched into Kansas in an attempt to gain control and make sure Kansas became a slave state.

On May 21, 1856, the town of Lawrence, Kansas was attacked by pro-slavery forces and one anti-slavery settler was killed.[7] Anti-slavery factions retaliated with more violence. They saw the Kansas-Nebraska Act as a reversal of the Missouri Compromise of 1820 that forbade slavery in the Louisiana Purchase north of the southern border of Missouri, except within Missouri itself.

In response to the sacking of Lawrence, abolitionist John Brown, with his sons and a small group of settlers opposed to slavery, abducted and killed five pro-slavery settlers near Pottawattamie Creek.[8]   The fighting in "Bleeding Kansas" went on for years and has been referred to by some historians as a prelude to the Civil War. Kansas was admitted to the Union as a free state in January, 1861.

James Lane, a militant anti-slavery U.S. Senator, led a brigade of Kansas volunteers he had recruited just after the beginning of the Civil War. On a September 1861 raid, Lane led his brigade in looting and burning the town of Osceola in western Missouri, executing nine of the town's citizens. Although a slave state, Missouri had remained in the Union. The Union commander in charge of Missouri, General Henry Halleck, stated that *a few more such raids will make this state unanimous against us.*[10]

In August 1862 Lane authorized the recruitment of a regiment of former slaves called the 1st Kansas Colored Infantry. In October of that year, the regiment was ordered to break up a Rebel guerrilla force based at Hog Island on the Osage River. Accompanied by scouts from the 5th Kansas Cavalry Regiment, 240 men of the 1st Kansas crossed into Missouri. When scouts identified a large party of Confederates about nine miles inside the Missouri line, the regiment occupied the farm of a known guerilla named John Toothman, two miles north of Hog Island.   Using split fence rails they built breastworks around the farm and named their fortifications *"Fort Africa"*. Realizing they were facing superior numbers they sent runners back to Kansas to request reinforcements and sent out skirmishers to give early warning in case the Confederates attacked.

The Rebels set a prairie fire outside the camp. In response, Captain Henry Seaman had his men "back burn", setting smaller fires close to the camp to prevent the larger fires from reaching the fortifications.   An attempt by the Confederates to create a diversion and isolate the two battalions of Union troops was unsuccessful. The Kansas troops were badly outnumbered but were able to resist the Rebel onslaught with several volleys of shot. The guerillas were forced to withdraw. The 1st Kansas Colored Infantry had lost eight killed and eleven wounded, but it was estimated that they had killed as many as forty Rebel guerillas.

A New York Times reporter accompanying the Kansans said they fought with *"desperate bravery"*. Richard Hinton, the 1st Kansas Colored Infantry's adjutant, said they had fought *"like tigers"*. The Battle of Island Mound, as it came to be called, was the first time an African American regiment launched an attack in a Civil War battle, and the first of many times black soldiers proved they were able and willing to perform effectively and courageously on the offensive.

Although not initially authorized by the War Department, the 1st Kansas Colored Infantry was mustered into the U.S. Army on January 13, 1863, after the Emancipation Proclamation was issued, and continued to see action in Kansas, Missouri, and Arkansas. The unit was eventually redesignated as the 79th U.S. Colored Infantry in December 1864.[11]

4. BLACK SAILORS IN BLUE

To a limited extent the United States Navy was integrated before the Civil War. During the War of 1812, a shortage of manpower led to African American men being recruited as sailors. After 1814 the number of black sailors was limited to 5% of the total enlisted population of the Navy, but during the Civil War as many as 20% of U.S. sailors were African American.[1] An estimated 2,400 black sailors that served between 1861 and 1865 were born in Virginia.

On enlisting in the Navy sailors were typically trained on a "receiving ship" anchored in port. Their Enlistment Date might be several months before their first muster date on the ship where they were permanently assigned to serve. On the receiving ship, they were trained in naval discipline, and began to learn the skills required to serve on a Navy vessel.

Black sailors were assigned a limited number of ratings. They were not allowed to serve as officers or petty officers.[2]

The rating of *Landsman* was given to men with no prior maritime experience or skills that might be relevant to the sailing of a ship. *First Class Boy* was a common rating for men who had been slaves before they enlisted. First Class Boys were paid $9 per month. Black sailors were paid the same wages as their white counterparts with the same rating.

An *Ordinary Seaman* had to have some nautical experience, at least basic sailing skills; a *Seaman* had to have two to three years of experience as a sailor.

A *Coal Heaver* hauled coal from the bunkers where it was stored to the boilers on a steamship. A team of Coal Heavers was called the "*black gang*" – a reference not to their race, but to the fine layer of coal dust they were covered with as they worked. Coal Heavers were paid pretty well, as they might have to make fifty trips in a day carrying a bucket with as much as 140 pounds of coal. A man had to be in good condition to be a Coal Heaver.

A *Fireman* also had to be in good condition and had to be knowledgeable about handling boiler fires and taking care of the equipment that powered steam vessels. U.S. Naval regulations read as follows:

"1023----No firemen or coal-heavers shall be shipped as such until they have passed a satisfactory examination by one or more medical officers of the navy in respect to their health and vigor, nor shall firemen be so shipped until they have passed a satisfactory examination by one or more engineer officers of the navy upon their ability to manage fires properly with different kinds of fuel, and to use skillfully smith's tools in the repair and preservation of steam machinery and boilers."[3]

Some sailors were listed as *Contraband*. Not an official rank, contrabands were often hired to perform various fatigue duties on board ship. George Diggs from Martin, West Virginia enlisted at New Bern, North Carolina in April 1863 and served as a Contraband on the *USS Hetzel*.[4]

Sailors who had been born in every part of Virginia enlisted from all parts of the United States. Landsman Archey Lane, born in Pittsylvania County, enlisted in August 1864 at Bridgeport, Connecticut, and served for the remainder of the war on the *USS General Thomas*, the *USS Great Western*, and the *USS Samson*.[5]

Walter Garner of Newport in Giles County enlisted on May 18, 1859. A coachman in civilian life, Garner enlisted as an Ordinary Seaman, so he must have had some maritime experience.[6]

Charles Cooper, a twenty-year-old Laborer from Carroll County, enlisted in Cairo, Illinois as a First Class Boy on the *USS Hastings*.[7] James Smothers of Sulphur Springs enlisted on the *Hastings*, from Cincinnati. Although he gave his occupation as Boatman, Smothers was assigned the rating of Landsman.[8]

York Gayton of Halifax County was thirty-six years old when he enlisted from White River, Arkansas, and serve as a First Class Boy on the *USS Red Rover*, a hospital ship.[9]

An eighteen-year-old named Virgin Williams, also from Halifax County, enlisted at Plymouth, North Carolina, and served on the *USS Miami*.[10] Samuel Robinson, born in Lee County, was listed as a Contraband when he enlisted from New Orleans to serve on the *USS Corypheus*.[11]

Born in Roanoke County, George Dandridge was twenty-five when he enlisted from Cincinnati to serve as a Second Class Fireman on the *USS Potomac*. Dandridge also served on the *USS Lafayette*, the *USS Grossbeak*, and the *USS Fearnot*.[12] Benjamin Haywood, also born in Roanoke County, served as a Third Class Boy on the *USS William Badger*, a stationary supply ship off the coast of the Carolinas.[13]

Robert Jackson of Bedford County enlisted at Cairo to serve on the *USS Springfield*, a stern-wheeled gunboat patrolling the Mississippi.[14] Daniel Mack, a blacksmith from Bedford County, enlisted at Monroe, Louisiana.[15] Mack served as a Landsman on the 720-ton side wheel steamer *USS Ouachita* and be present at the Battle of Fort Pillow.

Many men born in the counties that seceded to become the state of West Virginia enlisted in the Union Navy. Washington Johnson of Wheeling enlisted December 21, 1861 in Philadelphia as a First Class Boy and served on the *USS Potomac*. Johnson had been a carpenter.[16]

Perry Bowles of Greenbrier County enlisted at Vicksburg on July 4, 1863 on the day after the great battle and served as a Second Class Fireman on the *USS Judge Torrence*. Bowles had been a bricklayer.[17] Washington Brown of Kanawha County had been a Fireman in civilian life. Brown served on the *USS Silver Cloud* during the war as a Second Class Fireman.[18]

Joseph Stocks of West Virginia had been a boatman before he enlisted in Cincinnati to serve as a Second Class Fireman on the *USS Prairie Bird*.[19] John Tatson from Harrison County also enlisted from Cincinnati; he served on the *USS Great Western* as a Fireman.[20]

George Mathews and Gilbert Dawson, both born in Hardy County, West Virginia, enlisted from Island No. 82 in Arkansas on the same day, June 2, 1863. Mathews served on the *USS Prairie Bird*;[21] Dawson served on the *USS Marmora*.[22] Jacob Ludwick, also born in Hardy County, enlisted from New York in March 1864 and served on the *USS Stettin*.[23]

Just as in Union Army units, family members and friends sometimes enlisted and served together. Billy Jones[24], Fayette Jones[25], and Lewis Jones[26], born in Surry County, enlisted during the first week of August 1862 and served together on the *USS Winona* at the end of the war.

African American sailors born in Virginia served on many famous ships.

Siah Carter was born in Charles City County[27], Robert H. Cook in Gloucester County[28], and William Scott was born in Petersburg.[29] All three served on the famed ironclad, the *USS Monitor*, although they had not yet enlisted when the Battle of Hampton Roads occurred on March 8 and 9, 1862. During that fight, the *USS Monitor* was steaming to defend the *USS Minnesota*, which had been damaged by the *CSS Virginia* in an earlier fight and run aground.[30] Henderson Cruiser, a 37-year-old born in Lancaster County who had enlisted in September 1861, was a sailor on the *USS Minnesota* during that battle.[31] The *USS Monitor* and the *CSS Virginia*, also known as the *Merrimack*, shot at each other for three hours, often at point blank range, but neither inflicted much damage on their opponents.

Black sailors from Virginia served in most of the great naval battles of the war.

On November 2-3, 1861, the *USS Sabine* was involved in the rescue of 500 marines and the crew of the *USS Governor*, a troop transport ship, during a storm.[32] Landsman Robert J. Hern[33] and Landsman Daniel Jones[34], both born in Norfolk, served on the *Sabine* at the time of the the rescue.

On November 7, 1861, Union Navy ships sailed into Port Royal Sound in South Carolina to bombard Confederate fortifications at Hilton Head and Bay Point. The overwhelmed Rebel soldiers, and most residents of the area, fled; Union Army troops landed later and established a base.[35]

When Admiral David Farragut led a squadron of forty-three naval vessels up the Mississippi to capture New Orleans on May 1, 1862, Landsman William Davis[36], a baker from Norfolk, was serving on the *USS Kennebec*, and Landsman Cornelius Richardson[37], a waiter from Richmond, was serving on the *USS Itasca*, steaming nearby.[38]

James Cromell[39], a cook born in Norfolk, enlisted at Philadelphia on January 27, 1862, along with a barber named George W. Tynes[40] and a blacksmith named Elias E. Thomas[41], also born in Norfolk. The following day they were joined by another barber, Alexander Caine, born in Charlottesville.[42] All four men were rated as Landsman and were assigned to serve on the *USS St.*

Louis, one of the ironclad gunboats that participated in the capture of the city of Memphis on June 6, 1862.[43]

The *USS St. Louis* was later renamed to the *USS Baron de Kalb*. When Union naval and land forces won the Battle of Fort Hindman near the town of Arkansas Post, one of the ironclad gunboats that helped win the battle was the *USS Baron DeKalb*. Squire Henderson[44], Campbell Ligan[45], and Joseph Ligan[46], all born in Richmond, served on the *Baron DeKalb* during the battle.

John Stuart joined the Union Navy at Helena, Arkansas on October 1, 1862. Stuart had been born in Richmond. [47] Assigned to the *USS Benton*, Stuart served as a First Class Boy during the Battle of Vicksburg, which ended with a Union victory on July 4, 1863.[48]

Wilson Armistead, born in Norfolk, served on the *USS New Ironsides* during the Siege of Charleston Harbor from July to September of 1863[49] and was likely serving on board when the *New Ironsides* was rammed and torpedoed by the *CSS David* on October 5, 1863.[50]

When the *USS Housatonic* was rammed by the *CSS Hunley*, a Confederate submarine, on February 17, 1864, Landsman James Williams of Berkley County may have been one of the sailors abandoning the ship. Williams had enlisted in New York in June 1863 and had been a waiter in civilian life.[51] Williams worked and was likely acquainted with another Landsman on the ship, Theodore F. Parker of New York. Parker was killed during the battle.[52]

During the Battle of Fort Pillow on April 12, 1864, the *USS New Era* was one of the gunboats providing artillery fire for the embattled soldiers attempting to defend the fort.[53] Cannon and sniper fire became so intense during the fight that the *New Era* was forced to stop firing and close its gunports. First Class Boy Boyce Prince, born in Franklin County, served on the *New Era* during the battle. Prince was twenty-four years old.[54]

Landsman Charles Dennis[55], born on the Eastern Shore, was serving on the *USS Hartford* during the Battle of Mobile Bay in August 1864 when Admiral David Farragut gave the famous order *"Damn the torpedoes, full speed ahead!"* and led the ship through a Confederate minefield to a Union naval victory.[56]

Dennis's shipmate, Landsman John Lawson of Philadelphia, earned the Medal of Honor for heroism during that battle.[57]

Several sailors born in Virginia served on a number of vessels during the Second Battle of Fort Fisher near Wilmington, North Carolina in January 1865.[58] George Watson[59] and John T. Weaver[60] from Alexandria, Beaddy Carter[61] from Accomack County, Iveson Robinson[62] from King William County, Henry C. Bailey[63] from New Market, Thornton Puller[64] from Rappahannock County, and Stephen Jasper[65] from Norfolk, served on ships that were present during the climactic battle that resulted in a Union victory.

The Confederates made a desperate naval attack down the James River in late January 1865 in what became known as the Battle of Trent's Reach.[66] Port Royal Davis had been a mariner in civilian life and was serving as an Ordinary Seaman on the *USS Massassoit*; Davis had been born in Norfolk.[67] Thornton Smith, born in Frederick County, served on the same ship.[68] First Class Boy Moses Carey, born in York County[69], served on the *USS Hunchback*, with First Class Boy James Roots[70], born in Caroline County. These sailors born in Virginia had participated in the last great naval engagement of the war.

Black sailors born in Virginia served heroically and with distinction. When Confederates opened fire on the *USS Marblehead* near John's Island, South Carolina on the morning of December 25, 1863 Robert Blake was serving as Steward for the ship's captain, Lieutenant

Commander Richard Meade, who was still in his nightclothes. Blake brought Meade a fresh uniform, then went to the gun deck to help. When a powder boy was killed by an exploding shell, Blake took his place, and helped the gun crew continue firing at the enemy until the Rebels abandoned their position. Robert Blake, who had been born in Virginia, was awarded the Medal of Honor for his actions during this fight.[71]

James Mifflin, born in Richmond, was serving on the *USS Brooklyn* during the Battle of Mobile Bay on August 5, 1864 as an Engineers Cook. During the battle, assigned to help move powder from the ship's magazines to the guns firing at the enemy, exploding shells killed the men working with him two times, but Mifflin remained at his post and kept supplying the guns with powder until the Confederates defending Fort Morgan surrendered.[72]

Throughout the war, African American sailors born in Virginia served with courage and honor.

5. EMANCIPATION

On September 22, 1862, President Lincoln published the Emancipation Proclamation; its provisions were to go into effect on January 1, 1863.

Carefully worded, limited in scope, and intended for a specific purpose, the Proclamation only freed slaves in the areas of the rebellious South where, ironically, Emancipation could not be enforced. The document stated that only persons held as slaves in states that were 'in rebellion against the United States' were freed.

There were significant exclusions. In twelve parishes of Louisiana, which had been in rebellion against the United States but were in late 1862 administered by a Union military government, the status of slaves did not change. Also, the status of slaves in seven Virginia counties, formerly in rebellion but at the time of the Proclamation occupied by Union troops, did not change. The Virginia counties unaffected by the Emancipation Proclamation included Berkley, Accomack, Northampton, Elizabeth City, York, Princess Ann, and Norfolk. Slaves in the forty-eight counties of West Virginia, which had seceded from Virginia in 1861, were also excluded. Finally, slaves in the Union border states of Missouri, Kentucky, Maryland and Delaware were not affected by the Proclamation, as those states were not 'in rebellion.'[1]

While the President's declaration fell short of freeing all slaves, the Emancipation Proclamation was brilliantly conceived, perfectly timed, and forever changed the nature of the War Between the States. Until late 1862, President Lincoln had been careful to the describe intent of the war as restoration of the Union. Most Confederate leaders, on the other hand, characterized the Rebellion as an attempt to preserve "States Rights" – the alleged sovereignty of individual states over that of the Federal government.

By issuing the Emancipation Proclamation, Abraham Lincoln raised the stakes in the war. The President declared that the Federal government had the right to free the slaves, the authority to end slavery forever, and intended to exercise that authority in the areas currently in rebellion against the United States. Henceforth, the only way slavery could be preserved in those states was for the Confederates to win an absolute victory over the United States.

Before the Emancipation Proclamation was declared, African Americans had a more restrained interest in the Union cause. Many were willing to fight to preserve the Union, but until there was a real prospect of ending slavery, at least in the rebellious states of the south, African Americans had a limited interest in taking up arms. After the Emancipation Proclamation was declared, however, black Americans realized they could help change the world. Free persons of color, escaped slaves, and contrabands shared ties of kinship with the millions still held in slavery. If they could help the Union win the war, they could liberate slaves still held in bondage in the South, and exert influence to win freedom for the remaining slaves in the North.

Before the end of the war over 200,000 African American men would serve in the United States armed forces. Many served in combat; others served in support roles, freeing up other Union soldiers and sailors to fight the Rebels. Unquestionably, these African Americans helped win the war, restore the Union, and put an end to slavery.

TO COLORED MEN!

FREEDOM,

Protection, Pay, and a Call to Military Duty!

On the 1st day of January, 1863, the President of the United States proclaimed Freedom to over Three Millions of Slaves. This decree is to be enforced by all the power of the Nation. On the 21st of July last he issued the following order:

PROTECTION OF COLORED TROOPS.

"WAR DEPARTMENT, ADJUTANT GENERAL'S OFFICE,
Washington, July 31.

"General Order, No. 233.

"The following order of the President is published for the information and government of all concerned:—

EXECUTIVE MANSION, Washington, July 30.

"'It is the duty of every Government to give protection to its citizens, of whatever class, color, or condition, and especially to those who are duly organized as soldiers in the public service. The law of nations, and the usages and customs of war, as carried on by civilized powers, permit no distinction as to color in the treatment of prisoners of war as public enemies. To sell or enslave any captured person on account of his color, is a relapse into barbarism, and a crime against the civilization of the age.

"'The Government of the United States will give the same protection to all its soldiers, and if the enemy shall sell or enslave any one because of his color, the offense shall be punished by retaliation upon the enemy's prisoners in our possession. It is, therefore, ordered, for every soldier of the United States, killed in violation of the laws of war, a rebel soldier shall be executed; and for every one enslaved by the enemy, or sold into slavery, a rebel soldier shall be placed at hard labor on the public works, and continued at such labor until the other shall be released and receive the treatment due to prisoners of war.

"'ABRAHAM LINCOLN.'"

"'By order of the Secretary of War.
"'E. D. Townsend, Assistant Adjutant General.'"

That the President is in earnest the rebels soon began to find out, as witness the following order from his Secretary of War:

"WAR DEPARTMENT, Washington City, August 3, 1863.

"Sir: Your letter of the 3d inst., calling the attention of this Department to the cases of Orin H. Brown, William H. Johnston, and Wm. Wilson, three colored men captured on the gunboat Isaac Smith, has received consideration. This Department has directed that three rebel prisoners of South Carolina, if there be any such in our possession, and if not, three others, be confined in close custody and held as hostages for Brown, Johnston and Wilson, and that the fact be communicated to the rebel authorities at Richmond.
" Very respectfully your obedient servant,

" EDWIN M. STANTON, Secretary of War.

"The Hon. Gideon Welles, Secretary of the Navy."

And retaliation will be our practice now—man for man—to the bitter end.

LETTER OF CHARLES SUMNER,

Written with reference to the Convention held at Poughkeepsie, July 15th and 16th, 1863, to promote Colored Enlistments.

BOSTON, July 13th, 1863.

"I doubt if, in times past, our country could have expected from colored men any patriotic service. Such service is the return for protection. But now that protection has begun, the service should begin also. Nor should relative rights and duties be weighed with nicety. It is enough that our country, aroused at last to a sense of justice, seeks to enrol colored men among its defenders.

"If my counsels should reach such persons, I would say: enlist at once. Now is the day and now is the hour. Help to overcome your cruel enemies now battling against your country, and in this way you will surely overcome those other enemies hardly less cruel, here at home, who will still seek to degrade you. This is not the time to hesitate or to higgle. Do your duty to our country, and you will set an example of generous self-sacrifice which will conquer prejudice and open all hearts.

" Very faithfully yours,

"CHARLES SUMNER."

After the Emancipation Proclamation was issued, the war was irrefutably about slavery, and recruitment of black soldiers began in earnest. – *Image: Library of Congress*

For most Americans, the war was no longer just about preservation of the Union. After the Emancipation Proclamation, the war was clearly and indisputably about ending slavery.

By the President of the United States of America:
A Proclamation.

Whereas, on the twenty-second day of September, in the year of our Lord one thousand eight hundred and sixty-two, a proclamation was issued by the President of the United States, containing, among other things, the following, to wit:

"That on the first day of January, in the year of our Lord one thousand eight hundred and sixty-three, all persons held as slaves within any State or designated part of a State, the people whereof shall then be in rebellion against the United States, shall be then, thenceforward, and forever free; and the Executive Government of the United States, including the military and naval authority thereof, will recognize and maintain the freedom of such persons, and will do no act or acts to repress such persons, or any of them, in any efforts they may make for their actual freedom.

"That the Executive will, on the first day of January aforesaid, by proclamation, designate the States and parts of States, if any, in which the people thereof, respectively, shall then be in rebellion against the United States; and the fact that any State, or the people thereof, shall on that day be, in good faith, represented in the Congress of the United States by members chosen thereto at elections wherein a majority of the qualified voters of such State shall have participated, shall, in the absence of strong countervailing testimony, be deemed conclusive evidence that such State, and the people thereof, are not then in rebellion against the United States."

Now, therefore I, Abraham Lincoln, President of the United States, by virtue of the power in me vested as Commander-in-Chief, of the Army and Navy of the United States in time of actual armed rebellion against the authority and government of the United States, and as a fit and necessary war measure for suppressing said rebellion, do, on this first day of January, in the year of our Lord one thousand eight hundred and sixty-three, and in accordance with my purpose so to do publicly proclaimed for the full period of one hundred days, from the day first above mentioned, order and designate as the States and parts of States wherein the people thereof respectively, are this day in rebellion against the United States, the following, to wit:

Arkansas, Texas, Louisiana, (except the Parishes of St. Bernard, Plaquemines, Jefferson, St. John, St. Charles, St. James Ascension, Assumption, Terrebonne, Lafourche, St. Mary, St. Martin, and Orleans, including the City of New Orleans) Mississippi, Alabama, Florida, Georgia, South Carolina, North Carolina, and Virginia, (except the forty-eight counties designated as West Virginia, and also the counties of Berkley, Accomac, Northampton, Elizabeth City, York, Princess Ann, and Norfolk, including the cities of Norfolk and Portsmouth)], and which excepted parts, are for the present, left precisely as if this proclamation were not issued.

And by virtue of the power, and for the purpose aforesaid, I do order and declare that all persons held as slaves within said designated States, and parts of States, are, and henceforward shall be free; and that the Executive government of the United States, including the military and naval authorities thereof, will recognize and maintain the freedom of said persons.

And I hereby enjoin upon the people so declared to be free to abstain from all violence, unless in necessary self-defence; and I recommend to them that, in all cases when allowed, they labor faithfully for reasonable wages.

And I further declare and make known, that such persons of suitable condition, will be received into the armed service of the United States to garrison forts, positions, stations, and other places, and to man vessels of all sorts in said service.

And upon this act, sincerely believed to be an act of justice, warranted by the Constitution, upon military necessity, I invoke the considerate judgment of mankind, and the gracious favor of Almighty God.

In witness whereof, I have hereunto set my hand and caused the seal of the United States to be affixed.

Done at the City of Washington, this first day of January, in the year of our Lord one thousand eight hundred and sixty-three, and of the Independence of the United States of America the eighty-seventh.

*By the President: ABRAHAM LINCOLN
WILLIAM H. SEWARD, Secretary of State.*

More than 3,000 slaves living in Washington, D.C were freed on April 16, 1862 when Congress passed the Compensated Emancipation Act.[2]

A plan for the "gradual" emancipation of slaves was part of the constitution of the new State of West Virginia on June 20, 1863.[3] Children born after July 4, 1863 to enslaved women in West Virginia were to be free.

A new state constitution adopted on November 1, 1864 emancipated Maryland's slaves.[4] On January 11, 1865 an ordinance passed in a state convention freed slaves in Missouri.[5]

Ratified on December 6, 1865, the Thirteenth Amendment to the U.S. Constitution freed slaves in Kentucky, Delaware, and in the remaining areas of the United States where slavery existed.[6]

Neither slavery nor involuntary servitude, except as a punishment for crime whereof the party shall have been duly convicted, shall exist within the United States, or any place subject to their jurisdiction.

Section 2.

Congress shall have power to enforce this article by appropriate legislation.

Passed by Congress January 31, 1865. Ratified December 6, 1865.

The first battles in which U.S. Colored regiments fought set the stage for the experiences all African American soldiers would endure later in the war. It is not known whether former slaves born in Virginia were involved in the earliest fights in Louisiana, Oklahoma, or South Carolina but reports of these battles had a direct bearing on how U.S. Colored troops were perceived and how they would be utilized later when large numbers of Virginia-born soldiers enlisted in the Union Army.

Port Hudson – May 27, 1863

Louisiana Native Guard troops at Port Hudson. - *Photo: Wikimedia Commons*

Less than a month after the beginning of the Civil War, free African Americans in New Orleans formed a volunteer Confederate infantry regiment called the Native Guards, led by a white commander and several black officers. They trained for several months and actually marched in military reviews with other Confederate units. As they received no support from the Confederate government and had to buy their own uniforms and equipment; many became disillusioned.

54

In mid-1862 when white citizens of Louisiana expressed alarm at seeing African Americans organized and bearing weapons, the black Confederate regiment was disbanded.[7]

Union leaders realized that by gaining control of the Mississippi River, they could isolate the western states from the rest of the Confederacy and choke off the flow of supplies, reinforcements and commerce sustaining the rebellious states of the deep South.

On April 29, 1862, a determined naval attack led by Captain David Farragut resulted in the capture of New Orleans by Union forces. The Union Army of the Gulf was commanded by Major General Benjamin Butler. Born in New Hampshire and raised in Massachusetts, Butler was a lawyer and politician who had obtained his military commission by political appointment. He had only a limited amount of experience as an officer in the Massachusetts militia and in the past had been a supporter of slavery. Butler's ground forces occupied New Orleans immediately after the city's surrender.[8]

Desperate for more soldiers to strengthen Union occupation forces in Louisiana, General Butler decided to recruit black Louisianans to join the Union Army in late 1862. Butler did this on his own initiative; President Lincoln did not issue the Emancipation Proclamation allowing recruitment of black soldiers until January of 1863.

On Butler's orders, the 1st Regiment of Native Guards was mustered into service as a Union Army unit on September 27, 1862.[9] About a hundred of the recruits to the new Federal regiment had served in the Confederate Native Guards. Butler recruited two more regiments of Native Guards, composed mostly of slaves. Though white officers commanded each of the three regiments, most of the line officers and sergeants were African American. Controversy surrounded these regiments from the beginning. Many of Butler's own officers doubted the former slaves had the ability or will to fight in combat.

In December of 1862 Butler was replaced by General Nathaniel Banks, another political appointee. Skeptical of the abilities of black officers to lead men in battle, Banks replaced many of them with white commanders, and assigned the Native Guards primarily to garrison duty.

It was believed that securing the stretch of river running from Vicksburg to Port Hudson, 250 miles downriver, could allow the Federals to control the entire Mississippi. Beginning in April 1863, a Union army commanded by Major General Ulysses S. Grant began the Siege of Vicksburg.

In May 1863 Banks was ordered to take Port Hudson, a riverside stronghold about twenty miles from Baton Rouge, then march north to assist Grant's attack on Vicksburg.[10] Because Union forces controlled the river and land access was limited, Port Hudson was difficult for the Southerners to resupply. However, situated on an eighty-foot bluff overlooking a sharp bend in the Mississippi River and surrounded by rough terrain, the fort was occupied by a strong force of 7500 Rebels. Extensive trenches surrounded the Confederate position, and more than twenty pieces of artillery, about half of which were heavy coastal guns, were arranged to defend against attacks from the water or by land.

While part of the Union force marched southeast from Alexandria, the Native Guards set out from Baton Rouge, nineteen miles southwest of Port Hudson. On May 21, they came under fire for the first time in the Battle of Plains Store, holding the Union left against a Confederate attack. On May 26, Native Guards skirmished with a force of Rebels along the Telegraph Road north of Port Hudson while the men of a

Massachusetts unit built a pontoon bridge across Sandy Creek. Throughout that night, Union gunboats shelled the Confederate stronghold.

On May 27, 1863 the Union force attacked Port Hudson. The first Federal assault led by Brigadier General Godfrey Weitzel came from the northeast and started around 6:00 AM. Uneven terrain and effective enemy fire caused disorder among the advancing Federals as they neared the Rebel line. Subsequent waves of Union soldiers led by other brigade commanders were unable to breach the Confederate defenses.

The African American regiments, commanded by Brigadier General William Dwight, were stationed on the Union right flank. Dwight was not confident that the black soldiers would fight, and planned to test them at the first opportunity. When the first phase of the Union attack stalled, Dwight ordered the Native Guard regiments to cross the pontoon bridge constructed the day before and attack along the Telegraph Road. Around 10:00 AM, over a thousand troops from the 1st and 3rd Native Guards advanced towards the impregnable Confederate positions on the bluff.

The Rebels replied with withering rifle fire and cannister rounds shot from artillery. Still the determined Native Guards advanced, until they were blocked by a backwater below the bluff. Eight feet deep and over forty feet wide, the water obstacle was a barrier the troops could not cross. In just over a quarter of an hour, half of the attackers had been wounded or killed; the remainder were forced to withdraw into the nearby woods. Those who were able continued to fire on the Rebels.

Weeks passed before the Federals were able to take Port Hudson. The Confederates successfully defended the fortifications on the bluff until July 9, only surrendering after they learned of Grant's July 4 victory at Vicksburg. By that time, Port Hudson's Rebel defenders had been reduced to eating their mules, dogs, and even rats.

The attack by the Native Guards at Port Hudson was the first time African American soldiers participated in a major assault during the Civil War. In a letter to his wife, Banks wrote: *"They fought splendidly!"* Their courage and determination under fire gained them a measure of respect from their commanders, comrades, and even their enemies.

The praise they got in the Union press convinced more leaders that black soldiers would fight effectively and courageously, and that more black regiments should be raised to help defeat the Rebels. Thousands of African Americans were encouraged to enlist by the reports on the Battle of Port Hudson.

The Native Guards may not have won the battle that morning, but their bravery and resolve ultimately contributed to Union victory. In the next two years more than 186,000 black soldiers enlisted in the U.S. Army and over 25,000 black sailors joined the Navy. The Native Guards regiments helped lead the way.

Combahee Ferry– June 1-2, 1863

In 1849, a woman born with the name Araminta Ross escaped from the farm in Maryland where she had been enslaved. Growing up in slavery, Ross had been whipped and beaten; she suffered a traumatic head injury when an angry overseer threw a metal weight at another slave and missed, hitting her instead. The incident put her into a coma that lasted several days. Afterwards, she saw visions and experienced dreams she believed were premonitions from God.

When she married, Araminta changed her name to Harriet Tubman. Shortly after making her way to safety and freedom in Philadelphia, Tubman returned to Maryland to help several of her family members escape. Ultimately, she made more than a dozen dangerous trips leading others to freedom. Tubman led so many people to freedom she became known as a female "Moses".[11]

After the Civil War began, Harriet Tubman travelled to South Carolina to help refugees in the contraband camps there and support the Union cause. She worked as a nurse for the Union army, where she became acquainted with General David Hunter, who was recruiting former slaves for an African American infantry regiment.

In 1863, Colonel James Montgomery led an amphibious expedition from Port Royal up the Combahee River in South Carolina, intending to clear the river channel for Federal gunboats, capture supplies, and destroy several plantations that were supplying rice and other provisions to the Confederacy.

Montgomery's forces included 300 soldiers of the 2nd South Carolina Colored Infantry Regiment and a battery of artillery from Rhode Island. The troops started upriver in three Federal boats. After one of the boats ran aground, Montgomery disembarked troops from the *USS Harriet A. Weed* and had them advance upriver on foot.

Tubman's experiences helping slaves to escape made her skilled at moving covertly in hostile territory. She proceeded upriver with 150 men on the other boat, the *USS John Adams*, to a ferry crossing where the Confederates had built a pontoon bridge. Confederate soldiers on the bridge opened fire.

Tubman had the guns aboard the *John Adams* fire at the Combahee Ferry bridge, scattering the Rebels. She had her Union troops disembark on both sides of the river, set fire to the bridge and proceed upriver to the plantations. The overwhelmed Confederates withdrew.

The Union raiders captured several thousand bushels of rice along with other supplies. They burned seven plantations and freed more than 750 slaves. On their return to Port Royal, more than 100 of the freed men joined the Union Army. Harriet Tubman, a former slave, had become the first African American woman to lead United States Army soldiers in combat.[12]

A June 4, 1863 article in *The Charleston Mercury* reported:

We have gathered some additional particulars of the recent destructive Yankee raid along the banks of the Combahee. The latest official dispatch from Gen. WALKER, dated Green Pond, eleven o'clock Tuesday night, and which was received here on Wednesday morning, conveyed intelligence that the enemy had entirely disappeared. It seems that the first landing of the Vandels [sic], whose force consisted mainly of three 'companies, officered by whites, took place at Field Point, on the plantation of Dr. R. L. BAKER, at the mouth of the Combahee River. After destroying the residence and outbuildings, the incendiaries proceeded along the river bank, visiting successively the plantations of Mr. OLIVER MIDDLETON, Mr. ANDREW W. BURNETT, Mr. WM. KIRKLAND, Mr. JOSHUA NICHOLLS, Mr. JAMES PAUL, Mr. MANIGAULT, Mr. CHAS. T. LOWNDES and Mr. WM. C. HEYWARD. After pillaging the premises of these gentlemen, the enemy set fire to the residences, outbuildings and whatever grain, etc., they could find. The last place at which they stopped was the plantation of WM. C. HEYWARD, and, after their work of devastation there had been consummated, they destroyed the pontoon bridge at Combahee Ferry. They then drew off, taking with them between 600 and 700 slaves, belonging chiefly, as we are informed, to Mr. WM. C. HEYWARD and Mr. C.T. LOWNDES. The residences on these plantations are located at *different distances from the river, varying in different cases from one to two miles. On the plantation of Mr. NICHOLLS between 8,000 and 10,000 bushels of rice were destroyed. Besides his residence and outbuildings, which were burned, he lost a choice library of rare books, valued at $10,000. Several overseers are missing, and it is supposed that they are in the hands of the enemy.*[13]

The Combahee Ferry Raid resulted in a Union victory, largely due to Harriet Tubman's courage and leadership.

The 2nd South Carolina later participated in more actions against the Rebels, including the siege of Fort Wagner at Charleston and the Battle of Honey Hill. The regiment was redesignated as the 34th United States Colored Infantry Regiment in 1864. Soldiers born in Virginia are among those who served in the 34th later in the war; some may have been participants in the Combahee Ferry raid.

Milliken's Bend – June 7, 1863

In 1863 Milliken's Store was a village near a sharp bend in the Mississippi River fifteen miles northwest of Vicksburg. The Union Army had a supply base and recruiting hub at Milliken's Bend.[14]

Before the siege of Vicksburg, Grant moved his army to the east side of the Mississippi and opened a new supply base on the Yazoo River, north of the city. This reduced the Union Army's dependence on Milliken's Bend, but the supply depot on the west side of the river was kept operating and garrisoned in June 1863 by four USCT regiments and a white regiment from Iowa.

The 9th, 11th and 13th Louisiana Colored Infantry (African Descent), 1st Mississippi Infantry (African Descent) and about 120 white soldiers from the 23rd

Iowa Infantry guarded the post. The 1,500 Union troops at Milliken's Bend were commanded by Colonel Hermann Lieb, who had immigrated to the United States from Switzerland in 1854. Before the war Lieb had been a newspaper editor in Illinois. The Federal gunboats *USS Choctaw* and *USS Lexington* steamed nearby in the Mississippi River to provide artillery support.

In early June, patrolling Union troops had encountered Confederates less than ten miles away near Tallulah, Louisiana. Expecting the Rebels to attack, Lieb had his troops use cotton bales to build additional breastworks atop a levee on the west side of the river.

Brigadier General Henry McCullough commanded a Rebel brigade consisting of the 16th, 17th, and 19th Texas Infantry along with the 16th Texas Cavalry (Dismounted). McCullough had been assigned to attack the Federal supply base at Milliken's Bend and help relieve Union pressure on Vicksburg. Marching through the night, McCullough's 1,500 Confederates were less than a mile from the Union defenses by 3:00 AM on June 7, and attacked at dawn.

The Rebels approached from the southwest, emerging from a hedge of thorny Osage orange bushes beside the river. Both sides managed to get off a volley, but before the inexperienced Federals could reload, the Confederates reached the Union breastworks. Brutal hand to hand fighting ensued on top of the levee. Men stabbed each other with bayonets, swung their rifles like clubs, and fought with their fists. One casualty of the battle was Sergeant "Big Jack" Jackson, a former slave who had helped recruit many of the African American soldiers. Jackson swung his rifle at the Rebels until there was nothing left but the barrel, before he was shot and killed.

This engraving, depicting fighting on the levee during the Battle of Milliken's Bend, was featured in Harpers Weekly Magazine. - *Image: Library of Congress*

Overwhelmed, the Union troops withdrew to a second levee closer to the river with the Rebels in hot pursuit, then fell back to the riverbank, their last line of defense, still fighting. The *USS Choctaw* and *USS Lexington* opened fire on the Confederates from the river. Late in the morning, fearful that more Union reinforcements were on the way, McCullough withdrew his exhausted troops.

The Union and Confederate forces had been evenly matched in manpower. Some 101 Union soldiers were killed, 285 wounded, and 266 were missing. Colonel Lieb was among the wounded but survived the war. The Confederates had fewer casualties, losing forty-four killed, 131 wounded, and ten missing, but the Union troops had successfully defended Milliken's Bend against the Rebel attack. Expecting an easy victory, the Confederates were surprised and shocked at the determined resistance of the black soldiers, who just weeks before had been slaves working in cotton fields.

In a letter to President Lincoln later that year, Secretary of War Edwin M. Stanton wrote:

"Many persons believed, or pretended to believe, and confidentially asserted, that freed slaves would not make good soldiers; they would lack courage, and could not be subjected to military discipline. Facts have shown how groundless were these apprehensions."

Over time the site of the Battle of Milliken's Bend has been washed away by erosion of the west bank of the Mississippi River.

The 9th Louisiana Infantry, A.D. (African Descent) was reorganized and redesignated as the 5th U.S. Colored Heavy Artillery in 1864, still commanded by Colonel Lieb, and participate in more engagements before war ended.

The 11th Louisiana Infantry, A.D. was redesignated as the 49th U.S. Colored Infantry in 1864 and serve the remainder of the war in Vicksburg. The 13th Louisiana Infantry, A.D. was disbanded, and its remaining troops absorbed into other Colored Troop units.

The 1st Mississippi Infantry, A.D. became the 51st U.S. Colored Infantry and eventually took part in the Battle of Fort Blakely, the last major battle of the war. At least six men born in Virginia were serving the 11th Louisiana Infantry at the time of the battle.

Goodrich's Landing – June 29-30, 1863

In the Spring of 1863 Major General Ulysses Grant began assembling a large Union force along the Mississippi in preparation for his attack on the Confederate city of Vicksburg. Federal troops occupied several parishes in Louisiana on the western shore of the river.

Thousands of escaped slaves made their way to the area to seek protection from the Union soldiers. To help offset the costs of providing the former slaves with food and clothing, the U.S. Army seized several local plantations and put the refugees to work growing cotton and other crops. Regiments of U.S. Colored Troops were ordered to protect the plantations.[15]

In May, companies E and G of the 1st Arkansas Infantry (African Descent) were dispatched to Goodrich's Landing, a plantation on the western shore of the Mississippi River from which many of the crops were shipped. The African American soldiers were to occupy and defend a supply depot at a fort which Federal troops had constructed on an Indian ceremonial mound, five miles away.

On June 29 a Confederate force of more than 13,000 men commanded by Brigadier General James Tappan and Colonel William Parsons surrounded the fort. They had marched from Gaines Landing, Arkansas in an effort to disrupt the flow of supplies to Grant's army at the Siege of Vicksburg.[16]

The Confederates demanded that the Union troops surrender unconditionally. Realizing their small detachment of soldiers was hopelessly outnumbered, the officers of the 1st Arkansas agreed to surrender on the condition their rights as prisoners of war were respected. Under Confederate law, however, the 113 Black enlisted men at the fort were not to be recognized as prisoners of war. When the African American U.S. soldiers were captured, they were shipped to various points in Louisiana and Texas to be re-enslaved. The Rebels then destroyed the nearby plantations, withdrawing when they were attacked by Union reinforcements that had hurried to the area.

The Confederates were able to achieve a victory at Goodrich's Landing without a fight, but failed to achieve their objective of cutting off the flow of supplies to the Union army. The city of Vicksburg surrendered to Grant's forces on July 4, 1863.

Many of the prisoners captured at Goodrich's Landing who survived continued to be held in slavery until the end of the war.

In late 1864 the 1st Arkansas Infantry (AD) was redesignated as the 46th U.S. Colored Infantry. At least ten men born in Virginia were serving in the 1st Arkansas at the time of the fight at Goodrich's landing.

Cabin Creek – July 1-2, 1863

At the same time Confederate and Union armies were converging on Gettysburg in July 1863, a Federal wagon train loaded with supplies headed towards Fort Gibson, in what is now Oklahoma. Before they could cross Cabin Creek on the Texas Road, they encountered a large force of Confederate troops.

The Rebels were led by Brigadier General Stand Watie, a principal chief of the Cherokee nation. In 1835 Watie was one of four Cherokee leaders who signed the Treaty of New Echota surrendering tribal lands in Georgia and leading to the forced removal of the Cherokees west to Indian Territory, along what became known as the "Trail of Tears". Three other chiefs who signed the treaty were later murdered, but Watie survived and continued to lead the minority of Cherokees who favored the settlement. When the Civil War began, many Cherokees sided with the Union, but Watie, a slave owner, led a faction that supported the Rebels throughout the war. At Cabin Creek, Stand Watie commanded a force of 1,800 Confederate soldiers.[17]

About 1,500 Union troops were commanded by Colonel James Williams, and consisted of detachments from the 2nd Colorado Infantry, 3rd Wisconsin Cavalry, 6th and 9th Kansas Cavalry, 3rd Indian Home Guard, 1st Kansas Colored Infantry and the 2nd Kansas Artillery

When the Union supply wagons approached Cabin Creek on July 1, Williams was forced to call a halt because of shoulder high water in the creek, the result of recent heavy rains. That day, captured Confederate soldiers informed the Union officers of the planned ambush. The Rebels had formed lines extending a mile on each side of the crossing, and were concealed in the brush. Williams decided to delay his attack until the following day, and circled his wagons nearby to form a defensive perimeter.

On July 2, Williams ordered his artillery to bombard the Confederates for a half an hour before he had troops from the 3rd Indian Home Guard lead an attack. The water was now only waist high, but heavy fire from the Rebels prevented the Home Guardsmen from making the crossing. Williams next ordered the 9th Kansas Cavalry to charge the Confederates, covered by the 1st Kansas.

As the cavalry reached the other side, Williams led the men of the 1st Kansas Colored Infantry across the stream and up the opposite bank, forcing the surprised Rebels to withdraw. Colonel Williams had his wagons and men cross Cabin Creek, then continued on the trail, completing the resupply of Fort Gibson.[18]

Stand Watie continued to lead his Cherokee force against the Union Army for the remainder of the Civil War. His troops won a Confederate victory at a Second Battle of Cabin Creek in September 1864. Watie refused to recognize the Confederate defeat and did not surrender his troops until June 23, 1865, two and a half months after Lee's surrender at Appomattox.

The First Battle of Cabin Creek was the first time African American soldiers fought alongside white troops in a coordinated attack against a large Confederate force. The battle ended in Union victory, and the 1st Kansas Colored Infantry had distinguished itself in the fighting. The unit continued to fight in the west and eventually was redesignated as the 79th U.S. Colored Infantry Regiment.[19] A bronze statue at the Bates County Courthouse in Butler, Missouri commemorates the regiment.

A Gettysburg Story

While no United States Colored Troops fought at Gettysburg, some Confederate officers who fought in the battle brought enslaved men with them to work as cooks and personal servants. There were no African American combatants, but the Rebel invasion of the North had nightmarish consequences for free African Americans who lived near the battlefield.

On June 15, 1863, a Confederate mounted infantry brigade arrived in Pennsylvania, a few miles from Gettysburg. The Rebels were commanded by Brigadier General Albert Gallatin Jenkins, a graduate of Harvard Law School and politician who had been born in Cabell County, now part of West Virginia.

For the next two weeks Jenkin's men terrorized the local citizens. Black and white civilians living in the area attempted to resist the raiders, with some success, but eventually the Rebels abducted thirty free black men and an unknown number of women and children, taking them south into Virginia. The men were sent to Richmond, where most were imprisoned in Castle Thunder; the kidnapped women and children were sold into slavery.[20]

68

In a letter to his brother, a major in the North Carolina infantry complained:

"We have also captured thousands of horses and many hundred slaves. I have several negroes, free and slave, in my hands but negroes are worth nothing at all. No kind of negroes will sell for more than one hundred dollars."[21]

Reports of the raid appeared in Northern and Southern newspapers all around the country, many including transcriptions of letters from eyewitnesses. One letter printed in the *Daily Alta California*, said:

"During their stay among us, all the negroes that could be found were carried off by them; even children of four years of age were carried behind the soldiers on their horses, their parents having to leave them and make their escape to the grain fields and other places of refuge. Free men and women of color, raised in our town, were driven before the cavalry like cattle, while little children astride the horses clung to the riders to retain their seats."[22]

What the Rebels hoped to accomplish by the kidnapping of women and children during Lee's invasion of the North is not clear, but like the firing on Fort Sumter at the beginning of the war, the 1863 raids on Greencastle and Chambersburg ultimately hurt the Confederacy more than they helped.

By late July, Thomas Morris Chester, Philadelphia Press correspondent and recruiter for the U.S. Colored Troops, was soliciting volunteers for the 54th and 55th Massachusetts Colored Infantry regiments among the African Americans living in southern Pennsylvania, including many who had been born in Virginia. Now, unquestionably, the war was not just a *"white man's fight"*. This war was about freedom.

General Jenkins was in the Battle of Gettysburg. He recovered, but was wounded again during the Battle of Cloyd's Mountain at Pulaski, Virginia on May 9, 1864.[23] After his arm was amputated, Jenkins only survived for twelve days. He was thirty-three years old when he died.

A handful of the kidnapped men, like Amos Barnes, were released by the Confederates in December 1863 and were able to make their way back home to Pennsylvania. Most of the abductees would not return until after the war was over, if at all.[24]

In the Freedmen's Bureau archives, the following letter to Mrs. Priscilla Marshall reveals a poignant detail about the aftermath of Jenkin's Raid.[25] Marshall's young son Jack, and daughters Sallie and Rosa, had been kidnapped by the Rebel raiders:

Richmond, Va.
March 14th, 1866
Mrs. Priscilla
Greencastle, Franklin Co., Pa.

Madam,
Your communication of the 13th inst. is received –
If you get a statement from well known citizens in your neighborhood, that you lost the children Jack and Sallie, and the circumstances under which they were lost – the children will be sent to you. – Inquiries will be made for Rosa.

By order of
Col. O. Brown
Asst. Cmdr.
(Sgd.) James A. Bates
Capt. & a.a.a.g.

Priscilla Marshall's daughter Rosa was never found.

New York Draft Riots – July 11, 1863

On Saturday, July 11, 1863, the New York City Draft Board began drawing names of men between the ages of twenty and forty-five years old, complying with provisions of the Enrollment Act passed by Congress in March. The men whose names were selected were called up to serve in the Army, as part of the first Federal draft in U.S. history.

The Emancipation Proclamation had changed the nature of the war. What had begun as a fight to restore the Union was now perceived as a fight to free slaves.

Many Northern soldiers and officers protested at having to risk their lives to liberate slaves in the South. At a time when wages averaged less than $500 a year, most workers were too poor to pay the $300 to hire a substitute. Workers also feared freed slaves were about to flood the job market with low-cost labor, making it more difficult to get and keep jobs. Democrat politicians hoped to use the controversy to win more seats in Congress. For months, anti-war newspapers and Rebel sympathizers had raised tensions to a fever pitch, attempting to capitalize on the issue. The weekend passed quietly, but on Monday, July 13, the city exploded.[26] Hundreds of rioters filed into the streets. The 9th District draft office was set on fire; mobs attacked firefighters attempting to control the blaze. Soon the entire block was burning.

Protesters attacked draft officials, citizens, and police who attempted to restore order. Resentful of wealthy New Yorkers who could afford to pay for substitutes, rioters ransacked and set fire to several mansions on Fifth Avenue.

Black people were specifically targeted. Homes and businesses in African American neighborhoods were looted and burned. Black New Yorkers were brutally assaulted on the streets. Black men were lynched, their bodies burned.

The most vulnerable were attacked. Rioters set fire to the four-story Colored Orphan Asylum building on Fifth Avenue. Miraculously, the 200 children living in the orphanage survived.

The riots lasted for four days. City officials recalled the 7th New York Infantry Regiment from Gettysburg to assist police in breaking up the riot.

The official death toll was 119, but it is estimated that over a thousand New Yorkers were killed, many of them African Americans. More than 2,000 were injured, and at least 3,000 black New Yorkers were left homeless. The Colored Orphan Asylum had to be rebuilt in Harlem. By 1865, the African American population of the city dropped by twenty percent, as more than 2,500 persons of color moved out of the city.[27]

Honey Springs – July 17, 1863

In 1824 the United States had built an army post called Fort Gibson, at a point where a cattle trail called the Old Texas Road crosses the Arkansas River. The outpost in the Indian Territory was initially built to guard the western frontier against hostile Indian tribes, and later assigned to keep the peace in the land that eventually became the state of Oklahoma.

Union troops occupied Fort Gibson at the beginning of the Civil War. The Five Civilized Tribes living in the Indian Territory sided at first with the Confederacy. After defending the fort against a Confederate attack in 1862, Federal troops withdrew from Fort Gibson to Kansas but then reoccupied the post in April 1863.[28]

Confederate General Douglas H. Cooper commanded a force of about 3,000 soldiers based about twenty miles south of Fort Gibson on the Texas Road at a village called Honey Springs. His Rebel troops had attacked wagon trains attempting to resupply Fort Gibson, but Cooper wanted to capture the fort. Realizing he needed more men, he requested and received 3000 reinforcements from Fort Smith, Arkansas.

Cooper's troops included a brigade of three cavalry regiments and several detachments of artillery from Texas, along with a brigade comprised of two Cherokee regiments, one Choctaw regiment, and two Creek regiments from the Indian Territory. Native American troops made up the majority of Cooper's command.

Union forces at Fort Gibson were commanded by General James G. Blunt, who had arrived at the post with his men shortly after the Confederates failed to capture a 200-wagon Federal supply train at Cabin Creek. General Blunt's force included detachments from the 3rd Wisconsin Cavalry and 6th Kansas Cavalry, two batteries of artillery, two Indian Home Guard regiments, and the 1st Kansas Colored Infantry regiment. Most of the Union troops were Native American or African American soldiers.

Blunt got word the Confederates were planning to attack and decided to make a preemptive strike. As the Arkansas River was flooded, he ordered his men to build boats for the crossing. On July 16, though Blunt was suffering from a dangerous high fever, the Union force crossed the river. By 11:00 PM that night the Federal troops began their march towards Honey Springs. Early in the morning on July 17th, they arrived in the vicinity of the Rebel camp.[29]

Blunt formed his men into two brigades, which fought sporadically with the Rebels during the morning of the 17th. The main Union attack began in the mid-afternoon. It began to rain. Many of the Confederates had wet gunpowder, and were unable to fire their weapons. The 1st Kansas Colored Infantry made an attack but were repulsed by the Confederates, withdrawing in good order. Later they fought off an attack by the Rebels. Blunt later wrote of the men of the 1st Kansas:

"I never saw such fighting as was done by the Negro regiment...The question that negroes will fight is settled; besides they make better soldiers in every respect than any troops I have ever had under my command."[30]

Cooper had his men fall back to replenish their ammunition. The Confederates made a stand at Elk Creek, then again near the Honey Springs Depot, but by 2:00 PM the Rebels were in full retreat.

Union forces suffered seventy-seven killed or wounded at Honey Springs; the larger Confederate force had 134 killed or wounded and forty-seven taken prisoner. The outnumbered Federals had won a victory in the largest Civil War battle fought in the Indian Territory.

Fort Wagner – July 18, 1863

The American Civil War began in Charleston, South Carolina, when Rebel troops fired on the U.S. Army garrison at Fort Sumter on April 12, 1861. The rebellion of southern states had actually begun at a convention in Charleston, where South Carolinians voted to secede from the United States on December 24, 1860. The primary reason given in the South Carolina Declaration of Secession was *"increasing hostility on the part of the non-slaveholding States to the Institution of Slavery"*.[31]

President Lincoln gave orders that Charleston be taken. Recapturing the city where the rebellion originated could help undermine Rebel authority in

South Carolina and deal a devastating blow to Confederate morale.

Fort Wagner was located on Morris Island, about two miles southwest of Fort Sumter. Built of sand, earth, and sharpened palmetto trunks, surrounded by a moat with a line of abatis (rows of sharpened stakes embedded in the ground), and defended by sixteen large pieces of artillery, Fort Wagner was a formidable stronghold. Planks embedded with sharp spikes were submerged in the moat. The fort was positioned on the island in a way that limited the number of soldiers that could approach it on the land. A shelter or "bombproof" at one end of the fort could provide cover for as many as 2,000 men.[32]

In July 1863 the fort was defended by 1,800 Confederate troops, commanded by Brigadier General William Booth Taliaferro, an experienced veteran from Virginia who had fought in several engagements under Confederate General Thomas J. "Stonewall" Jackson. Taliaferro's command consisted of the 1st South Carolina Artillery, the Charleston Battalion, the 31st North Carolina Infantry, and 51st Carolina Infantry.

Union Brigadier General Quincy Gilmore was appointed commander of the Department of the South. From his headquarters in Hilton Head, South Carolina, Gilmore began putting together a plan to attack Charleston. The capture of Fort Wagner was essential to that plan, as the big guns in Battery Wagner were an important part of the defenses of Fort Sumter.

One of the Union units supporting the assault was the 54th Massachusetts Colored Infantry Regiment, organized earlier that year. Governor John Andrew had obtained permission from the U.S. War Department to form the regiment and asked Captain Robert Gould Shaw, son of a fellow Abolitionist, to command it. Initially reluctant, Shaw decided to accept the assignment and was promoted to Colonel, with Lt.

Colonel Edward Hallowell as his Assistant Commander. The 54th was organized in Boston with much publicity. Abolitionist and civil rights leader Frederick Douglass helped recruit for the unit, and two of his sons, Lewis and Charles, enlisted. Private James Caldwell of Company H was the grandson of another famous abolitionist, Sojourner Truth. More than 1,000 men enlisted in the regiment before it shipped out for South Carolina.

Shaw pressured quartermasters to provide the men of the 54th with the same quality of uniforms, weapons, and supplies as those being issued to white troops. When the men learned they were to be paid less than the $13 per month that the government had initially promised, they refused to accept the lower amount. Shaw supported them by writing to Governor Andrew to protest, and to ask that they be paid the same amount as white troops, as promised. Almost two years passed before they were be awarded equal pay, but the men were still willing to fight. Shaw quickly earned the respect of his men by leading firmly, fairly, and boldly advocating for their interests.

On May 2, Shaw married his fiancé, Annie Hagerty, in New York City. The newlyweds had very little time together; on May 28, the ship *USS DeMolay* left Boston loaded with the officers and men of the 54th. Five days later the Union force landed at Hilton Head, and made camp near Beaufort, South Carolina.

Shortly after arriving, the 54th Massachusetts was ordered to participate in a raid on the town of Darien, Georgia led by Colonel James Montgomery, a slaveowner from Kentucky with a reputation for cruelty. No resistance was encountered, as most of the inhabitants had fled, but during the raid, Montgomery had his men shell, loot and burn the town, and over Shaw's objections ordered some of the Massachusetts men to assist. This was not the kind of fighting the men of the 54th or their officers wanted to be involved with. In a letter to Annie, Shaw called the attack a *"dirty piece of business."*[33] He later protested to his superiors, objecting to being ordered to make war against women and children.

On July 10, Federal gunboats and artillery stationed on Folly Island shelled Fort Wagner for several hours while Brigadier General George C. Strong's brigade landed on the southern end of Morris Island. At dawn the next day, Strong's men attacked Fort Wagner but were unsuccessful and had to withdraw; the First Battle of Fort Wagner ended in a Union defeat.

In preparation for a second attack on the fort, Shaw and his men landed on James Island on July 16. The 54th Massachusetts came under fire for the first time on James Island when they were attacked by a large force of Confederate infantry. They successfully repelled the attackers, winning the praise of the Union generals commanding the expedition.

For the second attack on the fort, Union commanders decided to attack with two infantry brigades after an artillery bombardment lasting more than eleven hours. In preparation for the barrage they expected, the Confederates surrounded their smaller guns with sandbags, and buried the larger guns with sand. Most of the Rebels waited in the bombproof.

General Strong offered Shaw the opportunity to lead the attack with the men of the 54th Massachusetts. Shaw willingly agreed and marched his men onto the beach in front of the fort as the sun was setting. With fixed bayonets, 600 men and nineteen officers advanced toward the sixty-yard gap between the marsh and the

Colonel Robert Gould Shaw, commander of the 54th Massachusetts Colored Infantry Regiment. Shaw would lose his life leading his men during the Battle of Fort Wagner in 1863. - *Photo: Library of Congress*

Sergeant William Harvey Carney, hero of the Battle of Fort Wagner. Carney was awarded the Congressional Medal of Honor years after the war. - *Photo: Library of Congress*

ocean. The fort was silent and dark. It was thought that the all-day shelling had weakened the Confederate defenses.

At 7:45 PM Shaw gave the order to charge. Shaw commanded companies K, C, I, A and B on the right wing, while Hallowell commanded companies H, F, G, D, and E on the left. As they got closer, the Union guns fell silent. The 31st North Carolina Rebels were so terrorized by the bombardment that they refused to leave the bombproof. When the soldiers of the 54th Massachusetts were within 200 yards of the fort, the Confederates opened fire with artillery and muskets.

The determined Union soldiers continued to advance, crossing the moat and climbing up the parapet. When Shaw and about thirty soldiers reached the top of the wall, he raised his sword and yelled *"Forward, my brave boys! Come boys, come! Rally! Rally!"*[34] before he was shot multiple times and fell dead into the fort. The Confederates rolled hand grenades down the parapets. The soldiers on top of the wall began firing their muskets, then fought with bayonets, swinging muskets, and hand to hand.

Corporal Henry Peal, born in Virginia, managed to make it to the top of the wall with the Massachusetts state flag, but a Confederate on top of the parapet tore it off the staff. When an explosion killed John Wall, who was carrying the United States Flag, Sergeant William Carney, also born in Virginia, caught it before it could hit the ground. Peal and Carney held the flags aloft for more than an hour until reinforcements reached the Confederates, and the 54th Massachusetts was forced to withdraw. When he was finally able to walk back to the Union field hospital Carney said to the men around him, *"Boys, I only did my duty, the old flag never touched the ground!"*[35] and collapsed. He had been shot twice during the fighting.

General Strong was killed leading more regiments into the fight. When the shooting stopped at midnight, only 350 men of the 54th Massachusetts made it back to the Union lines. The rest had been killed, wounded, or captured. The Second Battle of Fort Wagner was over, and had resulted in another Union defeat.

The bravery and resolve shown by the men of the 54th Massachusetts, however, ultimately contributed to victory. The story of their performance at Fort Wagner was widely reported in the press and praised by their commanders, fellow soldiers, even some of their enemies. Many Union leaders who had doubted whether black soldiers would fight effectively were now convinced. Over the next few months, sixty more U.S. Colored Troop regiments were added to the United States Army.

Fort Wagner was eventually abandoned by the Confederates in September 7, 1863, after weeks of constant shelling, and occupied by Union troops.

6. COME AND JOIN US BROTHERS

As the war progressed the United States government had to strike a delicate balance between the need to recruit more soldiers to fight the war and the need to avoid alienating loyal slaveholders in the border states.

The Enrollment Act was signed into law by President Lincoln on March 3, 1863, and established procedures for drafting new recruits into the military. Volunteer enlistments and state levees were unable to supply all the manpower needed to win the war, so on February 24, 1864, an amendment to the Enrollment Act was signed into law by the President that allowed for the drafting of *"able-bodied male colored persons, between the ages of twenty and forty-five years"*[1] into the United States armed forces.

Another poster for the recruitment of African American soldiers. – *Image: Library of Congress*

Loyal Owners

Among other provisions, the 1864 Enrollment Act amendment provided for "loyal owners" to be paid $100 if their former slave had been drafted, or $300 if their former slave had volunteered. By enlisting, the soldier became free. When a slave enlisted, the former owner lost a capital asset.

Along with each claim, applicants had to submit proof of ownership of the slave, statements from witnesses that they were loyal to the Union, documentation that the statements were witnessed by a duly appointed official, and a deed of manumission backdated to the date of the soldier's enlistment.

Almost immediately, owners began filing claims for compensation.

Private Spencer Northern enlisted in Company F of the 9th U.S.C.I. on November 16, 1863. His former owner, Thomas Northam of Accomack County, submitted a compensation claim on February 29, 1864 – five days after the Enrollment Act amendment was signed into law – and was awarded $300 on August 31, 1864. Thomas Northam also filed a claim for Private Esaw Northern, on the same day. Spencer Northern survived the war and was discharged with his regiment on November 26, 1866 at New Orleans.[2] Esaw Northam did not survive and died of typhoid fever at Beaufort, South Carolina on July 19, 1864.[3]

Elizabeth Northam submitted a claim *"on behalf of her ward for life"*[4] – her daughter - for compensation for Private Erastus Northern of Company E, 9th U.S.C.I. on March 1, 1864. Erastus died of malarial fever at Point of Rocks Hospital on August 27, 1864.

Henry B. Northam submitted a claim on March 1, 1864 for compensation for Private Levi Northam, also of Company E, 9th U.S.C.I.[5] Levi survived the war and was discharged with his regiment on November 26, 1866 at New Orleans. Henry's claim for Levi was approved in August of 1864. Henry submitted another claim on March 31, 1864 for compensation for Private George T. Northam, also of Company E in the 9th Regiment.[6] George did not survive the war; he died of fever on December 19, 1863 after less than a month in the service.

James Northam of Accomack County filed a claim on March 1, 1864 for compensation for his former slave, Raymond, who enlisted under the name Raymond Northern on November 18, 1863.[7] Raymond Northern was an eighteen-year-old Private in Company G of the 9th U.S.C.I. Northern died on December 1, 1863 of "congestive chills" in the regimental hospital. A note on Northern's Compiled Military Service Record indicates that *'Col. Northern'* was a *'Strong Rebel'*, but James Northam was able certify his loyalty and collect his $300 claim on May 5, 1865.

The Northams of Accomack County submitted claims for compensation for the loss of services on six of their former slaves; four of these soldiers died of disease before the end of the war.

John P. Miller of Missouri submitted a claim for compensation for Private Jackson Haddox, a forty-three-year-old soldier in the Independent Battery of U.S. Colored Light Artillery, who had been born in Scott County, Virginia.[8] Another Missourian, Harvey Arnold, submitted a claim for Private James Arnold, who had been born in Franklin County, Virginia.[9]

Private Payton Tinsley was thirty-two years old when he enlisted in Company D of the 51st U.S.C.I. at Troy, Missouri on December 7, 1864.[10] His former owner, Rodney Tinsley of Pike County, Missouri, submitted a compensation claim on December 5, 1866. Tinsley's claim was handled by the Clarke and Coonley law firm of Saint Louis, Missouri. Payton Tinsley had been born in Bedford County, Virginia.

Sergeant William Bourdon of Company D, 9th U.S.C.I., was noted in his service records as being remarkable for neatness and soldierly bearing. Bourdon had been a 'private servant' before enlisting. When his former owner, William Bowdoin of Northampton County, submitted a compensation claim, he included a written affidavit from Brigadier General Henry H. Lockwood, commander of the Union 8th Army Corps First Brigade, which contained the following carefully worded statement: *"When the secession ordinance was submitted to the people in May 1861 Mr. Bowdoin in common with everyone in Northampton voted for the same to ratify it. I am informed that public opinion in that county did not make it safe to vote otherwise. With this single exception I know or have heard of no act of disloyalty in Wm. B's whole career and therefore regard him as a loyal man."*[11] Despite the ambiguity in this endorsement of Bowdoin's loyalty, his $300 claim, filed two days after the Enrollment Act amendment was signed into law, was approved in July 1864.

Private James Marshall of Company C, 9th U.S.C.I. had been dead for three years when his former owner, William J. Aydelote of Worcester County, Maryland submitted a compensation claim in January 1867. Private Marshall died of typhus at Benedict, Maryland less than two months after he had enlisted.[12]

On December 6, 1865 the Thirteenth Amendment to the Constitution of the United States was adopted, illegalizing slavery. The Amendment reads *"Neither slavery nor in voluntary servitude, except as a punishment for crime whereof the party shall have been duly convicted, shall exist within the United States, or any place subject to their jurisdiction. Congress shall have power to enforce this article by appropriate legislation."*[13]

84

Former owners continued to submit (and collect on) slave compensation claims until legislation discontinuing the practice was passed on March 30, 1867.[14]

Olustee – February 20, 1864

Until 1864 Florida had been the scene of very little fighting in the Civil War. The third state to secede from the Union, Florida provided the Confederacy with critical supplies including beef, pork, salt and sugar. Despite the Federal naval blockade, Florida was also able to contribute to the Confederate economy by raising and exporting high grade cotton.

In January 1864 President Lincoln asked Major General Quincy Gilmore, commanding the Department of the South, to devise a strategy for restoring Florida to the Union. At the time it was known that there were few Confederate forces in the sparsely populated state.[15]

Gilmore put together a plan designed to gain control of transportation routes in Florida, cut supplies off from the rest of the Confederacy, allow recruitment of freed slaves in the state for the Union Army, and allow cotton and timber to be shipped to the North. When Lincoln told him to proceed, Gilmore ordered Brigadier General Truman Seymour to lead the Florida expedition.

Seymour was a professional soldier, graduate of West Point, veteran of the Mexican and Seminole Wars and of a number of Civil War battles in Virginia. His command included the 54th Massachusetts Colored Infantry Regiment that had become famous during the July 1863 assault on Fort Wagner in Charleston. That attack had resulted in the death of the commander of the 54th, Colonel Robert Shaw, and had been unsuccessful, but their performance had convinced many Union commanders that African American soldiers would fight courageously and effectively, and helped in recruiting thousands of additional Black troops. Seymour was wounded by artillery shot during a subsequent charge on Fort Wagner and had just returned to active duty in December 1863.

Seymour led a force of 5,500 Federal troops on the Florida expedition, consisting of ten infantry regiments and four artillery batteries. Three of the infantry regiments were composed of African American soldiers: The 54th Massachusetts Colored Infantry, 1st North Carolina Colored Infantry, and the 8th U.S. Colored Infantry.

The 54th was commanded by Colonel James Hallowell, who had been second in command at Fort Wagner under Shaw and wounded during the battle. The 54th Massachusetts was an experienced, battle-hardened unit.

The 1st North Carolina was led by Colonel James Montgomery, known for cruelty both to his own men and to the enemy. The 1st North Carolina had performed mostly garrison and guard duty, and had limited fighting experience.

The 8th U.S. Colored Infantry was commanded by Charles Fribley, who had been promoted to Colonel when he took command of the regiment in November 1863. Fribley was a capable soldier, who had been appointed First Sergeant of his company when he enlisted in 1861, then commissioned as an officer in 1862. The only men in his new regiment who had any experience were the officers and sergeants. Most of the enlisted men in the 8th were new recruits and had never loaded, much less fired, their weapons. Since taking command, Fribley had made several requests that the men be trained with target practice, but he had been turned down.

Confederate forces west of Jacksonville were commanded by Brigadier General Joseph Finegan, a wealthy sawmill operator, lawyer and railroad builder who had immigrated to Florida from Ireland in the 1830s. Finegan led a force of about 1,200 men made up of regiments from Georgia and Florida.

Seymour's regiments were transported by ship from New York to South Carolina. Then, on February 4, 1864, his Federal troops were transported by ship from Hilton Head to Jacksonville. Rebel spies watched the Union force unloading at Jacksonville and notified Finegan, who sent an urgent request to General Beauregard at Charleston to send reinforcements. By February 19, Beauregard had sent more than 4,000 additional troops, the majority of them commanded by General Alfred Colquitt of Georgia, who had been a lawyer, preacher, and politician before the war. The Confederate regiments formed a defensive line near Olustee, sent cavalry towards Jacksonville to reconnoiter, and waited to see what the invading Federals were going to do.

On February 7, Seymour's force left Jacksonville, marching west on a route roughly parallel to the Florida Atlanta & Gulf Central Railroad that ran between Jacksonville and Lake City. The following day, Seymour's forces encountered a group of about 350 Confederate cavalry at Camp Finegan, eight miles west of Jacksonville, and after a short fight were able to capture 100 Rebels. On February 9, Seymour's advance guard was able to capture the town of Baldwin, about twenty miles west of Jacksonville.

Gilmore had ordered Seymour not to advance beyond Baldwin until further orders. Originally cautious, and skeptical as to whether or not the expedition could succeed, Seymour decided to disregard Gilmore's orders and advance beyond Baldwin towards Lake City. It may be that the relatively easy successes at

Camp Finegan and Baldwin boosted his confidence. During the afternoon of February 20, advancing through the pine forests and swampland along the railroad, troops of the 7th Connecticut Infantry ran into a Confederate cavalry regiment and two infantry regiments just west of the town of Sanderson.

The surprised Connecticut regiment was ordered to fall back, but the 7th New Hampshire and 8th U.S. Colored Infantry, misunderstanding orders, continued to advance. Under heavy fire from Rebel cavalry, the men of the 7th New Hampshire broke and ran. The inexperienced 8th Infantry, now exposed at the front, lost about 300 killed or wounded before ordered by Fribley to retreat. Fribley was killed before his unit could fall back, shot through the heart. Desperately trying to take cover, some of the inexperienced men curled up on the ground, others formed lines behind trees, trying to dodge the bullets.

Three New York Regiments, along with the 54th Massachusetts and the 1st North Carolina Infantry, advanced to try to stop the Confederates. The regimental band of the 54th played "The Star-Spangled Banner" to encourage the troops. Initially it appeared that the Union regiments might be able to hold the line, but recognizing that he was about to be outflanked on both sides, Seymour ordered a retreat at dusk. The 54th Massachusetts, 7th Connecticut, and 1st North Carolina were ordered to form a rear guard. Colonel Hallowell had to repeat the order to fall back three times to the determined veterans of the 54th. Seymour's men fell back all the way to Barber's Ford, near Jacksonville, that night.

Union forces suffered over 1,800 killed, wounded, and missing in the battle. The Confederates lost 900. The largest engagement fought in Florida during the Civil War, the Battle of Olustee, was a Union defeat.

Once again, however, African American troops received praise for their performance, which was comparable to that of the white units involved. The inexperienced 8th U.S. Colored Infantry did not panic and run, withdrawing only when Fribley ordered them to do so. The slightly more experienced 1st North Carolina Infantry handled itself well and the 54th Massachusetts had again distinguished itself as a reliable force of professional fighters.

Suffolk – March 9, 1864

In April 1863 a force commanded by Major General John J. Peck had established a strong Union Army garrison at Suffolk, just west of Norfolk, Virginia. Peck was successful in preventing an attempt to retake the town by a larger Confederate force under General James Longstreet in early May, but the large Federal force occupying Suffolk was needed elsewhere, and the Union garrison withdrew from the town later in the summer.[16]

During the spring of 1864, Union patrols frequented the area around Suffolk to forage for supplies and scout for Confederate activity. The Federals preferred to confiscate food items and livestock from Rebel citizens who had refused to take the oath of allegiance to the United States government. When the townspeople complained to Confederate authorities, a unit of Rebel soldiers was dispatched to the area to locate and attack any Union raiders they could find.

In March of 1864 troopers from the 2nd U.S. Colored Cavalry Regiment left their base at Camp Getty, four miles west of Portsmouth, to conduct reconnaissance in the Suffolk area.[17]

A Confederate infantry brigade commanded by General Matthew Ransom was encamped about three miles west of Suffolk. On the morning of March 9, they were alerted that a black Union cavalry unit was making a raid at Suffolk. Anxious to attack the black troopers before they could get away, the Rebels ran the entire distance to the town.

The surprised Federals were dangerously outnumbered; there were ten Rebels in the fight for every Union cavalryman. Confederate artillery opened fire, and house to house fighting ensued. Civilians shouted encouragement to the Rebel soldiers and brought them water to refill their canteens.[18]

The Union troopers were almost surrounded. Colonel George Cole, commander of the 2nd U.S. Colored Cavalry, ordered his men to stand their ground, and shot the Confederate commander from his horse. As the battle progressed, some of the men were fighting hand to hand.

When a group of black soldiers sought refuge in a nearby house, Confederate soldiers set the house on fire. Desperate, three Union troopers jumped from the flames, but were immediately cut down. Another three men stayed in the house, fought as long as they were able, and were burned to death.

Despite the overwhelming odds against them, Cole and most of his troops were able to fight their way clear of the town, escape from the angry Confederates, and make it back to their base at Camp Getty.

Lincoln Promotes Grant

On March 10, 1864, English Buffkin enlisted in Company H of the 54th U.S. Colored Infantry at Devall's Bluff, Arkansas. He was eighteen years old and had been a slave; he was married to Ann Buffkin, who lived in Little Rock. Private Buffkin had been born in Richmond, Virginia.[19]

In Knoxville, Tennessee that day, Thomas Washington enlisted in Battery D of the 1st U.S. Colored Heavy Artillery. Washington had also been born in Richmond and had been a slave.[20]

Charles Stopher enlisted in Company B of the 43rd U.S. Colored Infantry at Waterford, Pennsylvania. Stopher had been born in Richmond, but was free when he enlisted. He was hospitalized four times while in the service for chronic rheumatism but survived the war.[21]

On the same day these men enlisted, President Lincoln appointed Ulysses S. Grant as General-in-Chief of the United States Army.[22]

The war had been dragging on for nearly three years. Unlike most senior Union commanders, Grant had distinguished himself with a series of victories and had a reputation for aggressively pursuing the Rebels, battle after battle, constantly focused on depriving the enemy of the ability and will to fight.

Seeing little value in capturing cities and occupying enemy territory, Grant was determined to destroy the Confederate Army. When he took command, Grant coordinated the campaigns of Union armies operating in the field to support this strategic goal. His modern and comprehensive approach to fighting ultimately won the war. Both armies launched their spring campaigns as winter ended.

Fort Pillow – April 12, 1864

Tennessee was the last state to secede from the Union, joining the Confederacy only on June 8, 1861, nearly two months after the Civil War began with the Rebel attack on Fort Sumter. In February of that year, the state had voted to stay in the Union; when the state voted a second time in June, more than forty-four percent of the votes cast were against secession.[23] Many Tennesseans remained loyal to the United States, some even joining Union Army regiments that fought against the Confederacy.

Situated near the town of Henning, Tennessee, forty miles north of Memphis, Fort Pillow had been built by the Confederates in 1861 but abandoned by the Rebels in May 1862. United States forces then occupied the fort and used it as a base to secure a stretch of the Mississippi river north of Memphis.

Fort Pillow was of questionable value to either side. Situated on a high bluff, artillery in the fort could fire effectively at boat traffic over a long stretch of the river, but the surrounding terrain made the fort difficult to defend. Landward approaches to the east of the fort consisted of a series of ravines that could offer protection to attacking enemy forces, and nearby high knolls made troops occupying the fort vulnerable to enemy sharpshooters.

In 1864 Union Major General William Tecumseh Sherman had ordered his area commanders to abandon strategically insignificant positions like Fort Pillow, to free up men and officers for the upcoming campaign on Atlanta. Major General Stephen Hurlbut, for reasons that were never firmly established, sent troops to occupy the fort anyway. A regiment composed of Union men from Tennessee, the 13th Tennessee Cavalry, commanded by Major William F. Bradford, was ordered to Fort Pillow in February 1864. They were joined a few weeks later by detachments from the 6th U.S. Colored Heavy Artillery and the 2nd U.S. Colored Light Artillery. In March, Major Lionel F. Booth was dispatched by Hurlbut to take overall command of the 580 men garrisoned at the Fort.[24]

In May 1863 the Confederate Congress had passed a law stating that captured black Union soldiers were to be turned over to the state for trial and could face execution or a return to slavery.[25]

Major General Nathan Bedford Forrest, a former slave trader and Rebel cavalry leader, launched a raid through West Tennessee and Kentucky in March 1864 with more than 7,000 Confederates. In April, planning to capture horses and supplies, Forest ordered an attack on Fort Pillow by a force of about 1,500 Rebel troops led by Brigadier General James R. Chalmers. The Rebels left early on the morning of April 12, 1864 from Brownsville, Tennessee, thirty-eight miles away, and by 11:00 had surrounded the fort and captured two barracks buildings.

Sharpshooters deployed on the high ground nearby kept up a steady and deadly fire against the outnumbered defenders. A sharpshooter's bullet killed Major Booth, leaving Major Bradford in command. The parapets of the fort were so high, the artillerymen were unable to bring their guns to bear on the Confederate attackers in the ravines below.

At 3:30 in the afternoon, Forrest sent the following note: *"The conduct of the officers and men garrisoning Fort Pillow has been such as to entitle them to being treated as prisoners of war. I demand the unconditional surrender of the entire garrison, promising that you shall be treated as prisoners of war. My men have just received a fresh supply of ammunition, and from their present position can easily assault and capture the fort. Should my demand be refused, I cannot be responsible for the fate of your command."*[26]

Major Bradford replied, requesting an hour to respond. Believing Union reinforcements were close by, Forrest responded that he would only allow twenty minutes. When Bradford refused, Forrest ordered his troops to charge.

Sharpshooter fire was so heavy a Union gunboat on the river closed its gunports and stopped firing its cannons at the attackers.[27] Forrest's Confederates climbed the embankment around the fort, the first wave helping the second wave to climb up on their backs. The African American and Tennessean soldiers fought desperately, but after a few minutes the defenders broke and ran for the base of the bluff near the river.

What happened next was one of the most regrettable events in American history. Although many Union soldiers attempted to surrender, the frustrated Confederates continued to fire on the defenders, shouting *"No quarter!"*[28] Furious that many of the defenders were African American troops and others were loyal Tennesseans, the Rebels kept firing, until 231 were killed, 100 wounded, and 226 were captured or missing. Some Confederates insisted that they continued to fire in self-defense, as the Union soldiers continued firing as they withdrew, but the Rebels sustained relatively few casualties – only fourteen dead and eighty-six wounded.

A Confederate sergeant, in a letter to his sister two days after the battle, wrote: *"The slaughter was awful. Words cannot describe the scene. The poor deluded negros would run up to our men fall on their knees and with uplifted hands scream for mercy but they were ordered to their feet and then shot down. The whitte [sic] men fared but little better. The fort turned out to be a great slaughter pen. Blood, human blood stood about in pools and brains could have been gathered up in any quantity. I with several others tried to stop the butchery and at one time had partially succeeded but Gen. Forrest ordered them shot down like dogs and the carnage continued. Finally our men became sick of blood and the firing ceased."*[29]

After the war, Union Lieutenant Mack J. Leaming wrote a detailed eyewitness account of the battle, including the following statement: *"From where I fell wounded, I could plainly see this firing and note the bullets striking the water around the black heads of the soldiers, until suddenly the muddy current became red and I saw another life sacrificed in the cause of the Union. Here I noticed one soldier in the river, but in some way clinging to the bank. Two confederate soldiers pulled him out. He seemed to be wounded and crawled on his hands and knees. Finely one of the confederate soldiers placed his revolver to the head of the colored soldier and killed him."*[30]

Black and white Union soldiers were killed as they tried to surrender during the Battle of Fort Pillow in Tennessee. - *Image: Library of Congress*

Major General Nathan Bedford Forrest never acknowledged that he had given the order to take no prisoners, but whether or not he ordered the murders he failed to prevent the massacre.[31] Forrest's credibility is suspect. After the war the former slave trader became one of the first leaders of the Ku Klux Klan.

A few weeks after the battle of Fort Pillow, the U.S. Congressional Committee on the Conduct of the War collected testimony and depositions from more than fifty soldiers, officers, and civilians who survived the attack, as well as several doctors who treated many of the victims. The report of the committee, completed on May 5, 1864, records first hand testimony of black and white soldiers and officers being murdered after they surrendered, their bodies being mutilated, and soldiers being buried while they were still alive. Two black children who worked as servants for the fort's officers were murdered by the enraged Rebels. One white officer was nailed to the wooden floor of a building which was then set on fire, burning him alive.[32]

The murders at Fort Pillow were not the first atrocities Confederate soldiers committed against African American troops and white officers attempting to surrender and would not be the last. Rebel rage at armed black soldiers led to more inexcusable, unnecessary slaughter up to and beyond the end of the war. Fear and hatred between descendants of former slaveowners and descendants of former slaves continued to generate violence, resentment and division among Americans for decades to come.

Poison Springs – April 1864

In early 1864 the United States government was anxious to reestablish Union control over the western Confederate states of Texas, Louisiana, and Arkansas. A plan was developed in which forces under Major General Nathaniel Banks and Major General Frederick Steele could link up and attack the city of Shreveport, Louisiana. Steele's force could then build a Union garrison at Shreveport while Banks's force continued on to attack Rebel strongholds in Texas.[33]

96

Steele's force was based at Little Rock. Federal troops had taken the Arkansas capital on September 10, 1863, forcing the state government to move to a temporary capital at Washington, Arkansas. Steele planned to resupply at Camden, Arkansas, a port on the Ouachita River about halfway from Little Rock to Shreveport.

Steele set out with over 8,500 troops on March 23, 1864. As a diversionary attack, Colonel Powell Clayton conducted a cavalry raid to destroy a Rebel pontoon bridge at Longview, Arkansas. A detachment of Clayton's force captured more than 250 Confederates during the raid, then headed north towards Pine Bluff.

The Rebels decided to attack the Union force as it attempted to recross the Saline River at Mount Elba, Arkansas, but Powell's Federal cavalry successfully crossed the river and returned to Pine Bluff with their prisoners. Powell's casualties included two dead and eight missing.

When Confederate Major General Sterling Price learned of the Union activity in Arkansas, he ordered Brigadier John Marmaduke to attack the Federal column and prevent an attack on Washington.

Steele's force was attacked on April 3 at Elkin's Ferry as they attempted to cross the Little Missouri River, but the Union soldiers were able to drive away Marmaduke's smaller force and complete their crossing on April 4. Because of the delays caused by the attack, the Federals were forced to march on half rations.

The Union force was attacked on April 12 at Prairie D'Ane, a twenty-mile square of open prairie between Washington and Camden bordered by the Red River on the south, and again on April 13. Again they were able to drive away the Rebel attackers, but due to the repeated delays, they were forced to go on quarter rations as their supplies ran critically low.[34]

Reaching Camden on April 15 they encountered little resistance and were able to take the town, but were unable to resupply; the Confederates had taken most of the supplies with them when they evacuated. They also heard rumors from the citizens of Camden that Banks's force had been defeated.

Desperate to procure food for his men, on April 17 Steele sent a foraging party of nearly 1,200 men with 200 wagons to seize Rebels stores of corn they learned were located fifteen miles away. The foraging party was led by Colonel James Williams, commander of the 1st Kansas Colored Infantry Regiment. On April 18 the foragers had collected 5,000 bushels of corn and were headed back towards Camden when they found their way was blocked by a force of Marmaduke's Confederates at Poison Springs. The Rebel force consisted of over 3,600 soldiers from Missouri, Arkansas, Texas and a brigade of Choctaw Indians; the Federals were outnumbered three to one.

After shelling the Union troops with artillery for a half an hour, the Confederates began a series of attacks. By the third attack the Federals were running low on ammunition and Williams' horse had been shot from under him. During the third attack the 1st Kansas Colored Infantry troops were driven back through the wagon train, and some of the Rebels were observed killing wounded and surrendering Black soldiers in the chaos.

Williams decided to abandon the wagons and concentrate on saving his men. Confederates pursued them for about two miles but abandoned the chase when they thought Union reinforcements might be approaching.

The Confederates last 114 men killed, wounded or missing. The Union force suffered about twice as many casualties. In the 1st Kansas Colored Infantry, 117 men were killed and sixty-five were wounded. Rebels had been seen bayoneting wounded troops. The bodies of several black soldiers and white officers were desecrated. Some of the men had reportedly been scalped by men of the Choctaw regiment. The battle became known as the Massacre of Poison Springs.

A few days later, Steele's force received several wagonloads of supplies from Pine Bluff. Many of the wagons were driven by African American civilian teamsters, and the wagon train was guarded by a brigade of Union troops under the command of Lieutenant Colonel Francis Drake. The road over which they were travelling was muddy from recent rains. The wagon train stopped about 8 miles from Pine Bluff before crossing the Moro River the next morning.

On the morning of April 25 Drake's 1,800 troops and the civilian teamsters were attacked by over 8,000 Confederates commanded by Brigadier General James Fagen. Almost the entire Union column was killed, wounded, or captured. Additionally, the Rebels were reported to have killed as many as 100 Black civilian teamsters at the Battle of Marks Mills.[35]

As Steele's returning troops neared Little Rock, they planned to cross the Saline River at Jenkins Ferry.[36] The retreating Federals continued to be harassed by Rebel cavalry before they arrived at the river at 2:00 PM on April 29. The Saline was swollen by several days of heavy rain, so Steele's men needed to build a pontoon bridge to make the crossing. They completed the bridge and the Union cavalry crossed the river during the night. Early the next morning, the Confederates attacked before dawn. Visibility was limited by a thick fog hanging over the battlefield. Each side had roughly 10,000 men able to fight.

The Rebels were forced to attack on a narrow front in knee-deep mud, between a heavily wooded slope on one side and a swamp on the other. Union troops had quickly dug breastworks and set up barriers of sharpened sticks called abatis to further slow the enemy's advance. The difficulty of the approach and limited area to maneuver forced the Confederates to make piecemeal attacks. After repeated attempts to breach the Federal lines, the exhausted Rebels had suffered heavy casualties and several of their senior commanders had been wounded or killed. The remaining Confederates began to withdraw.

In past engagements, African American soldier's behavior towards Confederate prisoners had been restrained, but in this instance there were reports of soldiers from the 2nd Kansas Colored Infantry regiment bayonetting, shooting and cutting the throats of wounded Rebels on the battlefield, in retaliation for the murders of surrendering black soldiers and civilians at Poison Springs and Marks Mills.[37]

Steele's expedition had failed to accomplish his mission. His force had marched over 300 miles, much of it on short rations in cold, rainy weather, and suffered more than 2,500 casualties from multiple Rebel attacks. Shreveport's Confederate defenders refused to surrender to the Union until June 8, 1865, two months after Lee's surrender at Appomattox.

Substitutes

One of the most controversial provisions of the Enrollment Act of 1863 allowed drafted men to hire a substitute to take their place, or pay a commutation fee of $300 to the U.S. Government and avoid service. Hundreds of African American men, including many born in Virginia, were hired as substitutes all over the country by men wealthy enough to pay.[38]

James Henry Carter was born in New Kent County, Virginia in 1834. He enlisted in Company G of the 2nd U.S. Colored Infantry at Washington, D.C in August of 1863, as a substitute for Tracy Harris. Private Carter participated in actions at Clays Landing, Station Number 4, East Creek, Newfurt, and Natural Bridge, Florida during the first few months of 1865. He was discharged from Key West in January, 1866.[39]

Born in Fredericksburg, Peter Chisley enlisted in Company G of the 45th U.S.C.I. at Trenton, New Jersey in August of 1864.[40] He enrolled as a substitute for David Bainbridge. Peter Chisley was promoted to Corporal in September 1865 and be discharged that November with his regiment. Private Littleton Creath, born in Carroll County, Virginia, enlisted in Company E of the 23rd U.S.C.I. in Columbus, Ohio, as a substitute for Anthony W. Neal.[41] Creath survived the war. Born in Frederick County, Samuel Wallace enlisted in the 38th U.S.C.I. at Ellicott Mills, Maryland as a substitute for Benjamin H. Harris.[42] Wallace eventually earned a promotion to Sergeant, and survived the war.

James Saddler enlisted as a Private in Company D of the 8th U.S.C.I. at Columbus, Ohio on October 4, 1864, as a substitute for Robert M. Marshall of Jefferson County. Private Saddler had been born in Albemarle County, Virginia. He survived the war and was discharged with his regiment in Brownsville, Texas in November 1865.[43]

First Sergeant George Thompson of Company L, 2nd U.S. Colored Cavalry enlisted on February 2, 1865 in Lancaster, Pennsylvania as a substitute for George Nauman of Lancasters Northeast Ward. Thompson was born in Franklin County; surviving the war, he was discharged with his regiment from Brazos Santiago, Texas in February 1866.[44]

Private Carey Phillips of the 23rd U.S.C.I. was born in Lee County, Virginia. He enlisted in June 1864 at Greenfield, Massachusetts as a substitute for Albert S. Atkins of Southampton.[45]

Charles M. Ward enlisted in Company I of the 13th U.S.C.I. at Wabash in September, 1864, as a substitute for a drafted man from the 11th Congressional district of Indiana. Born in Pittsylvania County in 1832, Ward was a farmer.[46]

A bored copyist named "D.M. Kennedy" listed several soldiers who enlisted in Company I of the 39th U.S. Colored Infantry in Baltimore in July of 1864 as having been born in "Substitute, Virginia".

Private George Wilson was eighteen years old when he enlisted on July 9, 1864; he was only 5' 2 ¾" tall. He fought in the battles of Hatchers Run, Virginia, then at Sugar Loaf and Northeast Station in North Carolina, outside of Wilmington. Briefly hospitalized on March 16, 1865 for an unknown ailment, he enlisted as a substitute for a man named John T. Graham. Private Wilson survived the war and was discharged with his regiment at Wilmington, NC on December 4, 1865.[47]

Private Benjamin Allen, aged thirty-four, enlisted as a substitute for John H. James of the 3rd District in Maryland.[48] Private William Anderson, age nineteen, enrolled as a substitute for John Kermode of the 10th Ward in Northeast Baltimore.[49] While they were serving in Company I of the 39th, both were assigned to serve as cattle guards – and both were listed as having deserted on December 30, 1864 when ordered to return to their unit from that assignment.

Private William Ray enlisted on July 15 in Company I of the 39th, and was a substitute for a man named A. Brafmann and survived the war.[50]

Private Magnes Henderson was born in Amelia County. He enlisted in Company G of the 23rd U.S.C.I. on July 13, 1864 as a substitute for William Tucker. Henderson was wounded in action at the battle of the Crater in Petersburg just seventeen days later, but survived the war and was discharged at Brownsville, Texas on November 30, 1865.[51]

William Robinson of Augusta County enlisted in Company G of the 45th U.S.C.I. on August 1, 1864 as a substitute for E.P. Stewart, but died of disease on November 28.[52]

Born in Culpeper County, John Peck had been a slave in Prince George County. On July 29, 1864 he enlisted in Company K of the 28th U.S.C.I. at Ellicott Mills, Maryland, as a substitute for a man named John Meckle. John Peck was hospitalized at the Summit House Hospital in Philadelphia for laryngitis in August 1864 but survived the war and was discharged from Point Lookout, Virginia in June 1865.[53]

William Taylor enlisted as a Private in the 23rd U.S.C.I. at Washington D.C. in June 1864. Taylor had been born in Frederick County and enrolled as a substitute for John B. Warden. Private William Taylor fought in the Battle of the Crater and was discharged March 7, 1865 *by reason of amputation of left arm from gunshot wound received in action July 30th, 1864*.[54]

Corporal William Gordon, born in Rockingham County, Virginia, was serving in Company D of the 12th U.S.C.I. as a substitute when he was wounded in action at the Battle of Nashville in December 1864. Gordon survived the war.[55]

Joseph Marshall of Company H, 2nd U.S.C.I., died in the post hospital at Key West, Florida on March 26, 1864 of typhoid fever, and is buried in the military cemetery there. His personal effects were inventoried and turned over to his brother, Vincent; the Marshalls were born in

Spotsylvania County.   Joseph had enlisted from Washington on September 15, 1863 and was a substitute for Jonathan Ambler.[56]

Private John R. Green, born in Accomack County, was nineteen years old when he enlisted in Company K of the 23rd U.S. Colored Infantry at Greenfield, Massachusetts on June 3, 1864 as a substitute for John Clark of Hubbardston. Census records show a twenty-three-year-old shoemaker named John Clark living in Hubbardston in 1860. John Green was shot in the right lower jaw at the Battle of the Crater on July 30, 1864 and died of his wounds at L'Overture Hospital in Alexandria on September 21, 1864.[57]

Bermuda Hundred, Virginia - 1864

The town of Bermuda Hundred sits on a peninsula where the Appomattox River flows into the James. The area had been the site of several Indian villages in the past and was settled by English colonists from Jamestown as early as 1609. John Rolfe and his wife Pocahantas once lived on a plantation just across the James River to the north. The city of Hopewell lies across the Appomattox River to the south.

Bermuda Hundred was in a hotly contested battlefield during the Civil War. The Confederate capital city, Richmond, was fifteen miles away to the north. Petersburg, a critical Rebel supply hub, was only eight miles away to the south. The side that had control of Bermuda Hundred would have proximity to both of these strategic cities and a ready source of supplies that could be transported by boat up the James.

In the spring of 1864 Union General Grant planned to attack the Confederate Army of Northern Virginia near the city of Richmond. Grant, with Generals George G. Meade and Philip Sheridan, planned to attack from the north with over 100,000 Federal troops in a series of engagements that became known as the Overland Campaign.[58]

Grant ordered Major General Benjamin Butler, commander of the Union Army of the James, to attack towards Richmond from the southeast. Butler's primary objective was to cut the Richmond and Petersburg Railroad, reducing the flow of supplies to the Confederate capital and weakening Lee by forcing him to defend the railroad.

Grant ordered Butler to set up a Union supply base called City Point on a point of land that eventually became the town of Hopewell. Butler's headquarters and a Union Army hospital were located at Point of Rocks on the lower end of the peninsula. Surrounding Bermuda Hundred were landmarks with memorable names: Chaffins Bluff, Deep Bottom, and New Market Heights all became locations of hard-fought battles.

On May 5, 1864, Butler's 33,000 soldiers disembarked from transport boats at Bermuda Hundred. The next day Butler sent a brigade commanded by Brigadier General Charles Heckman to attack the railroad at Port Walthall Junction, seven miles due west of City Point. The attacking Federal brigade was repelled by Brigadier General Johnson Hagood's brigade of Confederates. On May 7, Butler sent a division commanded by Brigadier General William Brooks back to Port Walthall. The larger Union force was able to push back the Rebel brigade and damage some railroad track but was forced to withdraw. The Confederates were able to repair the minimal damage to the track.[59]

On May 9, Butler sent a force of 14,000 men and five U.S. Navy gunboats to attack towards Petersburg and destroy three bridges that crossed Swift Creek. A division of U.S. Colored Troops commanded by Brigadier General Edward Hincks was dispatched through the marshy wetland beside the river to attack the Rebel stronghold at Fort Clinton nearby. Two South Carolina regiments of Hagood's Confederates attacked the Union task force at Arrowfield Church, but the Federals were able to repel the Rebel onslaught with heavy fire.[60]

Butler had a bad habit of not following through when his troops had the advantage. His land forces had the upper hand against the Confederates, but Butler ordered his commanders to withdraw. The infantry attack on Fort Clinton was called off. The Union gunboats withdrew downriver when one of them, the *USS Brewster*, was sunk. Butler's task force had failed to destroy the bridges; Rebel communications between Richmond and Petersburg remained intact.

On May 10, Butler sent two divisions of troops to Chester Station, a stop on the Richmond and Petersburg Railroad, in another attempt to destroy the train tracks and cut the Rebel line of communication. The Union force was attacked by two brigades of Confederates. After hours of hard fighting, the outnumbered Rebels withdrew. Again, however, Federal commanders failed to follow up when they had the advantage, and the two Union divisions fell back to Bermuda Hundred.[61]

On May 12, Butler launched another land attack against the Confederate stronghold on the south side of the James at Drewry's Bluff, a ninety-foot cliff overlooking the river. The Union attack successfully turned back the Rebel right flank during an attack on May 13, but the overcautious Butler hesitated to drive home the advantage. Three days later, on May 16, a Confederate counterattack routed several of Butler's regiments and again he withdrew to Bermuda Hundred.[62]

Butler's force was spread out over several miles of the Bermuda Hundred peninsula. On May 20, a strong force of Confederates commanded by General P.G.T. Beauregard attacked Butler's advance pickets near Ware Bottom Church, about eight miles northwest of City Point. The Rebels inflicted 900 casualties on the Union troops, and suffered 600 casualties of their own. Butler's Union force was forced to fall back to safety. Beauregard's victorious Confederates were able to construct a line of defenses stretching from the James River to the Appomattox River that came to be known as the Howlett Line, and bottle up Butler's troops in the Bermuda Hundred peninsula. The five battles of the Bermuda Hundred Campaign ended in a Union defeat.[63]

Wilsons Wharf, Virginia – May 24, 1864

In preparation for an attack on the Confederate capital at Richmond, Grant ordered Butler to move his 33,000-man force close to the city, and to establish a Union supply base at City Point on the James River. On May 5, 1864, the bulk of Butler's Army of the James steamed upriver from Hampton Roads on a flotilla of 120 boats.

U.S. Colored Troops commanded by Brigadier General Edward A. Wild disembarked at Wilson's Wharf, a deepwater landing on the north shore of the James, fifteen miles from City Point. Wild's men were to build an outpost on high ground overlooking the wharf to help protect Federal shipments of troops and supplies on the river. Wild's landing force included the 1st and part of the 10th U.S. Colored Infantry regiments, and a few white troops from Battery M of the 3rd New York Light Artillery. The *USS Dawn*, a naval gunboat, provided additional support from the river.[64]

Edward Wild had already led an adventure-filled life.[65] Born in Massachusetts, he earned a medical degree from Harvard and studied homeopathic medicine in Philadelphia and Paris. During the Crimean War between Russia and the Ottoman Empire, Wild travelled to Turkey, and served as a medical officer in the Ottoman Army for a year before returning to Massachusetts. Wild was a committed abolitionist, firmly opposed to the institution of slavery. When the Civil War started, he joined the Union Army and became an infantry company commander. He fought in several engagements early in the war and was wounded at the Battle of Seven Pines. He was promoted to Colonel and commanded an infantry regiment at the Battle of South Mountain in September, 1862 where he was wounded so severely that his left arm had to be amputated.

When Wild recovered and returned to duty in 1863, he was promoted to Brigadier General and assigned duty as a recruiter. He was instrumental in helping recruit black troops and white officers for several U.S. Colored Troop units. Many of the African American soldiers he helped to liberate and recruit in North Carolina became members of the "African Brigade" that Wild later commanded.

Wild and his African Brigade developed a fearsome reputation. Once they captured a Rebel plantation owner who had recently whipped some of his female slaves. Wild's men tied the man up, stripped him, and allowed the beaten women to whip their former master. Wild was later court-martialed for exceeding his authority in punishing the civilian but was exonerated.

The men of the African Brigade worked hard over the next weeks, digging trenches and raising earthen walls, embedding sharpened sticks around the fort to form abatis, and positioning their cannons to provide effective artillery coverage. The Fort Pocahontas garrison in late

May consisted of 1,100 soldiers. Most were former slaves.

Rebels were alarmed at the presence of a strong outpost of armed black soldiers in such close proximity to Richmond. Confederate General Braxton Bragg ordered Major General Fitzhugh Lee's cavalry to *"surprise and capture if possible a garrison of Negro soldiers"*[66] at Wilson's Wharf. Fitzhugh Lee was the nephew of Robert E. Lee. The ambitious young general hoped to succeed General J.E.B. Stuart, who had recently been killed in combat, as senior commander of the Confederate cavalry. Rebel scouts had determined that only a third of the defenses around the fort were complete.

Lee's cavalry force included two brigades from Virginia, one brigade from North Carolina, and one regiment from South Carolina. The 2,600 troopers were accompanied by a single gun from a horse artillery battery. The Confederates rode all night from Atlee's Station, almost thirty miles away, and arrived at Fort Pocahontas around 11:00 AM on May 24.

A Confederate charge around noon drove in Wild's pickets. Lee sent a message to the fort offering to treat the black soldiers as prisoners of war if they surrendered, adding that he would not be answerable for the consequences if they did not. Wild and his men, aware of the massacre of black soldiers and white officers at Fort Pillow six weeks earlier, had no intention of surrendering. Wild sent a message back that said *"Present my compliments to General Fitz Lee and tell him to go to hell. Take the fort if you can."*[67]

Lee's enraged Rebels attacked from two directions. Some of his men got within thirty feet of the fort but were repelled by heavy rifle and artillery fire from the fort and from the *USS Dawn*. Repeated probes by the Confederate troopers were unsuccessful. Around 4:00

PM four more companies of the 10th U.S. Colored Infantry arrived to reinforce the Union defenders of Fort Pocahontas, and the defeated Confederates were forced to withdraw.[68]

Embarrassed at being beaten by a predominantly African American force, Lee overstated the number of Union troops and understated the number of Rebels. The U.S. troops lost six killed and forty wounded. The Confederates suffered a total of 200 killed and wounded. The Battle of Fort Pocahontas resulted in a Union victory.

7. NO POWER ON EARTH

A soldier was required to state his occupation when he enlisted. Depending on the demand, soldiers with skills might be given special duty assignments.

Private Joseph Diggs[1] of James City County and Corporal Mechlin Smith[2] of Surry County had both worked as carpenters before enlisting at Yorktown. Both served in Company G of the 36th U.S. Colored Infantry. In early 1864, Diggs and Smith were assigned to work on building a regimental hospital for the 36th.

The primary function of a musician was not to boost morale or provide entertainment but to communicate orders in the noisy environment of the battlefield. Men who were young or small in stature were frequently assigned to serve as musicians. Zachariah Taylor[3] of Lee County, Virginia was fourteen years old when he enlisted in Company I of the 36th U.S. Colored Infantry at Hampton in September of 1863. At 4' 10 ½" tall, Taylor had been a waiter before joining the Army. Private Henry Washington of Spotsylvania County was sixteen years old and 5' 2" tall when he joined Company I of the 29th U.S.C.I. at Madison, Wisconsin in September of 1864; he had been a musician by trade before he enlisted.[4] Private Alfred Wallack of Company I of the 19th U.S.C.I. was twenty-one years old, but only 4' 10" tall when he enlisted; Wallack was assigned to daily duty as a drummer.[5] Bugler George Jones of James City County served in Troop A of the 1st U.S. Colored Cavalry, enlisting when he was twenty years old. At 5' 6 ½" tall, Jones was of average height.[6]

Skilled blacksmiths tended to be older and were always in demand. Born in Franklin County, Private Edmund West was thirty-five years old when he enlisted in Company G of the 52nd U.S.C.I. at Vicksburg,

Mississippi in late 1864 and was appointed as regimental blacksmith.[7]   Sergeant Oscar Terry was born in Lunenburg County, had worked as a blacksmith, and was thirty-one years old when he enlisted in Company B of the 2nd Regiment Mississippi Infantry (African Descent), which was later redesignated as the 52nd U.S. Colored Infantry.[8] At forty-two years old, Private Carry Malone of Battery K, 3rd U.S. Colored Heavy Artillery, may have been unable to practice his skills as a blacksmith due to age and infirmity; he was appointed to serve as the company cook.[9] Malone had been born in Prince Edward County, Virginia and joined the Army at Fort Pickering, Tennessee in November of 1863. Private Willis Moore, born in Surry County, served in Company E of the 1st U.S. Colored Cavalry.[10] Moore was forty-one years old when he enlisted at Fort Powhatan in 1864 and listed blacksmith as his occupation; men who could shoe horses were especially valued in a cavalry regiment. In Company C of the 1st U.S. Cavalry, Private John Baily of Accomack County was on duty as their farrier, a type of blacksmith that specializes in shoeing horses.[11]

Not all skills were in demand. George Carter, born in New Kent County, Virginia, had been a railroad brakeman when he enlisted at Norfolk in late 1863.[12] He was put to work guarding cattle. John Edward Pine, a free person of color living in Accomack County, had been a chimney sweep as a civilian; he was assigned to help dig the Dutch Gap Canal on the James River in 1864.[13] Private Calvin Cooper[14] and Sergeant Richard Stamps[15] were born in Pittsylvania County, and were listed as painters. Thomas Kinney, born in Augusta County, gave his occupation as plasterer; Kinney was appointed to duty as a quartermaster sergeant for the 44th U.S.C.I.[16]

112

Private Jorden Roberts enlisted in Company G of the 52nd U.S.C.I. at Vicksburg, Mississippi in February 1864 and served until May of 1866.[17]

Private Grayson Jones of Company J, 27th U.S. Colored Infantry was forty-four years old when he enlisted and had worked as a cooper in civilian life.[18] As a skilled tradesman and a free man living in Ohio, Jones had been educated to the extent that he was able to sign his own name on his enlistment papers. Jones had been born in Bedford County. Another man born in Bedford County, also a cooper by trade, Corporal Payton Wilkes served in Battery B of the 9th U.S. Colored Heavy Artillery.[19] Wilkes enlisted from Pomeroy, Ohio.

Private Edward Arrington gave his occupation as 'engineer', and likely had skills that were in high demand during his time at Nashville with Company F of the 17th U.S. Colored Infantry.[20] Many African American soldiers stationed in Nashville were assigned to "fatigue duty," helping build fortifications and railroad lines around the city. Arrington had been born in Franklin County.

Aaron Callaway, born in Bedford County, gave his occupation as 'furnace stoker.'[21] Other soldiers were rope makers, miners, lumbermen, machinist, and millwrights.

At least five men born in Accomack County serving in Company D of the 10th U.S. Colored Infantry identified themselves as 'oystermen'. Some had lived on Chincoteague Island, where they enlisted. Eleven men from Accomack County served in Company I of the same regiment and had identified themselves as 'sailors'. William Elliott, born in Surry County and serving in the 1st U.S. Colored Cavalry, identified himself as a 'waterman'.[22]

Born in Winchester, Virginia, two waiters enlisted in the U.S. Navy from New York City in 1863. Landsman Edward C. Grant served on the *USS Mount Vernon*[23];

Landsman George H. Smith served on the *USS Fort Jackson*.[24] Waiter was a frequently listed occupation.

Private Thomas Gaskins, born in Augusta County, gave his occupation as 'weaver'.[25] Sergeant Josephus Miller from Lee County gave his occupation as 'wheelwright'.[26] Private Dawson Wright, born in Franklin County, identified himself as a 'coal digger'.[27] Private Stephen Cox, born in Amelia County, gave his occupation as 'field hand' when he enlisted in the 3rd U.S. Colored Cavalry at Haines Bluff, Mississippi in February 1864.[28] Corporal Joseph Anderson, also in the 3rd U.S. Cavalry, gave his occupation as 'gardener'.[29]

The most common occupation listed for U.S. Colored soldiers is 'farmer'; the second most common is 'laborer'. Farmers and laborers were born in all parts of Virginia, worked all over the states, and served in every U.S.C.T. regiment. Many had been slaves, but some had been free before the war.

The Crater – July 30, 1864

Located near the Appomattox and James Rivers and at the junction of five railroads, Petersburg, Virginia was an important supply and communications hub for the Confederacy, just twenty-six miles from Richmond. Union forces reached the vicinity of Petersburg in early June 1864 and launched several inconclusive attacks in the area over the next two months. General Grant recognized that the fall of Petersburg would weaken the Confederacy and open the way for an attack on the Rebel capitol. However, many of Grant's subordinate generals were political appointees, not professional soldiers, and failed on several occasions to follow up on strategic advantages gained on the battlefield. By mid-July, Union commanders were desperate to break the stalemate outside the heavily defended city.[30]

Lt. Colonel Henry Pleasants, a former coal mining engineer commanding the 48th Pennsylvania Infantry regiment, suggested secretly digging a tunnel directly under a Confederate strongpoint, filling it with explosives, and blowing a gap in the Rebel lines through which Union forces could advance. Grant and other generals had reservations about whether or not the plan was feasible, but allowed work on the mine to begin, assigning Major General Ambrose Burnside to command the attack. By late July, Pleasants and his men had secretly dug a 511-foot tunnel, and placed four tons of gunpowder in a T-shaped chamber under the Rebel entrenchments.

Burnside had assigned the 4th Division of United States Colored Troops, commanded by Major General Edward Ferrero, to lead the attack. Ferrero may have been one of the least capable general officers in either Army during the Civil War. Prior to the war, he had been a dance instructor, and he was known to have a drinking problem. Officers of the eight USCT regiments that made up the 4th Division trained their men for the assault, ordering them to attack around the rim of the crater created by the explosion.

Days before the battle, however, Major General George Meade ordered Burnside to pick a white division to lead the attack. After the war, Meade testified that he made this decision because the white units were more experienced, not because he lacked faith in the African-American troops. Burnside, petulant at having his orders overridden, decided to have white unit commanders draw straws to determine the unit that was to lead the assault. Brigadier James H. Ledlie drew the short straw. It would have been difficult to pick a more ill-suited leader for such a vital mission. Ledlie's division was weak and undermanned, and during his one prior combat experience at Cold Harbor a few weeks before, he had run for cover instead of leading his men during the battle. Ledlie did not brief his officers before the attack, and his troops were untrained. The result was a tragedy.

At 4:44 AM on July 30, 1864, the fuse was lit to ignite the mine, detonating an explosion that threw dirt, debris and bodies 100 feet into the air and created a crater 200 feet long, sixty feet wide, and thirty feet deep. A Union soldier said *"The earth trembled under our feet and an enormous mass sprang into the air."* Ledlie's unprepared soldiers waited at least ten minutes before beginning their charge. They stopped when they reached the edge, then many climbed down into the crater instead of fanning out to the left and right sides to continue the assault. The surprised Rebels soon recovered and began returning fire. Before the assault, many soldiers in the U.S. Colored Troop Regiments were heard shouting, *"Remember Fort Pillow!"* referring to the massacre of over a hundred black troops by Rebel General Nathan Bedford Forrest's men in a battle that had occurred two months earlier.

The Union commanders responsible for leading the attack, Ferrero and Ledlie, remained behind the lines in a bunker, sharing a bottle of rum, while their superior officer, Burnside, remained in his headquarters. Recognizing that the assault had failed, Grant sent an order to Burnside to end the attack. Still believing the battle could be won, Burnside ignored Grant's order and commanded Ferrero's United States Colored Troops to attack.

In the confusion of battle and lacking proper leadership, the African American regiments charged with the white soldiers into the crater, then were unable to climb out when they tried to withdraw. Confederate forces led by Brigadier General William Mahone, who had moved forward from a position two and a half miles away when they heard the explosion, mounted a determined counterattack, firing artillery and rifles into and around the pit.

A number of black soldiers were murdered when they tried to surrender, and others were killed after they were disarmed and led to the rear as prisoners of war.[31] Mahone tried to stop the atrocities, but it was some time before he could regain control of his men. The Battle of the Crater was a disaster for both sides, but resulted in a Confederate victory. More than 500 Union soldiers were killed, 1,800 wounded, and 1,400 captured in the failed attack. The Confederates lost 361 killed, 727 wounded, and 403 missing or captured.

Mahone later expressed remorse over the killings. After the war he campaigned in Virginia for African American education and voting rights, led the "Readjusters", and served a term in the U.S. Senate from 1881 to 1887.[32]

Burnside, Ferrero and Ledlie were removed from their commands but were otherwise lightly punished, due to their political connections.

Grant later described the Battle of the Crater as *the saddest affair I have witnessed in this war.*[33] The July 30 attack on Petersburg resulted in a Union defeat. Hancock's infantry and Sheridan's cavalry withdrew back across the pontoon bridge at Deep Bottom on July 31.

Fathers and Sons

Robert (Bob) Stokes[34] and Enos Stokes[35] both enlisted in Battery B of the 13th U.S. Colored Heavy Artillery at Smithland, Kentucky on January 18, 1865, and both were discharged from the same place on November 18, 1865. Bob was forty-two years old, Enos was nineteen. The

Stokes may or may not have been father and son; it was not uncommon for fathers and sons to enlist together. The Stokes were both born in Franklin County, Virginia.

George Polson was forty-five years old when he enlisted in Battery B of the 2nd U.S. Colored Light Artillery Regiment at Camp Hamilton on January 28, 1864.[36] William Polson, twenty-two years old, was likely his son and enlisted in the same unit on the same date.[37] Both were 5' 8" tall; their descriptions were identical.

William Polson served out his full enlistment and was discharged from Brownsville, Texas with the regiment on March 17, 1866. George, however, was discharged October 29, 1865 from Ringgold Barracks in Texas for chronic rheumatism after several hospitalizations. George's wife was named Wealthy Polson. The Polsons lived in Onancock on the Eastern Shore of Virginia.

William[38] and Samuel Jubilee[39], also from the Eastern Shore, appear to have been father and son. They enlisted within a few days of each other in Company I of the 2nd U.S. Colored Cavalry Regiment. William was forty-four years old, Samuel was twenty-six. Samuel served his entire enlistment, mustering out with his regiment from Brazos Santiago, Texas on February 12, 1866. Samuel was allowed to purchase his service revolver for $20.00 when he was discharged, but died in the hospital at New Orleans of pneumonia on October 26, 1865.

First Battle of Deep Bottom – July 27-31, 1864

In 1864, General Ulysses S. Grant planned a massive assault against the city of Petersburg, Virginia. Railroads leading to Petersburg carried troops, ammunition and rations into Virginia from sources throughout the South. Controlling Petersburg would allow Union forces to choke off the flow of supplies to the Rebel army defending the Confederate capital at Richmond.

Defensive fortifications around Petersburg and Richmond included more than thirty miles of trenches, hundreds of cannons, and thousands of Confederate soldiers.

In preparation for the planned July attack on Petersburg, Grant needed to draw more Confederate soldiers away from the city. He ordered Major General Winfield Scott Hancock and Major General Philip Sheridan to lead an attack towards Richmond, twenty-five miles away.[40] Grant hoped the Federal attack would compel General P.G.T. Beauregard, commander of the Rebel force defending Petersburg, to dispatch some of his men to reinforce the Confederate capital.

Southeast of Richmond, the James River meanders through Henrico County, in a tortuous series of bends. At one of these river bends, Jones Neck, the river is only about 400 feet wide. Bailey Creek empties into the river from the north in an area called Deep Bottom. In June, Union engineers had managed to tie twenty-five boats together under cover of night to build a bridge across the river, without alerting the Confederate pickets nearby. The pontoon bridge at Deep Bottom was to be controlled and maintained by the Federals for the rest of the war.

Grant ordered Hancock, leading the Army of the Potomac's II Corps, and Sheridan, leading two divisions of cavalry, to cross the James at Deep Bottom. Hancock's troops were to attack the Rebels at Chaffin's Bluff, three miles west of the river crossing, and keep the Confederates pinned down while Sheridan's cavalry galloped towards Richmond.

The Union force crossed the pontoon bridge at 3:00 AM on July 27. The three divisions of II Corps overran Rebel positions guarding the New Market Road that led to Richmond and deployed along the east side of Bailey's

Creek. Union cavalry was able to capture high ground near Fussell's Mill, northeast of Deep Bottom, but were unable to hold off a Confederate counterattack. Rebels on the west side of Bailey's Creek blocked further Federal progress towards Richmond. In the meantime, Confederate General Robert E. Lee shifted troops from Petersburg and elsewhere to bolster the defenses of Richmond, as Grant had expected.[41]

On the morning of July 28 Union forces were unsuccessful in a joint attack on the Confederate left flank, and the Rebels counterattacked. Some of Sheridan's troops dismounted and fired from prone positions at the attacking Rebels. The remaining mounted cavalry chased the enemy away from the Federal positions on the high ground and took almost 200 Confederate prisoners.

Union forces were unable to achieve all their objectives during the First Battle of Deep Bottom, but were successful in drawing Confederate forces away from Petersburg before the attack planned for July 30. Union forces suffered sixty-two killed, 340 wounded, and eighty-six soldiers missing or captured. Confederate forces lost eighty killed, 391 wounded, and 208 missing or captured.

Second Battle of Deep Bottom - August 14-20, 1864

In early August 1864, General Robert E. Lee dispatched two divisions, one of infantry and one of cavalry, to Culpeper, north of Richmond. From there the two divisions could reinforce Lt. General Jubal Early's forces operating in the Shenandoah Valley or support the defense of the Confederate capitol at Richmond as needed.

Believing that a larger element of the enemy had been withdrawn from Richmond, Grant planned another

Union pontoon bridge across the James River at Deep Bottom. A U.S. Colored Troop soldier stands guard in the foreground. - *Photo: Library of Congress*

Today, there is a boat ramp at Deep Bottom Park where the pontoon bridge once crossed the James River. - *Photo by the Author*

attack on the city for late August. Major General Winfield Scott Hancock would again be in command. On the 13th, Union Major General David Birney's X Corps crossed the James River at Deep Bottom, along with a cavalry division commanded by Brigadier General David Gregg and a detachment of artillery from Hancock's II Corps. That night and the next day, the rest of Hancock's force steamed upriver and disembarked near Deep Bottom.[42]

On August 14 Birney's X Corps deployed on the Union left, Hancock's 3rd Division commanded by Brigadier General Gershom Mott in the center, and Hancock's 1st and 2nd Divisions commanded by Brigadier General Francis Barlow deployed on the right. Birney was to attack from the south towards New Market Heights. Mott's division was to attack along the New Market Road, and Barlow's two divisions were to attack along the Darbytown Road towards Richmond. Gregg's cavalry was to circle wide around the Union right, then turn northwest and attack towards the city.

The heat and humidity were oppressive. Men from both sides collapsed, and many died, from heatstroke. Hard fighting during the day resulted in limited Union successes. The Federals encountered more Rebel resistance than they expected to find, and they became bogged down in the heavily wooded terrain. That night, Hancock ordered Birney's X Corps to move to the opposite end of the Union lines. Even though it was raining, a third of Birney's soldiers fell out from the heat during the march.

A brigade of Black soldiers commanded by Brigadier General William Birney took up positions near Fussell's Mill. The USCT brigade included the 29th Connecticut along with the 6th, 7th, and 8th United States Colored Infantry regiments.

Birney's X Corps was unable to reach Fussell's Mill until the afternoon of August 15 because of the difficult terrain. They were unable to attack that day.

Gregg's cavalry attacked along the Charles City Road northwest to Richmond on the morning of August 16, but after fighting all day they were pushed back to Fisher's Farm, five miles northeast of the crossing at Deep Bottom. At the same time a division from X Corps was able to break through the Confederate line but were repulsed by a Rebel counterattack.

A truce was called on August 17 while soldiers from both sides retrieved their dead and wounded. By August 18 Confederate resistance had weakened, but the Union attack had run out of momentum. On the night of August 20, Hancock's forces withdrew back across the James River.

The Union loss at the Second Battle of Deep Bottom was costly. Union casualties included 327 killed, 1,851 wounded, and 721 soldiers missing or captured. Confederate losses included 200 killed, 900 wounded, and 400 missing or captured. The Federal attack accomplished little other than preventing Lee from adequately reinforcing Early's forces in the Shenandoah Valley.

The pontoon bridge at Deep Bottom continued to be a vital strategic crossing for the remainder of the war.

Athens – September 23-25, 1864

In late 1864, soldiers from the 106th U.S. Colored Infantry Regiment were among those dispatched to Athens, Alabama to defend the town and a nearby railroad bridge from an anticipated Confederate attack.[43]

In September, 3,500 Confederate troops commanded by Major General Nathan Bedford Forrest moved towards Athens in an effort to cut the railroad line and disrupt the flow of troops and supplies supporting General William Tecumseh Sherman's march through Georgia.

On September 23, 1864 Forrest attacked, forcing the Union troops commanded by Colonel Wallace Campbell to retreat to Fort Henderson, just outside the town.

The morning of the 24th the Confederates began shelling Fort Henderson with artillery. During a personal meeting under a flag of truce, Forrest convinced Campbell that there were more than 8,000 Rebels ready to storm the fort. Believing his force was hopelessly outnumbered, Campbell surrendered to Forrest around noon.

On September 25, Forrest's Confederates attacked Union troops guarding the Sulphur Creek Trestle, a railroad bridge across the Tennessee River a few miles Athens. The Union position guarding the railroad trestle consisted of an earthen fort and two strong blockhouses. Surrounded by ravines, the position was difficult for Rebel infantry to storm. However, the fort was constructed at a lower elevation than the surrounding hilltops, where Forrest set up his artillery. The gunners had an unobstructed view of the inside of the fort.

Rebel guns lobbed shells down into the fort, killing more than 200 of the defenders in two hours, including the Union commander, Colonel William Hopkins Lathrop. The remaining 800 troops guarding the trestle were surrendered by Colonel George Spalding.

White Union soldiers taken prisoner in these engagements were sent to Castle Morgan, also known as Cahaba Federal Prison, near Selma, but Black prisoners were sent to Mobile, Alabama to provide slave labor, building up Confederate earthworks around the port city.

Lewis Gill was born in Franklin County, Virginia in 1835 to Abe and Jane Gill.[44] He had two sisters, Sarah and

Ann Matilda, and a brother, David Gill. By August 19, 1864 he was in Pulaski, Tennessee, where he joined Company B of the 106th United States Colored Infantry as a Private and was assigned to guard duty along the Nashville and Decatur railroad line. He was likely recruited from a 'contraband camp' that had been set up in Pulaski for slaves that had been freed by the Union Army. Just over a month after Private Gill joined the army, his regiment was forced to surrender in the fighting near Athens, Alabama.

Gill, who had escaped from slavery and served a little more than a month in the Union army, was once again a slave, taken prisoner by Forrest's victorious Rebels. The prisoners remained at Mobile in captivity until the Confederates surrendered on April 9, 1865.

Gill rejoined his unit after the Confederate surrender. On November 7, 1865, the 106th USCT consolidated with the 40th Regiment, US Colored Troops. Gill was assigned to Company G and promoted to Corporal that same day. On January 11, 1866, Lewis Gill was promoted to Sergeant, and mustered out of the Union Army with the rest of his regiment on April 25, 1866.[45]

Sergeant Lewis Gill would make a new home with his wife Lethe and daughters Mary Jane and Caledonia in Madison, Alabama after the war, only twenty-one miles from where he had been captured. When he registered to vote in Madison in 1867, Gill owned twenty-three acres of land, several mules, and raised corn on his farm. He had a bank account in Morgan, Alabama.

Sometime after 1870 the Gills had moved to Chickasaw, Mississippi. By the time of the 1900 Census Gill and Lethe had another daughter, Ann Eliza, and had moved to Tunica, Mississippi. In 1910 the Gills were living in Coahoma, Mississippi and had a grandson, Lewis Gill Jr., twelve years old.

Sergeant Lewis Gill died December 12, 1910, having lived seventy-five years. Lethe Gill filed for a widow's pension that year, and died in Coahoma in 1915.[46] During his life, Lewis Gill had twice been a slave and twice been a soldier.

While they were involved in battles all over the South, the fighting around Petersburg would continue to involve U.S. Colored Troops until the very last days of the war.

New Market Heights – September 28-30, 1864

In the late spring of 1864 Petersburg was still under siege by Union troops. Union General Grant attempted to attack the Confederate capital of Richmond from the north while diversionary attacks were being conducted by General Benjamin Butler and the Army of the James from the south. Repeated attempts by Butler's troops to cut the rail line from Petersburg to Richmond had failed. The Confederate Army of Northern Virginia was spread thin as General Robert E. Lee ordered troops back and forth in an effort to defend both cities. Grant continued to probe for a weakness, hoping by his attacks towards Richmond to provoke a pitched battle with Lee's outnumbered Rebel forces.

The Confederates had set up strong defenses all along the James River south of Richmond. Butler hoped to secure more Rebel territory upriver from the Bermuda Hundred peninsula his troops had occupied in the spring. At a bend in the river around Farrar's Island, the Rebels had scuttled a number of ships to block the approach Union gunboats. Three heavy artillery batteries guarded the river on the west bank of the bend. The channel was heavily mined with underwater explosives. To sail upriver around Farrar's Island, Union

126

boats had to navigate these obstacles under heavy fire for more than five miles.

However, the "neck" of the river bend, at a point called Dutch Gap, was less than 200 yards across. Butler's engineers determined that a navigable canal could be dug across Dutch Gap, that could allow Union gunboats to sail upriver while completely bypassing the dangerous five miles of water around Farrar's Island. In mid-August 1864 Butler ordered construction on the canal to begin. The work was to be performed by soldiers from U.S. Colored Troop units of the Army of the James.[47]

U.S. Colored Troops working on the Dutch Gap Canal. - *Photo: Library of Congress*

Grant planned another offensive against the Confederates in the fall of 1864. The southern end of the Richmond defensive line was located west of a farm belonging to the Chaffin family. This time, a Union corps attacking from the south was to cross the James River on pontoon bridges and attack fortified Rebel positions east of Chaffins Farm. Another corps was to attack the Rebel defenses at Fort Harrison, Fort Gregg and Fort Gilmer, a few miles to the west. A Federal cavalry division would cross the river at the same time and attack towards Richmond.[48]

The men were to travel light. Grant's orders to Butler included these instructions on what the men were to carry: *"They will take only a single blanket rolled and carried over the shoulders, three days rations in haversacks and sixty rounds of ammunition in box and on the person. No wagons will be taken. They will be supplied, however, with six days rations, half forage for the same time, and forty rounds of extra ammunition for men, to follow if they should be required. No wagons will cross the James River till ordered by you."*[49]

Brigadier General William Birney's X Corps was to cross the James at the Deep Bottom pontoon bridge and lead the attack against fortified positions at New Market Heights a little over a mile away. The high ground across the New Market Road was held by over 1,800 Rebel soldiers in four regiments of infantry, one of cavalry and battery of artillery.

The Confederates had prepared slashes – trees cut down with the limbs facing the enemy – and abatis to slow the expected Union advance. Cannon of the Rebel 1st Rockbridge Artillery were able to fire shells over the marshy ground where the Federals were to approach. Butler shifted U.S.C.T. soldiers from the Dutch Gap Canal excavation as he gathered his forces for the upcoming battle.

On the night of September 28, 1864 Major General Edward Ord's engineers built another pontoon bridge at Aiken's Landing, about two miles upriver from Deep Bottom. The new bridge took sixty-seven pontoons and was in place by 2:00 AM. The platform on the bridge was covered with dirt and straw to muffle the sound of marching troops. Ord's men crossed the bridge by 4:30 AM.

On September 29, 1864 the fields between Deep Bottom and the New Market Heights Road were covered with a thick fog. Before the assault soldiers were ordered to remove the priming caps from their weapons and fix bayonets; their officers intended for them to reach the Rebel lines before firing their rifles.

At 5:30 A.M., the Union attack began when Union Colonel Samuel Duncan led the 4th and 6th U.S. Colored Infantry regiments in the first assault on the Confederate positions.[50] The Confederates held their fire until the Union soldiers reached the first of two lines of obstacles arranged on the South side of the New Market Road, then opened with a withering mix of rifle and artillery fire. The initial Union assault was repulsed with 387 casualties.

At 7:30 AM, two hours after the first attack, the fog had been burned away by the rising sun, and the 5th, 36th, and 38th U.S. Colored Infantry Regiments led by Colonel Alonzo Draper attempted a second charge. The 22nd U.S. Colored Infantry was to advance on their left. Despite being bogged down for a half hour by the obstacles and heavy Rebel fire, the second assault was successful, and Union troops were able to take control of the positions along the New Market Road when the Confederates withdrew, having received orders to support their comrades defending Fort Harrison.

The attack against Fort Harrison began at the same time as the first attack on New Market Heights. Fort Harrison's earthen walls were eighteen feet high, reinforced with logs on the inside, and partially surrounded by a dry moat. Four operable cannon and 200 Rebel troops commanded by Major Richard Cornelius Taylor defended the fort. Notably, the field to the east of the stronghold, where the attacking Federals were expected to approach, was clear of obstacles. There were no barriers to slow down an enemy advance. Taylors men were also critically low on ammunition.

Ord's two divisions of 2,500 Union soldiers marched up the Varina Road from the pontoon bridge at Aiken's Landing, and encountered the Confederate pickets just east of Fort Harrison. U.S. soldiers were ordered to remove the percussion caps from their rifles until they reached the fort. Learning of the attack, Lee dispatched reinforcements, but they did not arrive until late in the day. The few Rebel reinforcements that arrived from New Market Heights could not save the fort from the overwhelming Federal onslaught.

The Union attackers climbed the walls of the fort, so close that men on both sides got powder burns from enemy rifle fire. Hand to hand fighting ensued, but by mid-morning, Ord's superior numbers were able to take control of Fort Harrison.[51]

Brigadier General William Birney, brother of the Corps commander, led his brigade of Colored Troops towards Richmond. When they reached the intersection of the New Market Road and Varina Road, they were stopped by fire from a Confederate artillery battery stationed at Laurel Hill Church. As they attacked the battery, they began drawing fire from two cannons stationed at Fort Gilmer, about a mile away. Two Federal attacks on the strong Rebel position had already failed when Birney ordered an attack by Companies C, D, G and K of the 7th U.S. Colored Infantry. Birney was later criticized for assuming a smaller force could capture Fort Gilmer when assaults by a larger force had failed.

The attack by the men of the 7th U.S. Colored Infantry began at 3:00 PM. They were under heavy artillery fire from two directions. As they charged, many tumbled into the twenty-seven-foot ditch in front of the fort, then helped each other climb up to the base of the parapet. The Confederates fired from point blank range, hurling grenades and lighted artillery shells into the attacking federals. Of the 120 men who made it into the moat, all were killed, wounded, or captured but one. Fighting at Fort Gilmer was over by nightfall. The Federals also failed to capture Rebel strongpoints at Fort Gregg, Fort Johnson and Fort Hoke.[52]

Fort Gilmer was one of the Confederate fortifications near New Market Heights. To prevent Union troops from tunneling under the walls, the Rebels constructed this 27-foot ditch in front of the fort. During the battle, Rebel soldiers lit artillery shells and rolled them down into the ditch as Union troops attacked. - *Photo: Library of Congress*

The next day, the Confederates counterattacked at Fort Harrison, but were repulsed with heavy casualties. The Union attacks, initially successful, were stalled just seven miles from Richmond. Federal troops kept possession of Fort Harrison until the end of the war.

One of the organizers of the Union X Corps Hospital at Jones Neck was a nurse named Clara Barton, who eventually became the founder of the American Red Cross. Many of the soldiers wounded at New Market Heights were treated there.[53]

Sixteen Union soldiers were eventually awarded the Medal of Honor for their heroism during the Battle of New Market Heights; fourteen were U.S. Colored Troops, and two were white officers.

Proud of his men and awed by their courage, Butler felt that more should have been decorated for their valor. At his own expense, the general commissioned a medal from the Philadelphia Mint, and awarded it to 197 members of the U.S. Colored Troop regiments for their heroism. The Latin motto on the Army of the James medal reads *"Ferro iis libertas perveniet,"* which translated means *"Freedom will be theirs by the sword."*[54]

U.S. Colored Troop units played a significant role in the battles at New Market Heights, Fort Harrison, Fort Gilmer, and Chaffins Farm on September 29-30, 1864. The X Corps, 3rd Division, 1st Brigade consisted of the 27th Connecticut Infantry Regiment and the 7th, 8th, 9th and 45th U.S. Colored Infantry Regiments.

The XVIII Corps Third Division 1st Brigade consisted of the 1st, 22nd, and 37th U.S. Colored Infantry Regiments. The 2nd Brigade consisted of the 5th, 36th, and 38th U.S. Colored Infantry Regiments. The 3rd Brigade included the 4th and 6th U.S. Colored Infantry Regiments. Troops from the 2nd U.S. Colored Cavalry also participated in the battle.

The Union attacks around New Market Heights failed to reach Richmond but succeeded in weakening Rebel defenses around Petersburg, as Lee was forced to move 10,000 men from the Petersburg garrison to help protect the Confederate capital.

During the war a total of 144 days of work were performed on the Dutch Gap Canal, much of the time under heavy Confederate sniper and artillery fire. After the fighting at New Market Heights work on the canal was resumed. On January 1, 1865, all that remained was a "bulkhead" barrier of land separating the excavation from the river. Engineers blew the bulkhead with six tons of blasting powder, but the explosion sent much of the debris into the ditch. As a result, the Dutch Gap Canal was not finished until after the war.

Saltville – October 2-3, 1864

Before refrigeration, one of the more common methods of preserving meat was to pack it in salt. Salt pork and salt beef were staple food items for Rebel troops. Salt was also used to help cure leather. During the Civil War, Saltville, Virginia produced as much as sixty-six percent of the salt used by the Confederacy.

In September 1864 an expedition of Union troops left Prestonburg, Kentucky with the objective of destroying the Virginia salt works 250 miles away.[55] Brigadier General Stephen Burbridge commanded a force of almost 5,000 men, including two cavalry and seven infantry regiments from Kentucky, a Michigan cavalry regiment, an Ohio cavalry regiment, and the recently formed 5th U.S. Colored Cavalry, a regiment composed primarily of former slaves.

The 5th was added to the expedition almost as an afterthought. The new regiment was shorthanded and had received almost no training. They had been rushed into service without being organized.

Although they were a cavalry regiment, they were mounted on untrained horses and equipped with Enfield infantry rifles.[56] The heavy muzzle loaders were too long and cumbersome to be loaded by a man on horseback. The mounted troopers had to dismount every time they needed to reload.

White troops harassed and abused the black soldiers, shouting insults at them when they passed, pulling off their hats, even stealing their horses. The men of the 5th U.S. Colored Cavalry did not respond to the provocation. One of their officers, Colonel James Brisbin, said *"these insults, as well as the jeers and taunts that they would not fight, were borne by the colored soldier patiently...but in no instance did I hear colored soldiers make any reply to insulting language used toward [them] by the white troops."*[57]

Born in Kentucky, Burbridge had attended the Kentucky Military Institute. When the war began, he organized an infantry regiment and was made its commander, distinguishing himself in several engagements. Promoted to Brigadier General, Burbridge was appointed commander of the District of Kentucky in June 1864 and tasked with putting a stop to Confederate guerilla activity in the state.

Burbridge's heavy handed leadership quickly generated controversy. Declaring martial law in the state in conformity with President Lincoln's orders, he abused his authority for political purposes, arresting political opponents and newspaper editors who criticized the president. He also issued Order Number 59, which stated: *"Whenever an unarmed Union citizen is murdered, four guerrillas will be selected from the prison and publicly shot to death at the most convenient place near the scene of the outrages."*[58] More than fifty people were executed without trial under Order No. 59, earning the general the nickname "Butcher" Burbridge and enraging many Kentuckians on both sides.

Confident in the numerical superiority of the forces at his disposal and perhaps overconfident in his abilities as a commander, Burbridge was in no hurry during the Saltville expedition. Slowed by encounters with Rebel units after they got underway in late September, the Federals had to set up camp in a severe storm on the

134

night of the 29th. The following morning, Burbridge allowed his troops to rest until noon before resuming their journey. When they got within two miles of Saltville in the afternoon, Burbridge ordered the men to set up camp for the night, rather than proceed with the attack. The repeated delays gave the Confederates time to bring more reinforcements into the area.

The morning of October 2 was foggy and cold, when Burbridge's troops dismounted and attacked the Confederates dug in on the hills around Saltville. The Rebels were able to withstand repeated Federal attacks. Confederate reinforcements continued to arrive at Saltville throughout the day.

The troops of the 5th U.S. Colored Cavalry made three assaults against the Confederates, capturing the Rebel earthworks on the third attack. Despite their inexperience, they were able to maintain their position for more than two hours before a shortage of ammunition forced them to withdraw.

The next day, Burbridge ordered his army to return to Kentucky. The opportunity to seize the saltworks had been missed. In flagrant violation of accepted Army policy, Burbridge left his wounded troops behind. The resulting incident was one of the most shameful episodes in American history.

On the morning of October 3, Confederate soldiers searched the battlefield and the surrounding area for wounded Union troops, shooting those that were still alive.[59] A Confederate officer wrote in his diary: *"Our men took no negro prisoners. Great numbers of them were killed yesterday & today."*[60]

Some of the wounded had been taken to a hospital at Emory and Henry College nearby. William Gardiner, a Union surgeon who had been left behind to care for the wounded, said *"there came to our field hospital several armed men, as I believe soldiers in the Confederate service, and took 5 men, privates, wounded (negroes), and shot them."* He added that on October 7, *"several armed men entered the said hospital about 10 p.m. and…shot 2 of them (negroes) dead in their beds."*[61]

On October 8, a guerilla leader from Tennessee named Champ Ferguson returned to the hospital and murdered Lieutenant Elza Smith, a white officer of the 13th Kentucky Cavalry, in his bed. It is estimated that fifty wounded Union soldiers were murdered by Rebel guerillas after the First Battle of Saltville, most of them African American troops from the 5th U.S. Colored Cavalry Regiment. Champ Ferguson became one of only two Confederates tried for war crimes. He was found guilty and executed by hanging in October, 1865.[62]

Two months after the battle, soldiers from the 5th U.S. Colored Cavalry and 6th U.S. Colored Cavalry returned to Saltville as part of a force commanded by Brigadier General George Stoneman. In their second raid on Saltville, Union troops defeated the Confederate defenders and succeeded in burning the salt works.[63]

Darbytown Road – October 7-13, 1864

One week after the battles of New Market Heights and Fort Harrison, General Robert E. Lee was determined to dislodge the Union forces threatening Richmond from positions they now occupied along the New Market and Darbytown Roads. Union General Ulysses S. Grant was equally determined to hold the territory Federal troops had already gained and ultimately to capture the city.

Union Major General David Birney's X Corps consisted of three infantry divisions and one cavalry division. Birney's First and Third divisions held the Union line along the New Market Road, while cavalry under Brigadier General August Kautz held the

Darbytown Road a few miles to the north. The Third Division was commanded by Birney's brother, Brigadier General William Birney, and was composed of African American soldiers. Colonel Alvin Voris commanded the 1st Brigade, which included the 7th and 9th U.S. Colored Infantry Regiments. Colonel Ulysses Doubleday commanded the 2nd Brigade, made up of the 29th Connecticut Colored Infantry along with the 8th and 45th U.S. Colored Infantry Regiments. A few days earlier, many of these African American units had sustained high casualties capturing the positions they now defended.[64]

On October 7 Lee sent a task force of two Confederate divisions commanded by Major General Robert Hoke and Major General Charles Field to take back territory the Rebels had lost in the fighting a week earlier.

The initial attack was conducted against the Federal line on the Darbytown Road, where Kautz's cavalry was routed and retreated from the field. As the first phase of the battle was successful, the attacking Confederates turned their attention to Union infantry defending the New Market Road. When one of the senior Rebel commanders, Brigadier General John Gregg of Texas, was killed, the attack was repulsed and the Confederates withdrew to their lines near Richmond. The failed Rebel attack on the 7th was the last time Lee's army initiated a major offensive north of the James River.[65]

Defensive positions around Richmond included two lines of trenches southeast of the city. Anxious to protect the Rebel capital, Lee ordered Hoke and Field to dig and fortify a third trench between the existing lines.

General Grant, had already ordered four separate offensives against Richmond in 1864, probing and attacking from multiple directions throughout the summer and fall. He now ordered Major General Benjamin F. Butler, commanding the Army of the James, to lead a fifth offensive before the Rebels could complete their third defensive line south of the city.

Butler ordered Major General Alfred Terry, the new commander of X Corps, to lead the attack. Terry, who had lost a lot of soldiers during the previous weeks of fighting, asked Butler for additional troops but was turned down. Scheduled for dawn on October 13 the attack was delayed by several hours when Kautz's cavalry was late in arriving. Because of the postponement, the element of surprise was lost. When the assault by 550 men of the First Brigade was repulsed by the Confederates with heavy casualties, Terry retreated, pursued by the Rebels until they were stopped by Union cannon fire. Grant's fifth offensive against Richmond had failed.[66]

Boydton Plank Road – October 27-28, 1864

Frustrated, Grant devised an elaborate plan for a sixth offensive. The two-pronged attack involved more than 50,000 Union soldiers. Butler's Army of the James would attack Richmond, and Major General Winfield Scott Hancock would lead the Army of the Potomac in a massive attack at Petersburg.

Butler's X Corps, still commanded by Alfred Terry, was to attack towards Richmond from positions near Fort Harrison, advancing along the Darbytown Road. To Terry's right, the main assault against Richmond was to be made by Major General Godfrey Weitzel's XVIII Corps along the Williamsburg Road, roughly parallel to the Darbytown Road and a few miles to the north.[67]

Objectives for the simultaneous attack on Petersburg by the Army of the Potomac included severing Rebel communications along the Boydton Plank Road, then cutting the South Side Railroad. Major General John Parke's IX Corps was to attack the Confederate lines east of Boydton Plank Road, then turn north and continue the attack towards Petersburg if opportunity permitted.

Major General Gouverneur K. Warren's V Corps was expected to secure Parke's left (southern) flank. If Parke's attack on the Boydton Plank Road stalled, Warren was to attempt to flank the Confederates and attack them from their rear.

Hancock's two divisions of II Corps were to cross Hatcher's Run, a small stream south of Petersburg, feint north towards the town along the Boydton Plank Road, then turn west to cut the South Side Railroad, while Brigadier General David Gregg's cavalry division protected Hancock's left flank from the south.

On October 27, the Union troops moved out at 3:00 AM. It was raining and cold; the roads along which the soldiers advanced were quickly churned into mud, slowing their progress. Weitzel attempted to turn the Confederate left flank near Richmond with an attack by only two brigades, and was unsuccessful. Terry attacked the strong Rebel lines along the Darbytown road with only one brigade, and failed. Terry's 3rd Division of U.S. Colored infantry, still short of manpower from losses incurred during the previous month's battles, lost more men when they ran into a brigade of Confederate cavalry.[68]

The attack against Petersburg was delayed by the bad weather and quickly bogged down when Parke's men were unable to break the Rebel lines east of the Boydton Plank Road. Parke ordered his men to dig in. Warren's troops were also delayed by the bad weather and terrain.

Closely monitoring the progress of the Petersburg attack, Grant and General George Meade realized that neither Parke nor Warren could attain their objectives, and ordered Warren to send one of his divisions south to reinforce Hancock's right flank.

Hancock's attack started off well. His men were able to secure a stretch of the Boydton Plank Road south of Petersburg. Around 1:00 PM Meade ordered Hancock to extend his lines to the east to link up with the division sent by Warren, to keep from being cut off from the remainder of the Union army. When Grant visited Hancock's position that afternoon, he concluded that the Confederates defending Petersburg could not be defeated by Hancock's corps, and called off the attack. As Hancock's men started to withdraw, they found their way north blocked by a Rebel division commanded by Major General Henry Heth. Another Rebel division commanded by Major General William Mahone blocked Hancock's forces from turning east, and a cavalry division led by Major General "Rooney" Lee was rapidly approaching from the south.

Hancock's army was surrounded. More than 600 of the Federal troops were taken prisoner, but Gregg's cavalry was able to hold off Lee's division. When Mahone attacked in the late afternoon, the Union force rallied and was able to break out and cut off Mahone's force. Running low on ammunition, Hancock's force withdrew after dark, leaving 250 wounded soldiers on the battlefield.

The Army of the James suffered more than 1,600 casualties, while inflicting only 100 casualties on the Confederates defending Richmond. The Army of the Potomac lost 1,750 men in the Petersburg attack, while the Confederate defenders suffered 1,300 casualties. The Union army had failed to attain either of its objectives in the battles of Darbytown Road and Boydton Plank Road.

Honey Hill – November 30, 1864

After the fall of Atlanta to Union forces on September 2, 1864, Major General William Tecumseh Sherman came up with a plan to disrupt the Confederate army's remaining sources of supply and demoralize Rebel civilians and soldiers. He planned to march his army from Atlanta through the Southern heartland, capturing the supplies they needed and burning the rest, to the port of Savannah, South Carolina. Sherman believed that foraging for supplies on such a large scale and destroying what they did not need would deprive the Confederate Army of those supplies and undermine Rebel determination to continue fighting the war.

President Lincoln and General Grant were initially skeptical of Sherman's plan, but on November 2, 1864 Grant sent Sherman a message that said, *"Go as you propose."*[69]

Sherman commanded four Union army groups. He sent two of these armies, under General George Thomas, to fight Confederate Lieutenant General John Bell Hood's army in Tennessee and divided his remaining forces into two columns of infantry and artillery supported by a cavalry division. Marching roughly 30 miles apart, the two columns would march through the most prosperous areas of Georgia and South Carolina and converge on Savannah, 285 miles away. As his 62,000 soldiers planned to forage for supplies as they marched, Sherman's staff used crop and livestock data from the 1860 Census to select the best route for the campaign.

Union forces had established a strong presence in Beaufort, South Carolina, forty miles northeast of Savannah, early in the war. The port of Savannah was blockaded by the Federal navy but food, ammunition and troops could still be shipped into the city via the Charleston & Savannah Railroad, which ran roughly north to south about twenty miles west of Beaufort. If the rail line from Charleston could be destroyed,

Savannah would be weakened by the loss of a critical source of supplies and reinforcements.

In late November 1864 Brigadier General John P. Hatch left Hilton Head in command of 5,000 men, steaming up the Broad River on naval transports towards Boyd's Neck, near the rail line west of Beaufort. Hatch's command included thirteen regiments of infantry. The 54th and 55th Massachusetts and the 32nd, 34th, 35th and 102nd U.S. Colored Infantry Regiments were made up of African American soldiers.

The Federal troops had to spend an extra night on the crowded transports as a dense fog prevented them from disembarking. Finally, on the morning November 30, they were able to begin marching northwest towards Grahamville, a village about two miles from the railroad.[70]

Near a low ridge called Honey Hill, the Union soldiers encountered a Confederate force of 1,500 men commanded by Colonel Charles J. Colcock. The Confederates were able to maintain a deadly fire from well dug in positions. An artillery battery of seven Rebel guns straddled the road. Swampy ground and heavy undergrowth in front of the low ridge restricted the ability of the Union troops to maneuver. Again and again, the Federal soldiers attacked, but were repulsed. Three Union officers were awarded the Medal of Honor for their actions in the fight.[71]

At one point in the battle, the flag bearer of the 55th Massachusetts Colored Infantry was killed by an exploding artillery shell. Corporal Andrew Jackson Smith, a former slave, picked up the flag and carried it for the remainder of the battle. He was nominated for the nation's highest honor in 1916, but Smith's Medal of Honor was awarded posthumously in 2001.[72]

The fighting went on all day. The Union force outnumbered the Confederates, but in this instance the

142

Rebels had a decisive advantage in the terrain where they had chosen to make a stand. Despite repeated, determined attacks by the Union regiments, Hatch knew he could not overcome the Rebel defenses. At dark, Hatch withdrew his battered force and sailed back downriver towards Hilton Head.

Federal casualties included eighty-nine men killed, 629 wounded, and another twenty-eight men missing. The Southerners lost only eight killed and thirty-nine wounded. The Battle of Honey Hill was a victory for the Confederates.

Deveaux Neck – December 1864

In late 1864 Brigadier General E.E. Potter set out with a force of 5,000 Union troops on an expedition up the Broad River in South Carolina. Potter's objective was to blow up a bridge on the Charleston and Savannah Railway, severing a vital communication route between the Rebel cities of Savannah and Charleston. The Federal force included soldiers from the 32nd, 33rd, 34th and 102nd U.S. Colored Infantry Regiments.[73]

General William Tecumseh Sherman's 62,000-man army had left Atlanta on November 15, planning to capture the port city of Savannah by Christmas. On the way, Sherman's troops confiscated livestock and crops, destroyed railroad tracks, and burned buildings in an effort to weaken the Confederate economy and undermine support for the rebellion. By cutting the railroad line, Potter planned to isolate Savannah before Sherman's arrival, reduce the flow of supplies to the city and cut off a potential Rebel line of retreat.

Potter's troops steamed from Beaufort, South Carolina on a flotilla of twelve U.S. Navy transports. The Union soldiers disembarked on a peninsula called Deveaux Neck between the Coosawatchie and Tulifinny

Rivers, tributaries of the Broad, at around 8:00 AM on December 6, 1864. The Federals advanced up the peninsula and encamped a short distance from the railroad.

Major General Samuel Jones, a graduate of and former instructor at West Point, was commander of the Confederate Department of South Carolina, Georgia, and Florida. On learning of the Union landings, Jones hurriedly assembled a makeshift force of infantry and cavalry units from Georgia and South Carolina, including two companies of cadets from the Citadel in Charleston and the Arsenal in Columbia, commanded by Major James B. White, Superintendent of the South Carolina Military Academy. Jones's defensive force consisted of fewer than 1,000 Confederates.[74]

The 343 cadets arrived by train at Pocotaglio on December 6, and marched "double quick time" to the bridge across the Tulifinny, four miles away. Assigned to guard the train trestle, the cadets began to dig in and fortify their position.

The next morning, two lines of infantry and cadets moved towards a nearby hill where Federal troops had dug in and began firing from the woods. The Union force was surprised by the intensity of the attack by the outnumbered Confederates and withdrew several hundred yards under heavy fire. Firing with deadly accuracy from under cover, the Rebels were able to inflict nearly 1,000 casualties on the Union troops on December 7, while suffering fewer than fifty killed and wounded.

On December 8th it rained for much of the day. Both sides regrouped, improved their fortifications, and tended their wounded. Reinforcements arrived to bolster the Confederate defenders.

The Union task force counterattacked on December 9 but was repulsed by the Confederates. Again, the Rebels incurred fewer than 100 casualties in the fighting, but more than 200 Federals were killed, wounded or missing. Low on ammunition, Potter's force was compelled to withdraw.

The Battle of Deveaux Neck had resulted in a Confederate victory. Union troops were unsuccessful in destroying the train trestle. As a result, more than 10,000 Rebel soldiers were able to evacuate from Savannah to Charleston on the railroad before Sherman's troops arrived. Despite the failure of the raid on Deveaux Neck, Sherman's army was able to capture Savannah. Mayor Richard Arnold surrendered the city on December 21, 1864.

Sherman sent the following message to President Abraham Lincoln: *"I beg to present you, as a Christmas gift, the city of Savannah, with 150 heavy guns and plenty of ammunition, and also about 25,000 bales of cotton."*[75]

8. STORIES OF SOLDIERS AND SAILORS

For most of recorded history, more people have died from disease during war than from battlefield injuries. More than 25,000 Americans died in the Revolutionary War; 17,000 of those deaths were caused by disease. Eight times as many British soldiers died from disease during the Napoleonic War that rocked Europe at the beginning of the 19th century than were killed by Napoleon's army.[1]

The Common Enemy

During the American Civil War, soldiers found themselves serving in all parts of the country, frequently in unfamiliar climates and in all weather. They lived in unsanitary camps, drinking filthy water, eating inadequate and sometimes rotten food, and were exposed to a variety of diseases for which they had no immunity.

Medical science was still in its infancy. The concept of diseases spread by germs or bacteria was unknown, the relationship of cleanliness to health unrecognized. Smallpox vaccination had been invented decades before, but few soldiers had been vaccinated. Diseases were often misdiagnosed. There were no antibiotics, limited availability of anesthetics, and few effective medicines to treat any illness. Even the mildest disease could turn deadly.

The closest parallel our generation has experienced was the COVID-19 pandemic that began in 2020. During the early stages of the outbreak, no one was immune, there was no vaccine, and few effective treatments. A person might have light, cold-like symptoms one week and be fighting for his life the next. Millions would die around the world before the plague could be brought under control.

At the time of the Civil War, almost every infectious disease was deadly. There were no cures. If a soldier became so ill he was unable to function but lived long enough to be sent to a regimental hospital, he was likely to die there.

Dysentery or chronic diarrhea was one of the most prevalent killers. Pneumonia, typhoid, cholera, measles, malaria and smallpox were also common.

A soldier languishing in a regimental hospital had to think: this was not the way things were supposed to end. For many soldiers who experienced it, it was not the end, at least not right away.

Corporal Jeremiah Sanders, born in Franklin County, Virginia, was hospitalized twice for disease, once in New Bern, North Carolina and once at Folly Island near Charleston, but he survived the war, presumably to go back to his job as a waiter in Massachusetts, where he had enlisted.[2] Private John James, also from Franklin County, was hospitalized in Camp Casey, Virginia for 'chronic bronchitis', but was back on duty three weeks later.[3]

Some soldiers were recognized as being unfit for battle due to health reasons when they enlisted and assigned to an "invalid unit" where they could expect to perform guard duty and light manual labor. Private Henry Pulliman enlisted at Chattanooga and was assigned to the Company A of the 42nd U.S. Colored Infantry, an "invalid unit", but soon went absent without leave, possibly due to his poor health.[4] Private Richard Giles, who enlisted at age fifteen and was assigned to Company H of the same "invalid" regiment, spent four weeks in the regimental hospital due to illness, but was released from the hospital.[5] Giles served until he was mustered out in Alabama in 1866, after the war ended, and lived until 1896.

Sergeant Richard Vons, was listed as "a good soldier" on his service records.[6] A Sergeant in Company I of the 39th U.S. Colored Infantry, Vons was severely wounded at the Battle of the Crater on July 30, 1864 when a bullet broke his left scapula. He recovered from his wound to fight again in the battle of Sugar Loaf in North Carolina, but died of 'intermittent fever' (malaria) at the post hospital at New Bern on September 23, 1865. Vons was born in Franklin County, Virginia.

Private Paul Pearson died of dropsy (edema) in Arkansas only 133 days after joining the Union Army.[7] Private Smith Holloway died of pneumonia less than two weeks after he joined.[8]

Private Josiah Taitt[9] died in Alabama in 1864; his brother, Private Granville Taitt[10], signed for his belongings, then followed him in death five months later. Both brothers died of pneumonia. The Taitts had been born in Franklin County.

John Mason, a farmer from Accomack County serving in the 9th U.S.C.I., was hospitalized for smallpox in April 1864 but recovered.[11] Private Mason fought in the battles of John's Island, Deep Bottom, and Chaffins Farm.

Private Richard Smith of Frederick County was hospitalized twice for sickness while he served in the 41st U.S.C.I., but survived.[12] A former slave with the illustrious name of General Scott, born in James City County, enlisted in Company A of the 35th U.S.C.I. when he was sixteen years old in May, 1863.[13] Private General Scott fought in the battles of Olustee, John's Island, and Honey Hill. Scott was hospitalized four times for illness while he was in the service, but survived and was discharged from Charleston on June 1, 1866.

Private William Moore enlisted in the 54th Massachusetts Infantry a few months after the battle of Fort Wagner.[14] Born in Rockbridge County, Moore was sick in hospital when his service ended. Private Washington Ray of Salem was described as a "very dark mulatto", with "two single scars on his right cheek".[15] Hospitalized for illness in September 1864, he survived until the end of the war. Elisha Boggess, born in Smyth County, was a Sergeant serving in Company E of the 43rd U.S.C.I. described as "a good soldier."[16] Hospitalized at City Point in August of 1864, Boggess returned to duty on September 27 – just in time to fight in the Battle of New Market Heights.

Diarrhea and dysentery were frequently listed as causes of death. Private John Q. Adams, born in Page County, died of diarrhea while serving in the 47th U.S.C.I. in Mississippi.[17] Born in Richmond, Private Henry Lee of the 33rd U.S.C.I. died of diarrhea in Savannah, a month after Robert E. Lee's surrender.[18]

Robert Ardis, born in Surry County, enlisted at Fort Powhatan on June 29, 1864 in Company E of the 10th U.S.C.I.[19] Ardis died of diarrhea forty-six days later and twenty miles away at the Point of Rocks Hospital.

Born in Amelia County, Joseph Anderson served in G Troop of the 3rd U.S. Colored Cavalry.[20] He fought in the action at Roaches Plantation on March 31, 1864 two months after he was promoted to Corporal. Joseph Anderson died of dysentery in Memphis on April 13, 1865, four days after Lee's surrender.

Soldiers were involved in accidents. John Green, born in Bedford County, was thirty-three years old and serving in the 5th U.S. Colored Heavy Artillery when he was crushed and killed by an overturned wagon near Vicksburg in November 1863.[21] Two soldiers from Accomack County[22], one a boatman[23], drowned after the war while serving in Texas. Private James Tatman, a teamster from Augusta County serving in the 53rd U.S.C.I., died of an accidental gunshot wound.[24] Private William Williams of the 45th U.S.C.I. had been born in Bedford County; Williams was gathering firewood when he wandered in front of a practice target and was shot by accident.[25] Private Benjamin Jones was killed at Fort Powhatan in February 1865 when a pistol held by one of his comrades accidentally discharged.[26]

Far away from home, soldiers sometimes become the victims of crime. Private Samuel Parker of the 9th U.S.C.I. was killed in Texas after the war, *"Supposed to have been murdered by Mexicans March 15/66 near Brownsville"*.[27]

A thirty-nine year old private in the 42nd U.S.C.I. with the likely name of Napoleon Bonaparte was taken to the insane asylum after being wounded in action.[28] Private Bonaparte had been born in Shenandoah County.

Private Joseph Lacy was born a slave in New Kent County. He joined Company A of the 4th U.S. Colored Infantry in July of 1863 when he was twenty-four years old. Wounded in the joint of his hip by a bullet in October of 1864, Lacy as taken to the government insane asylum in Washington when he was discharged. He remained there until he died of phthisis pulmonalis and chronic dementia on September 19, 1876.[29]

While serving as military governor of the Commonwealth after the war, Union General Edward Canby recognized the need for greater access to mental health services and treatment for African Americans living in Virginia.[30] In 1869 Canby ordered that temporary space be provided for an asylum for treatment of black persons diagnosed with lunacy. In 1870 the Virginia legislature took ownership of the Central Lunatic Asylum for Colored Insane, which was moved to a new facility constructed in Dinwiddie County in 1885. The facility would be the only mental

150

institution serving African American patients in Virginia until it was integrated in 1967.

Soldiers died from a myriad of diseases. Of 608 U.S.C.T. soldiers whose records show they were born in Accomack County, at least twenty-three died of typhoid fever, eighteen of pneumonia, and seven of cholera. By contrast, just seventeen of these soldiers were known to have died from wounds received in battle.

Disease was an enemy shared by soldiers from both armies. Two thirds of the 660,000 recorded deaths of soldiers during the American Civil War were from disease, rather than from combat injuries. If neither army had fired a shot, the war would still have been a humanitarian disaster.

Samuel H. Smothers

On August 31, 1864, an educator living in the peaceful community of New Garden, Indiana left his pregnant wife and young son and made his way to Troy, Ohio, to enlist in Company C of the 45th U.S. Colored Infantry Regiment.

Samuel H. Smothers was a teacher and principal at the Union Literary Institute, a private school founded by Quakers and free African Americans living in the area for the education of black and white children. The school's Board of Directors included black and white members.[32]

At 6' 1 ½" tall, Smothers was an imposing figure. He was described on his enlistment papers as thirty-one years old, with black skin, black eyes, and dark hair.[33]

Smothers had been born in 1833 in Franklin County, Virginia to a free woman of color named Jane Smithers, who baked cakes for a living. Making his way to Indiana, Smothers worked hard to obtain an education and was hired as a schoolteacher. In 1857 he married Eunice

Crane. When he left to join the Army they had a four-year old son, and Eunice was pregnant with their second child.[34]

Founded in 1846, the Union Literary Institute offered an education to children and adults, without discrimination with regard to race, sex, or financial status. This was a radical concept at the time. When the Institute was founded, public schools in Indiana only allowed white children to attend.

Every student at the Institute was required to work a few hours each day helping with the upkeep of the school, growing food, and performing other tasks. This work taught valuable skills to the students and helped keep tuition costs affordable.

The Union Literary Institute. Samuel H. Smothers, born in Franklin County, Virginia, taught and served as principal at this integrated school in Indiana. - *Photo: Union Literary Institute Preservation Society*

The school was an important stop on the Underground Railroad. In 1860 the Institute built a new

152

two-story brick building. The first principal was Reverend Ebenezer Tucker, a white clergyman and committed abolitionist. Smothers was the second principal of the school.

During 1863 and 1864, the school published a magazine, *"The Student's Repository: A Quarterly Periodical, Devoted to Education, Morality & General Improvement,"* which featured articles by students and adult contributors and was edited by Smothers, who was also a regular contributor.[35]

Distinguished alumni who studied at The Union Literary Institute include Hiram Revels, the first black U.S. Senator, and James S. Hinton, the first black man to be elected to the Indiana House of Representatives.[36]

In Volume 1 of "The Student's Repository", published in July 1863, Smothers included the following essay:

My Grandfather

There are few things upon which I reflect with more regret than the fact that I know so little of my ancestors. And this is the case with most of our race. Slavery has almost destroyed the family relation among its victims. But few of us know anything of our ancestors any further back than our great-grandparents, and some of them not even that far. I am one of the latter class. My knowledge of my ancestors (on my father's side,) commences at my grandfather.

My grandfather's name was Harry Hunter. He was a native of Virginia. I don't know when he was born but he has been dead about forty years. The leading facts in his history are briefly these:

He was born and raised a slave. He was doomed to all the hardships and cruelties of the slave's wretched and unhappy life. He had a large family of children, (the oldest of whom was my father, who is still a slave if he is living,) of whom he was passionately fond. The love of liberty was also deeply implanted in his soul. So conscious was he of his manhood, so vivid were his conceptions of the natural rights of man, that he suffered no man to whip him. Being a man of wonderful courage, and great physical strength, he frequently combatted with and whipped five or six white men at a time.

His desire for freedom at last became so intense that he made up his mind to flee to the Free States, and after many hardships and privations, he at last reached the State of Ohio. He was now beyond the reach of his fiendish oppressors; for, although he was not entirely safe in Ohio, he could have gone on to Canada, where they never could have got him. But alas! His children whom he loved as clearly as he did his life, were still in slavery. The thought of his children still being in the awful house of bondage, caused his heart to bleed afresh, and he resolved to make a desperate effort to deliver them. He accordingly went back to his old neighborhood for the purpose, if possible, of getting his children away. But while he was secreted in the forest and mountain, waiting for an opportunity to have an interview with his children, and to make arrangements for their contemplated flight, lo! The white people found him out. They chased him through the forest and swamps, but he succeeded in baffling all their fiendish stratagems for several days, till he at last became exhausted with fatigue and alarm, and laid himself down to sleep.

"There is a healing in the angel wing of sleep, even to the toil-worn bondman," and never was its balm more welcome than it was to him! He, no doubt, had forgotten his toils and sufferings, and visions of freedom were passing over his mind. Yes, he doubtless was dreaming of the time when he expected to again reach a land of liberty, and have his children with him. But oh! How soon these visions were blasted forever. His pursuers came upon him, and with a bludgeon they struck him a fatal blow on the head, and killed him outright.

Yes, grandfather, thou wast murdered,
Thou wast killed by ruffian hands,
But thy spirit's gone to the heavenly land

154

Bright angels stood ready to receive thee
And waft thee to thy Eternal home.
Yes, thou art high up in heaven!
In that land above the sky-
Oh! May I strive to meet thee
When I am called to die.
Samuel H. Smothers[37]

In 1864, Smothers felt that he should personally join the fight for freedom, and enlisted in the U.S. Army. During the next few years, Samuel Smothers witnessed and participated in a number of the most important events in our nation's history.

Companies from the 45th U.S. Colored Infantry Regiment fought in the battles of New Market Heights, Chaffins Farm, and Fort Harrison September 28-30, 1864, Darbytown Road October 13, 1864, and Fair Oaks on October 27 and 28, 1864. On March 4, 1865, the 45th U.S.C.I. marched in the parade at President Abraham Lincoln's Second Inauguration, the first African American regiment to be assigned that duty.[38]

Later that month the regiment moved back to Virginia near Richmond, fighting in the battle of Hatcher's Run March 29-31, helping bring about the fall of Petersburg on April 2, and helping pursue Confederate General Robert E. Lee's army to Appomattox. The 45th was present at Appomattox when Lee surrendered to Union General Ulysses S. Grant on April 9, 1865. The regiment was stationed in Petersburg and City Point in the two months following the surrender, then on June 5 boarded steamers bound for New Orleans, on the way to guard the Mexican frontier in Texas.

Smothers may not have known them, as they were assigned to other companies, but at least three other men from the 45th had been born in Franklin County. Private

Robert Atkins[39] of Company H survived the war, as did Corporal Wesley Wades[40] of Company E. Private James Monroe[41] of Company E did not survive but died of smallpox in Virginia in 1865.

His term of service having expired, Smothers was honorably discharged on September 30, 1865.

By 1870 Smothers was living with his wife and three children in Shreveport, Louisiana, where he taught at The Union School, which had been established by the Freedmen's Bureau. Many of his students became teachers, helping others attain a better life. He wrote letters and articles for publications around the United States.

Eventually the family moved to Texas, where Smothers was elected as the Tax Assessor of Harrison County. By 1880 they were living in Dallas, where Smothers started a newspaper for the black community and founded the first high school for black students in Dallas. Smothers edited and published the *"Baptist Missionary and Educational Journal"* and founded the Harrison County Normal School for educating future teachers.

In an 1880 speech, Smothers expressed his strong belief in the value of a good education:

"We should remember that knowledge is power and ignorance is weakness. The protection which we most need is the power which education and prosperity gives. For my own part all I ask of any man is an equal chance, and then if he can outstrip me in the race of life let him do it."[42]

The life and career of Samuel H. Smothers were testimony to this belief. Smothers dedicated his life to enabling others to obtain an education and unlock the opportunities doing so would provide. His lifelong commitment to education invites comparison to a more famous educator born in Franklin County, Virginia – Booker T. Washington. One can only wonder whether the two men were familiar with each other's work.

Starting from humble beginnings, Smothers overcame tremendous challenges and inspired others to do so. As a leader in his community and an educator for more than thirty years, Samuel H. Smothers made a positive difference in thousands of American lives.

After Eunice's death, Samuel Smothers married Mariah Lyles in 1892. He continued working as an educator and community leader until his death in Brazoria, Texas in 1901, when he was sixty-nine years old.

No image of Samuel Smothers survives and the place of his burial is not known, but the educator from Virginia left a significant legacy in his writings and efforts to provide an education for others.

Dalton – October 13, 1864

In September 1864 the 44th Regiment of U.S. Colored Infantry commanded by Colonel Lewis Johnson was assigned to garrison duty at Dalton, Georgia, a town that had been the scene of two prior Civil War battles. There were 751 soldiers assigned to the regiment. More than 600 of those soldiers were African Americans. Most were former slaves who had joined the Union Army just weeks before.

Confederate General John Bell Hood's Army of Tennessee had been badly beaten by Union General William Tecumseh Sherman's army during the Battle for Atlanta, but Hood managed to convince Confederate President Jefferson Davis that he could capture the city of Nashville, Tennessee, then held by Federal troops. As the Rebels marched northwest, Hood intended to destroy part of the Western and Atlantic Railroad and disrupt the flow of supplies to Union forces in the south. Choosing to bypass a better fortified Union Army stronghold in Renata, Georgia, Hood decided to attack the lightly defended Union garrison at Dalton, surrounding the town with more than 35,000 Confederate troops.[43]

Learning from pickets posted outside the town that they were about to be attacked by a powerful Rebel force, the Union garrison at Dalton sheltered inside Fort Hill, a stronghold on the site of what is now a school. The African American troops in the fort were anxious to fight. They were aware of the law passed by the Confederate Congress in 1863 stating that black troops could be returned to slavery or executed as insurrectionists, and they had heard stories of atrocities committed by Confederates against black Union soldiers after battles at places like Fort Pillow and Petersburg.

Hood sent a message to Johnson, demanding the Dalton garrison surrender immediately, and promising no quarter to soldiers of either color if he had to attack. Faced with an overwhelming number of Confederates, Johnson surrendered the garrison. He later stated that his small garrison could not have lasted fifteen minutes against such a superior Rebel force. Confederate Private William Bevins later wrote, *"While the artillery made ready the Texans passed the word down the line as though it came from General Cheatham, 'Kill every damn one of them,' which would have been carrying out their own threat of 'no quarter'."*[44]

Confederates from Major General William Bate's division made prisoners of the small Union force. The Union defeat at Dalton resulted in the largest surrender of African American troops during the Civil War. The Union officers were paroled, but Black soldiers were segregated and their personal belongings, shoes, and overcoats were taken by the Rebels, who put them to work tearing up track along the Western and Atlantic Railroad line.

When a sergeant from the 44th refused to participate in the destruction of the railroad, he was immediately shot. Five more soldiers from the 44th were summarily executed for failing to keep up. The Rebels sent 250 men of the regiment back to their former masters, and forced another 350 to work as personal servants or perform hard labor around the Confederate defenses at Mobile, Alabama. By December, 1865 only 125 of these men were still living, and most in poor condition.

Private Charles Lawrence, born in Franklin County, Virginia in 1840, enlisted in Company K of the 44th United States Colored Infantry at Rome, Georgia, on September 8, 1864.[45] Just thirty-five days later he was captured when the Union garrison surrendered at Dalton, and forced to serve as a slave until he was able to escape his captors at Thomasville, GA in May, 1865, a few weeks after the war ended. He returned to duty with the 44th and remained with his unit until they mustered out at Chattanooga on April 30, 1866.

Nashville – December 15-16, 1864

By late 1864, the Confederate States had been weakened by a series of Union victories. In September, Union General William Tecumseh Sherman had taken the city of Atlanta, an important supply hub for the entire Confederacy. After the fall of Atlanta, General Ulysses Grant sent Major General George Thomas to command Union forces defending Nashville from an expected attack by the Confederate Army of Tennessee, commanded by Major General John Bell Hood.

John Bell Hood was born in Kentucky. At only thirty-three years old, Hood had risen rapidly through the ranks and had a reputation for aggressiveness and courage. Hood paid a high price for his reputation. He was shot in the hand by a Comanche arrow in Texas in 1857, he was injured in the arm by cannon fire at Gettysburg, and during the Battle of Chickamauga he had a leg amputated after another wound almost cost him his life. Five months later he was back in action, often riding as much as twenty miles a day with his cork prosthetic leg dangling from his saddle.[46]

Hood's reckless daring had also been costly for his men. At Gaines Mill in 1862 more than 400 enlisted men and almost all the officers of his brigade became casualties after he led a charge that broke the Union lines. An assault led by Hood during the Second Battle of Bull Run resulted in the loss of more than 1,000 men from his command. At Antietam, almost half of the 2,000 soldiers in Hood's division were killed or wounded.

Despite General Robert E. Lee's doubt that Hood was ready to lead a large army, Confederate President Jefferson Davis promoted Hood in July to full General, commanding the forces defending Atlanta from Sherman's siege. When Hood's attempts to break the siege were unsuccessful, the result was a catastrophic failure for the Confederacy. His evacuating Rebels set fire to the city in an effort to prevent Union troops from capturing valuable warehouses filled with supplies.[47]

Hoping to cut Sherman's lines of communication and divert the Union army from its destructive advance through Georgia, General Hood and President Davis came up with a desperate plan to divide and destroy the Union forces guarding Nashville, a critical supply center for Union forces operating throughout the South.[48]

Commanding the Union forces at Nashville, General George H. Thomas had been Hood's Artillery professor at West Point. A mature, seasoned veteran, Thomas had fought in Mexico, Florida, and Panama. Like Hood, Thomas had been wounded by an arrow fighting

Comanches in Texas prior to the war. He also had a bad back, injured during a fall from a train platform at Lynchburg.[49]

Though a Virginian, at the beginning of the war Thomas remained loyal to the United States, and accepted a command in the Union Army. As a result, much of his family refused to have anything to do with him during the war and for most of the rest of his life.[50] Thomas had distinguished himself commanding troops during several engagements in Kentucky and by his steady leadership in keeping the Union lines from being routed during the Battle of Chickamauga in 1863. Later, the "Rock of Chickamauga", as he was nicknamed, won an important victory at the Battle of Chattanooga, and defeated the first of Hood's four unsuccessful attempts to break the siege of Atlanta. Thomas was as deliberate and methodical as Hood was reckless and impulsive. Expecting an attack by the Confederates on Nashville, in November Thomas began shifting additional divisions to reinforce the 30,000 soldiers guarding the city.

In an ironic turn of history, the competing armies in the Battle of Nashville were commanded by a Confederate general born in a Union state, and a Union general born in a Confederate state.

In late November it became evident the Rebel attack on Nashville was imminent. Thomas ordered Major General John Schofield to move his 25,000 troops from Columbia, Tennessee, southwest of Nashville, to reinforce the city's defenses.

Aware that Schofield's army was on the move, Hood hoped to attack Schofield's divided force. Some of Schofield's units were camped thirty miles south of Nashville, while the main body of Union reinforcements were still moving north from Columbia. On November 29, Schofield's advance party encountered Hood's

Confederates at Spring Hill, but neither side was able to secure a conclusive victory.[51]

That night, as Hood's army camped within a few yards of the Columbia-Nashville Turnpike, Schofield marched the main body of his troops north along the road just beyond the glow of the Rebel campfires, and rejoined the rest of his army near Franklin, Tennessee, only fifteen miles from Nashville. In bypassing Hood's army and reconsolidating his forces, Schofield denied Hood a critical advantage that could have resulted in a decisive Confederate victory.[52]

The next morning Hood was furious to learn his army had been outmaneuvered. He ordered his officers to attack Schofield's army at the town of Franklin. At one point during the battle, several of Hood's divisions charged two miles across an open field under heavy Union artillery and rifle fire. Once again, Hood's impetuous aggressiveness led to disastrous casualties among his men: More than 6,000 Rebels were killed or wounded at Franklin. Schofield's army suffered 3,000 casualties but was able to escape and join Thomas in the defense of the Tennessee capital.[53]

Hood's Confederates, already numerically inferior to the Union forces defending Nashville, were critically weakened by the defeat at Franklin. Still, Hood believed he could secure a strategic victory with his remaining 25,000 soldiers. Hood arrived near Nashville December 2 and began building fortifications south of the city.

With more than 55,000 troops defending Nashville, Union forces had a numerical advantage, but about 13,000 were African Americans serving in United States Colored Infantry units. Until this point, they been assigned as laborers in constructing the railroads and defenses surrounding the town, and performing guard duty. Most were former slaves, were not battle tested and had little training. Thomas and his officers were unsure they would fight effectively when faced with actual combat conditions.[54]

Almost as soon as Hood's army reached the Nashville area, General Grant and President Lincoln began urging Thomas to launch an attack. A careful planner, Thomas replied he would attack as soon as his army was ready. Days passed, then a week, until on December 9 temperatures dropped to near zero and the area was hit with ice storms and snowfall. Both armies were immobilized as Tennessee experienced the coldest winter in decades. Frustrated that Thomas still had not attacked the Rebels, Grant dispatched another commander to relieve him. Finally, on December 12, the storm ended. Temperatures stated to rise. The snow melted, covering roads and fields with mud. By December 14, George Thomas was ready to attack.[55]

The morning of December 15th dawned with a thick fog as temperatures continued to climb. At 8:00 AM Major General James Steedman's Provisional Detachment, including two brigades of United States Colored Infantry, attacked the gun battery guarding the eastern end of Hood's line near Rains Hill on the Confederate right flank. At 9:00 Union artillery started bombarding the Rebel position, and at 10:00 Steedman's brigades attacked, eventually forcing the Confederates to withdraw to the southwest. Although Hood sent reinforcements from his left, Steedman's attack kept a Rebel corps pinned down for most of the day.

That afternoon, Thomas ordered a powerful assault on the Confederate left, leading with a charge on Mongomery Hill, about a mile south of Nashville. A series of attacks on other positions on the weakened Confederate left flank continued until nightfall, when Hood's army was forced to fall back to a line about three miles south of the city, between Shy's Hill on his left and Overton's Hill on the right.

On December 16th Union artillery pounded the Rebel positions. The 2nd Colored Brigade commanded by Colonel Charles Thompson again led with an attack on the Confederate right flank at Overton's Hill. Attacking at an angle to the Rebel lines, the 100th US Colored Infantry's progress was obstructed by fallen trees. The 12th US Colored Infantry was halted by a dense thicket – but the 13th U.S. Colored Infantry Regiment continued its charge to the top of Overton's Hill, suffering severe casualties and retreating only when units to its left and right were pushed back by withering Confederate fire.

Union Major General A.J. Smith's forces then attacked the Confederate left, nearly wiping out Colonel William Shy's regiment. Observing the success of the attack on Shy's Hill, other Union units quickly captured Overton's Hill. The Confederate force collapsed, and Hood's Army of Tennessee suffered another 6,000 casualties.

The victorious Union army pursued Hood's defeated troops to the Tennessee River as bitter cold weather returned. Thomas called off the pursuit on December 29. The remnants of Hood's army continued to retreat until they reached Tupelo, Mississippi, where on January 13 Hood asked to be relieved of his command.[56]

During the Battle of Nashville, Thomas's brilliant left-right-left-right series of attacks and the Union army's overwhelming numerical superiority led to one of the most complete Union victories of the Civil War. Hood's Army of the Tennessee was destroyed, no longer effective as a fighting force, and Sherman's lines of communication to Nashville remained intact. When General Thomas viewed the bodies of dead black and white American soldiers after the battle he said to his commanders: *"Gentlemen, the question is settled; negro soldiers will fight."*[57]

A Cavalry Soldier

Henry Helm was born in Franklin County, Virginia in 1839. In 1864 he was in Haines Bluff, Mississippi, and joined Company H of the 3rd US Colored Cavalry. He gave his occupation as 'field hand'. His owners in Virginia had probably sold him to slave traders, who sold him to new owners in Mississippi.[58]

Cavalry during the Civil War was used for scouting the enemy's position, screening the movements of troops, providing security for units on the move and performing picket duty for encamped forces. Highly mobile, cavalry units could travel as much as thirty-five miles in a day without tiring horses or their riders. Cavalry troops were frequently used by both sides to conduct long distance raids to disrupt enemy supply lines.[59]

A cavalry soldier represented a significant investment. Union cavalry troopers were issued a sword, revolver, and usually a short-barreled Spencer carbine rifle. Cavalrymen were issued a dark colored horse that typically ate ten pounds of hay and fourteen pounds of feed each day.

Cavalry units in both armies learned to fight on horseback and on foot, employing tactics that had been developed during fights with Native American tribes on the western frontier. On horseback, troopers used their revolvers and swords; when fighting on foot, every fourth trooper held the horses of the other three while they fired their carbines.[60]

Private Helm's cavalry uniform was probably the nicest and most complete set of clothing he had worn in his life up to that time. He would have been issued a blue kepi-style hat, a dark blue blouse (shirt), and light blue trousers with a yellow stripe up the side of each leg, and knee length black boots. A wide leather belt with a brass buckle, supported by a strap across his chest, held his sword and pistol. On his horse he carried a tent, blanket, poncho, canteen, and saddle bags for his rations and personal effects.

In February 1864 Private Helm's regiment joined an expedition led by Colonel James Coates that had been ordered to raid through the Yazoo City area and link up with General Sherman's army at Meridian. As Coates' force travelled, they confiscated several hundred bales of valuable cotton from plantations along the river. Reaching Yazoo City on February 28, the cavalry disembarked first to reconnoiter and secure the town.

On March 5 Confederate forces commanded by Brigadier General Lawrence Ross attacked the Union detachments guarding Yazoo City. The day before, Ross's force had been reinforced and now outnumbered the Union troops defending the town. Men from Helm's unit were dug in, fighting from rifle pits. The Union infantry used cotton bales to barricade the streets. Three times Ross demanded that the U.S. force surrender, but the commander refused, as Ross offered no guarantee that black Union troops and their officers would be treated as prisoners of war rather than executed. After a six-hour battle, Coates was able to mount a counterattack that drove the Rebels away.[61]

The 3rd U.S. Colored Cavalry also participated in Brigadier General Benjamin Grierson's raid on Egypt Station, Mississippi in December 1864. The Union division captured more than 600 prisoners, destroyed ten miles of railroad track, several locomotives, dozens of freight cars, warehouses and other supplies. Grierson's raid was so successful that when the remnants of Confederate General John Bell Hood's Army of Tennessee reached Tupelo, Mississippi after being defeated at the Battle of Nashville, there weren't enough supplies to feed them. Hood had to furlough many of his men so they could fend for themselves.[62]

When the war ended, Private Henry Helm travelled to Memphis with his unit. By the time he was twenty-six years old, he had escaped from slavery and survived the war. He had to have cut a dashing figure in his cavalry uniform. He met and married a twenty-one-year-old woman named Elizabeth, but their time together was short lived; Private Henry Helm died of typhus in the regimental hospital on September 14, 1865, another victim of disease, the shared enemy of all soldiers.

In late 1864 the Confederacy was stretched to its limits on every front. Rebel soldiers and civilians were hungry and tired. Confederate troops were decimated by battlefield casualties and disease, while the Union seemed to have an inexhaustible supply of new recruits.

A successful Union attack at Mobile Bay in Alabama had deprived the South of a vital seaport, and most of what remained of its Navy. Lee's Army of Northern Virginia was pinned down in fighting around the capitol at Richmond, Virginia. The fall of Atlanta in September and Sherman's subsequent march to Savannah had split Rebel armies fighting in Virginia and the Carolinas from vital sources of supply in the South, and deprived the Confederacy of another seaport. General John Bell Hood's Army of the Tennessee had been destroyed by decisive Union victories at the battles of Franklin and Nashville.

North Carolina was home to the South's only remaining seaport. A 20-mile strip of land guarded the approach along the Cape Fear River to the port of Wilmington. The entrance to the river was protected by Fort Fisher, an L-shaped series of earthworks, obstacles, bombproof shelters, land mines and artillery emplacements guarded by 1,900 Rebel soldiers.

Confederate Colonel William Lamb commanded the garrison.[63]

First Battle of Fort Fisher – December 23-27, 1864

Recently promoted to Lieutenant General, Grant knew that controlling the port of Wilmington could help bring about a quick end to the war. Grant assigned the Army of the James, veterans of several engagements in Virginia, to attack Fort Fisher and take Wilmington.[64] Grant originally intended for Major General Godfrey Weitzel, second in command of the Army of the James, to lead the attack. Weitzel had immigrated to the U.S. from Germany, and was an experienced military professional who had graduated second in his class at the West Point military academy. Since joining the army at the beginning the war, he had earned several rapid promotions for "gallant and meritorious services" in a number of successful engagements.

However, Weitzel's commanding officer, Major General Benjamin Butler, insisted on personally commanding the Fort Fisher attack. Butler was not a professional soldier but an influential political appointee. While he had some battlefield successes, he also had some notable failures. Butler's hesitancy during multiple attacks on Petersburg earlier in 1864 had failed to result in Union victory, even though he had commanded better trained, better equipped and numerically superior forces in several engagements against the Confederate defenders. Despite misgivings, Grant reluctantly allowed Butler to lead the Fort Fisher expedition as he was senior in rank to Weitzel.

Some 6,500 soldiers of the Army of the James embarked on transports at Hampton Roads on December 14, 1864. They were joined in the attack by sixty-four U.S. Navy warships commanded by Rear Admiral David D. Porter.

Butler planned to have a ship, the *USS Louisiana*, loaded with 200 tons of gunpowder and detonated near the fort just prior to the attack. He was confident the explosion would damage the walls of the fort. Due to stormy weather, Butler's troop transports had to withdraw from the area around Fort Fisher. Near midnight on December 22, 1864, Porter decided to begin the attack by having the *USS Louisiana* towed near to the walls of the fort and fire the charges, but the explosion went off prematurely, nearly a mile from the beach, and caused no damage. The next morning, Porter ordered his gunboats closer to shore and launched an all-day barrage. Union gunners fired more than 10,000 rounds at Fort Fisher during the day, but the U.S. Navy suffered more casualties from on-board explosions of guns than the Confederates suffered in the fort.[65]

Near nightfall on December 23, the seaborne transports returned with the troops. Initially, Butler hesitated, thinking the explosion of the powder ship and the lengthy barrage had given the Confederates too much time to prepare for the Union assault. He finally decided to proceed, and on Christmas Day had a division of troops land to scout the defenses and determine whether a full attack could succeed.

On the beach, Union troops captured a Rebel artillery battery north of the fort. Two Confederate Junior Reserve battalions from North Carolina surrendered to the Federals. Brigadier General Adelbert Ames men set up a defensive line. A brigade of Federals commanded by Brigadier General Newton Curtis was sent forward to reconnoiter and reported that the walls of the fort appeared to be lightly defended. Curtis prepared his men for the attack, but contrary to Grant's orders, Butler ordered the Federals to return to the ships.

Expecting Confederate reinforcements and more bad weather, Butler declared that Fort Fisher was "impregnable" and on December 27 ordered the U.S. invasion force to return to Hampton Roads. The First Battle of Fort Fisher had resulted in an embarrassing and expensive defeat for the Union.

Frustrated, Grant relieved Butler of his command on January 8, 1865. He appointed Major General Alfred Terry to take command of the Army of the James and ordered him to lead a second expedition to take the fort.

Second Battle of Fort Fisher – January 13-15, 1865

Although Alfred Terry was a political appointee he had established a solid record as a competent soldier. He had experience with siege warfare at Charleston and at Petersburg. His troops had captured Fort Wagner in September 1863 after a hard summer of fighting. He had been one of the senior commanders at the battle of New Market Heights, so had experience working with U.S. Colored Troop units and their officers. Terry developed a good working relationship with Rear Admiral Porter.[66]

Terry planned to use an overwhelming force of 10,000 Union soldiers and fifty-three Navy ships in the assault on Fort Fisher. Almost a third of the ground troops involved in the expedition were African American soldiers. On January 13, 1865, Terry landed a division of U.S. Colored Troops commanded by Brigadier General Charles J. Paine on the peninsula north of the fort, to block reinforcements from coming to the aid of the Rebel defenders. Again, Porter's ships planned to bombard the fort with thousands of rounds of naval gunfire. Terry's two other divisions of Union infantry were to attack the short north wall of the fort. A strike force of 1,600 sailors and 400 marines were to land on the beach to attack the long wall of the fort that faced the Atlantic.[67]

Confederate General W.H.C. Whiting, commander of the District of Cape Fear, joined Colonel Lamb at the fort. Whiting asked General Braxton Bragg to send reinforcements to the fort, as he expected another Union attack. A large force of Confederates under Major General Robert Hoke were stationed just south of Wilmington, but Hoke was unwilling to release his troops, as he felt he needed them to defend the city.

On January 15, Porter's gunboats opened fire on Fort Fisher. The heavy bombardment disabled most of the Confederate guns within a few hours. The sailors and marines landed and attacked from the Atlantic beach. While the Rebels were distracted by the assault from the sea, Terry's infantry divisions attacked and breached the north wall of the fort.

The U.S.C.T.s were successful in blocking all but 400 Confederate troops from reinforcing the fort. At one point Rebel artillery at the south end of the fort began firing shells at the Union attackers inside the north perimeter. In the evening the Confederate commander, Colonel Lamb, was wounded and turned over command of the garrison to Major James Reilly.

Repeated requests to Bragg for reinforcements were ignored. After the first Union attack on Fort Fisher failed, Bragg believed the fort could not be taken. He dispatched General Alfred Colquitt to take command.

By the time Colquitt and his staff landed at the fort, however, the Confederate wounded were being evacuated, and the remaining defenders were preparing to surrender. Around 10:00 PM General Terry took the surrender of Fort Fisher from General Whiting. The Second Battle of Fort Fisher had resulted in a decisive Federal victory. The last Confederate seaport was cut off. A month later the city of Wilmington fell to Union forces.

Simpsonville – January 25, 1865

The ground was covered with snow on January 24, 1865 when a group of eighty soldiers from Company E of the 5th U.S. Colored Cavalry regiment camped for the night at a farm near Simpsonville, Kentucky. They had driven a herd of 900 cattle northwest from Camp Nelson, a Union supply depot and base south of Lexington. The cattle were to be delivered to Louisville, twenty-five miles west of Simpsonville on the Old Midland Trail, now U.S. Route 60.[68]

Although the men of Company E were cavalry soldiers, on this mission they were dismounted; only their commander, Second Lieutenant Augustus Flint, rode horseback. Flint made arrangements with the farmer to spend the night in the farmhouse, and to have his men pen the cattle in a fenced enclosure for the night before they bedded down in their tents. The temperature was near zero.

Sometime in the night, a stranger knocked on the door of the farmhouse. He told Flint that about a hundred of the cattle had gotten loose, and were doing damage at his farm nearby. He offered to awaken some of Flint's men to have them round up the cattle but said he didn't have proper boots. Flint, warm and dry in the comfort of the farmhouse, offered to loan the stranger his boots, and went back to bed.

The stranger was a spy for a group of Confederate guerillas. Earlier he had removed some of the rails from the fence where the cattle were penned and herded some of the cattle outside of the enclosure. Now, wearing Flint's boots, he awakened some of the soldiers and sent them to round up the straying cattle in the snow. They were awake far into the night. The stranger disappeared, still wearing the unsuspecting Lieutenant's boots.

The next morning, Flint borrowed shoes from the farmer to proceed on his mission. As the men got the cattle in motion, Flint stopped by the dry goods store in Simpsonville to purchase a new pair of boots more suitable for the winter weather.

Suddenly, fifteen Rebel guerillas rode into town. They were armed with six-shot Navy revolvers; some carried two pistols. Alerted by a citizen, Lieutenant Flint ran out of the store and hid in the storeroom crawl space until the guerillas left. The Rebels stole $1,200 in currency and merchandise, then galloped off to catch up with the cattle herd.[69]

Of the eighty soldiers, forty-one were at the back of the herd. Without their commander present, they were moving along casually, unaware of any danger. The guerillas galloped up behind the soldiers, firing as they attacked. They stampeded the cattle; the frightened horse team capsized the supply wagon. Most of the soldiers never got off a shot. Due to the bad weather, the powder in their muskets was damp. The men in front of the herd were able to escape.

Of the men behind the herd, at least twenty-two were shot dead on the spot by the guerillas, several were wounded, and only two were able to escape – one by playing dead, the other by hiding under the overturned wagon. The fight took less than an hour. The guerillas gathered all the muskets and ammunition from the dead and wounded soldiers, and galloped away. After the attack, Flint ran from his hiding place and rode his horse to Louisville, abandoning his men.

That afternoon a group of citizens gathered up as many wounded men and bodies as they could find, and buried some of the dead in a mass grave. The next day they found more bodies and buried them along with some wounded that had died after the battle in a second mass grave. More wounded died days later as they were being carried on ambulances to Louisville.[70]

The following news account was published shortly after the massacre:

THE CINCINNATI DAILY GAZETTE
Cincinnati, Ohio
Saturday Morning, January 28, 1865
Vol. 76 No. 183
Horrible Massacre by Guerrillas — Thirty-five Colored Soldiers Murdered — Eight More Dangerously Wounded

From The Louisville Journal, 26th

A drove of Government cattle, about nine hundred head, was on the way to this city yesterday from Camp Nelson, guarded, by eighty negro soldiers detailed from various regiments. The day being cold, and no danger being apprehended, the soldiers were allowed to straggle along by themselves, while their officers stopped to warm at various houses on the road. One half of the command marched in front of the cattle, while the other portion kept in the rear of the drove. The cattle and the guards were not yet out of sight of Simpsonville when fifteen guerrillas, headed by the desperate Colter, dashed into the town. Three of the negro officers were loafing in the tavern at the time, but they succeeded in making their escape from the outlaws. The guerrillas robbed the citizens of the place of goods amounting to about twelve hundred dollars when they started in pursuit of the negro troops guarding the cattle. They were not long in over-taking them as the citizens of Simpsonville, soon after their departure from the place, heard rapid firing down the road. In about half an hour the guerrillas returned; loaded down with booty, and stated that they had killed twenty-five of the negroes. They gave no further explanation, but moved off in the direction of Shelbyville. A gentleman who was detained at Simpsonville by the outlaws, after they were out of sight, resumed his journey toward Louisville. Not more than half a mile this side of the village a terrible scene was presented to view. The ground was stained with blood and the dead bodies of negro soldiers were stretched out along the road. It was evident that the guerrillas had dashed upon the party guarding the rear of the cattle and taken them completely by surprise. They could not have offered any serious resistance, as none of the outlaws were even wounded. It is presumed that the negroes surrendered and were shot down in cold blood, as but two of the entire number escaped-one of them by secreting himself behind a wagon, the other by running, as he was met several miles from the scene of tragedy, wounded and nearly exhausted. Thirty-five dead bodies were counted lying in the road and vicinity. It was a horrible butchery, yet the scoundrels engaged in the bloody work shot down their victims with feelings of delight.

The cattle stampeded, and as soon as the advance guard learned of what was going on in the rear, each individual in blue made a tall scamper for a place of safety. Colter, Berry and Sue Mundy were the leaders of the murderous gang. The outlaws were but fifteen in number-one of them a black scoundrel, who boasted on the return of the band to Simpsonville that he killed three of the soldiers. In making the attack, the guerrillas were only armed with navy revolvers. After the wholesale murder, they took good care to secure the arms and ammunition of the slain. The officers in command of the negro troops should be held responsible for the slaughter, for it is certain that if they had been with their men, and enforced a proper discipline, the outlaws would have been whipped with ease.

If the soldiers had not been straggling, Colter would never have ventured to make the attack. A heavy responsibility rests with some one, and we trust that the facts of the case will be fully inquired into by the authorities.

LATEST: A gentleman who left Simpsonville at 8 o'clock last evening, and arrived in the city at a late hour last night, states that the citizens, up to the time he left, had collected and buried fourteen dead bodies of the murdered soldiers. Eight negroes, so severely wounded that many of them will die, were receiving medical treatment. It was thought that several more bodies would be found this morning scattered about the fields, as after they were shot many of the negroes ran in different directions and fell and died. The guerrillas were traveling towards Shelbyville at last accounts.[71]

Henry MacGruder was convicted as a spy and terrorist for other offenses and hanged late in 1865, but although the other guerillas were identified, no one was ever punished for the murders committed during the Simpsonville Massacre. Lieutenant Augustus Flint was never held accountable for his carelessness or for abandoning his wounded and dying men.

The Simpsonville Massacre was largely forgotten until 2008, when the Kentucky African American Heritage Commission and the Shelby County Historical Society launched an effort to investigate the slaughter, locate the mass graves and memorialize the murdered soldiers. An African American cemetery at the site of the incident was determined to be near the location of the two mass graves.

In 2010, two columns of gravestones were erected along Highway 60 near the site of the massacre, with a U.S. flag and a historical marker. The stones are engraved with the names of the twenty-two soldiers buried nearby.

Mount Elba – January 1865

In June 1864 a twenty-year-old former slave named John Henry enlisted in Battery H of the 2nd United States Colored Artillery regiment as a Private in Pine Bluff, Arkansas. It is not known how John Henry made his way to Arkansas from Franklin County, Virginia, where he was born March 10, 1844. He gave his occupation as a farmer. He was likely sold by his original owner; had he escaped from captivity in Virginia, he probably would not have made his way to another southern state. He occasionally used an alias, sometimes giving his name as John Henry Jones.[72]

The 2nd US Colored Artillery was a 'Light Artillery' regiment, a designation which referred to the regiment's mobility, not the size of its cannon. In a light artillery unit, gunners were mounted on horses as the army moved, so they could keep up with the cavalry units to which they were assigned. The cannons they fired and the caissons carrying powder and shells were drawn by six-horse teams.[73]

In January 1865 Private Henry's unit was assigned to join a large cavalry raid on Mount Elba, Arkansas, thirty-six miles away from Pine Bluff, commanded by Brigadier General Eugene A. Carr, a career Army officer. Carr was a veteran with many years of experience; his first combat assignment had been in the Battle of the Diablo Mountains in Texas, where he was wounded by an Apache arrow. Carr's force set out from Little Rock, Arkansas on January 22, and stopped at Pine Bluffs to pick up more troops and the six cannon that were to provide artillery support during the raid. All told 3,519 Union soldiers participated in the expedition.[74]

The Union force set out from Pine Bluff at daylight on January 26. They arrived at Mount Elba the following day, after their advance party had skirmished with a party of about sixty Rebels, capturing ten. One Union trooper and two Confederates were killed. At Mount Elba the Federal troops built a pontoon bridge over the Saline River. Leaving his infantry units to guard the river crossing, Carr led his cavalry across the bridge to continue the raid farther south, at one point approaching within two miles of the town of Camden, Arkansas where they engaged another small Confederate force.

They returned to Little Rock on February 4, 1865, marching much of the way through cold rain on muddy roads, having captured thirty-four Confederate prisoners and killed three Rebels. One of the Union raiders was killed, and three were wounded.

On mustering out of the Army in 1866 Private John Henry made a home in Gould, Arkansas - only forty-five miles from Pine Bluff – and lived to be seventy-six years old. John Henry died on August 14, 1920.[75]

9. MEDALS OF HONOR

The Congressional Medal of Honor is the highest military decoration for valor awarded by the United States, and is awarded by the President on behalf of Congress. Eight African American men born in Virginia were awarded the Medal of Honor for heroism during the Civil War.

William H. Carney - July 18, 1863:

When the color sergeant was shot down, this soldier grasped the flag, led the way to the parapet, and planted the colors thereon. When the troops fell back he brought off the flag, under a fierce fire in which he was twice severely wounded.[1]

His Compiled Military Service Records indicated he was born in New Bedford, Massachusetts but William Carney had been born into slavery in Norfolk, Virginia in 1840. He made his way to Massachusetts, where other members of his family were living. On February 17, 1863, at age twenty-two, Carney joined Company C of the 54th Massachusetts Volunteer Infantry regiment, giving his occupation as 'Seaman'. He was promoted to Sergeant on March 30, 1863 at the mustering of his regiment.[2]

In Civil War regiments, the duty of a flagbearer was more than symbolic. The flag of a regiment and company guidon signaled where soldiers of a particular unit were supposed to be. In the confusing smoke and dust of a battle, the regimental flag was often the only identifiable rallying point for soldiers in the chaos. The flagbearer's role was vital. The flag needed to be kept aloft and identifiable, near the unit commander. If the flagbearer was wounded or killed, it was critical for another man to step in and raise the colors, so the soldiers in the company could rally together and continue to fight as a cohesive unit.

During the attack on Fort Wagner on July 18, 1863, an explosion killed John Wall, who was carrying the United States flag. Sergeant William Carney caught the flag before it could hit the ground. Seriously wounded twice during the battle, Carney continued to carry the flag until he was relieved. As he walked back to the field hospital, he said to the men around him: "Boys, I only did my duty; the old flag never touched the ground!" before he collapsed. He spent the next few months in hospitals. With a serious gunshot wound in his left hip that partially paralyzed his leg, Carney was discharged from the Army for disability on June 30, 1864. Carney was awarded the Congressional Medal of Honor on May 23, 1900. He died on December 9, 1908 from injuries sustained in a tragic elevator accident, and is buried at the Oak Grove Cemetery in New Bedford, Massachusetts.[3] In Norfolk, Virginia, the town where he was born, a monument to African American veterans of the Civil War and Spanish American War at the West Point Cemetery includes a statue of Sergeant William H. Carney.[4]

Robert Blake - December 25, 1863:

On board the U.S. Steam Gunboat Marblehead off Legareville, Stono River, 25 December 1863, in an engagement with the enemy on John's Island. Serving the rifle gun, Blake, an escaped slave, carried out his duties bravely throughout the engagement, which resulted in the enemy's abandonment of positions, leaving a caisson and one gun behind.[5]

Born in Virginia, Robert Blake escaped from slavery before joining the U.S. Navy to serve as a steward for

Lieutenant Commander Richard W. Meade, commander of the gunboat Marblehead.

When the ship came under heavy Confederate artillery fire near John's Island, Blake brought Lieutenant Commander Meade a uniform – so he could change out of his nightclothes – then walked to the gun deck to help there.

Technically Blake was a non-combatant, and could have returned to safety below decks, but when a powder-boy manning one of the Marblehead's guns was killed by an exploding shell, Blake took his place, and kept firing at the enemy until the Rebels abandoned the fight.[6]

James Mifflin - August 5, 1864:

On board the USS Brooklyn during successful attacks against Fort Morgan, rebel gunboats, and the ram Tennessee in Mobile Bay, 5 August 1864. Stationed in the immediate vicinity of the shell whips, which were twice cleared of men by bursting shells, Mifflin remained steadfast at his post and performed his duties in the powder division throughout the furious action which resulted in the surrender of the prize ram Tennessee and in the damaging and destruction of batteries at Fort Morgan.[7]

Born in Richmond, Virginia in 1839, James Mifflin was twenty-five years old when he enlisted in the United States Navy in April 1864.[8] In September of the same year, Mifflin was serving as an Engineer's Cook on the USS Brooklyn during the Siege of Fort Morgan at Mobile Bay, Alabama. Mifflin was assigned to operate the 'shell whips', crane-like devices used for moving powder and ammunition from the hold of the ship to the gun deck.

During the battle, exploding enemy shells killed the other men on the deck around him two times, but Mifflin stayed at his post, carrying ammunition to the gunners until the Rebels defending Fort Morgan surrendered.

Powhatan Beaty, September 29, 1864:

Took command of his company, all the officers having been killed or wounded, and gallantly led it.[9]

Born into slavery at Richmond, Virginia on October 8, 1837, Powhatan Beaty joined Company G of the 5th U.S. Colored Infantry Regiment on June 7, 1863 in Cincinnati, Ohio, where he had been living. He gave his occupation as "Turner".[10] Beaty was appointed as First Sergeant when he enlisted at Camp Delaware. During the Battle of New Market Heights on September 29, 1864, Beaty ran 600 yards through withering enemy fire to retrieve the flag when the flagbearer was killed by enemy fire. When Company G's commanding officer was killed in the fighting, Beaty took charge, and commanded the company for the remainder of the fierce battle. Major General Benjamin Butler recommended Beaty for the Congressional Medal of Honor, which was awarded to him on April 6, 1865.[11]

First Sergeant Beaty remained with his unit until he was discharged at Carolina City, North Carolina on September 20, 1865. He returned to Cincinnati and resumed his old job as a turner. He became a popular public speaker, began acting in amateur theater and eventually performed as a professional actor. His most notable performance occurred on May 7, 1884 at Ford's Theater in Washington D.C., where he acted in a production of Shakespeare's works. Frederick Douglass was in the audience that night.[12]

Born in Richmond, Virginia, Sergeant Powhatan Beaty was one of the heroes of the Battle of New Market Heights. He was awarded the Congressional Medal of Honor for his actions during the battle. - *Photo: Library of Congress*

Powhatan Beaty passed away on December 6, 1916 and was buried in the Union Baptist Cemetery in Cincinnati, Ohio.

James Daniel Gardiner, September 29, 1864:

Rushed in advance of his brigade, shot a rebel officer who was on the parapet rallying his men, and then ran him through with his bayonet.[13]

Born on September 16, 1839 in Gloucester County, Virginia, James Daniel Gardiner joined Company I of the 36th U.S. Colored Infantry Regiment on September 15, 1863.[14] A little over a year later he took part in the vicious fighting around New Market Heights outside of Richmond. Charging ahead of his regiment, Gardiner ran to the top of the Confederate fortifications along New Market Road, and killed a Rebel officer that was trying to rally his men for a counterattack. Gardiner was promoted to Sergeant on the day after the battle, and awarded the Medal of Honor on April 5, 1865

Sergeant James Gardiner was awarded the Congressional Medal of Honor for heroism during the Battle of New Market Heights. - *Photo: Congressional Medal of Honor Society website*

After his regiment transferred to Texas he was hospitalized twice for illness, reduced in rank back to private, and at one point confined for disciplinary issues, but Gardiner remained with his unit until he was discharged on September 20, 1866.

James Gardiner died on September 29, 1905, forty-one years to the day after earning the nation's highest award for bravery. He is buried at Calvary Cemetery in Ottumwa, Iowa. A memorial to Gardiner was erected by Gloucester County in 2005.

Miles James, September 29, 1864:

Having had his arm mutilated, making immediate amputation necessary, he loaded and discharged his piece with one hand and urged his men forward; this within 30 yards of the enemy's works.[15]

Miles James was born in Princess Anne County, Virginia in 1829. At age thirty-nine, he joined Company B of the 36th U.S. Colored Infantry Regiment on November 16, 1863 at Norfolk, giving his occupation as "Farmer."[16]

During the charge on New Market Heights, Corporal James' left arm was mangled by rifle fire. Despite his wounds, he kept firing on the enemy with his right hand, and urged his men to keep moving forward against the Rebel works along the New Market Road.

In February 1865 his commanding officer, Brigadier General A.G. Draper, wrote the Surgeon in Charge at Fort Monroe asking that he allow James, then a Sergeant, to remain in the service.

Draper wrote: "He is one of the bravest men I ever saw; and is in every respect a model soldier. He is worth more with his single arm, than half a dozen ordinary men."[17]

Edward Ratcliff, September 29, 1864:

Commanded and gallantly led his company after the commanding officer had been killed; was the first enlisted man to enter the enemy's works.[18]

Edward Ratcliff was born a slave in Virginia and worked on the Hankins family farm in James City County until he was liberated when the Union Army occupied Yorktown.

Ratcliff was married to Grace Randall, also a slave, and they had a daughter named Hannah, born in March 1861. He was twenty-nine years old when he enlisted in Company C of the 38th U.S. Colored Infantry Regiment on January 1, 1864 at Norfolk.

Ratcliff was promoted to First Sergeant when he enlisted, likely for his maturity and stability.[19] When his commanding officer was killed during the assault on the Confederate earthworks at New Market Heights, First Sergeant Edward Ratcliff took command of Company C and led his unit in the attack. He led from the front – Ratcliff was the first enlisted man to reach the Rebel strongpoint.

In December, 1864, because of his bravery, Edward Ratcliff was promoted to Sergeant Major of his regiment, and on April 6, 1865, he was awarded the Congressional Medal of Honor.

Edward Ratcliff remained with his unit until he was discharged in January 1867 from Indianola, Texas. He was eighty years old when he died on March 10, 1915 in York County. He is buried in the cemetery at the Naval Station in Lackey, Virginia.

186

Charles Veal, September 29, 1864:

Seized the national colors, after two color bearers had been shot down close to the enemy's works, and bore them through the remainder of the battle.[20]

Born in Portsmouth, Charles Veal was free when he joined Company D of the 4th U.S. Colored Infantry on July 21, 1863 at Baltimore. He gave his occupation as 'Fireman'.[21] Veal was promoted to Corporal shortly after enlisting, on August 28, 1863.

During the attack on the Confederate lines at New Market Heights on September 29, 1864, Sergeant Alfred Hilton, born in Maryland, was carrying the American flag. When the soldier carrying the regimental flag was wounded, Hilton picked up the regimental flag and kept moving forward. When Hilton was wounded, Corporal Charles Veal picked up the regimental flag, and Sergeant Major Christian Fleetwood, a Maryland soldier, picked up the American flag.

Hilton, Veal, and Fleetwood were all awarded the Congressional Medal of Honor for their heroism at New Market Heights. Major General Benjamin Butler promoted Veal to Sergeant shortly after the battle.[22]

Sergeant Veal was seriously wounded in action at the battle of Fort Fisher on January 13, 1865, but spent only a week in the hospital. Veal died young, at age thirty-four, on July 27, 1872.

10. THE OTHER SHORE

On the Eastern Shore of Virginia are Accomack County in the north and Northampton County in the south. A native American settlement in what is now Accomack County was first visited by European explorers in 1603, four years before a permanent settlement was established in Jamestown.[1]

The Chesapeake Bay is on the western side of Accomack County; the Atlantic Ocean washes the eastern beaches. The name Accomack is derived from a native word meaning "*the other shore*".[2]

The peninsula is composed of coastal salt marshes, beaches, forest, and farmland, and is rich in wildlife. Wild ponies graze Chincoteague Island in the northeast across from the Assateague Island National Seashore; Martin National Wildlife Refuge is found on the Chesapeake side.

Before 1860 many Accomack farmers raised peanuts, vegetables, and tobacco. The Chesapeake Bay supported a thriving trade in oysters and fish. The Eastern Shore was, and is, remote and peaceful compared to the mainland across the Chesapeake.

During the war oystering in the bay was suppressed by Federal military authorities to keep Confederates from profiting from the industry and to limit the number of potential enemy boats from sailing the Chesapeake.[3]

More than 600 African American men born in Accomack County joined the Union Army. Some who listed their occupation as 'Oysterman' or 'Sailor' may have been out of work when they enlisted. Most, as evidenced by their subsequent conduct, were committed to fighting for their freedom. All would suffer and sacrifice. The stories of the Accomack County men reflect the experiences of thousands of black soldiers born in Virginia who served in the Union Army during the war.

In late 1863 Union Colonel William Birney was assigned to raise several regiments of United States Colored Troops. Born in Alabama in 1819, Birney had an adventure-filled past before joining the United States Army.[4]

His father, James G. Birney, had moved from Kentucky to a plantation in Alabama. A lawyer by profession, James Birney had a highly developed sense of justice, defending the legal interests of members of the Cherokee Indian tribe in the 1820s, when it was highly controversial to do so.

Living and working on his plantation, Birney became disillusioned and began to feel slavery was exerting a malignant influence on his children.

At first, Birney believed in the gradual emancipation of slaves. He was an early supporter of the American Colonization Society. Elected to the legislature, James Birney helped pass a resolution barring importation of slaves into Alabama from other states, although the practice was later resumed. Sensing his anti-slavery stance might be putting his family at risk, Birney moved back to Kentucky in 1833, freed his remaining six slaves, and hired his former slave Michael to work for wages. Deciding to support the immediate emancipation of slaves, Birney became a leader of the abolitionist movement and was one of the founding members of the Republican Party.

William Birney was educated as a lawyer and professor of English literature. He was a strong and vocal supporter of his father's abolitionist views. After marrying in 1846, William moved to Europe. When the French Revolution of 1848 began, he was teaching English literature at the University of Bourges. William Birney took an active part in the Revolution against King

Louis Philippe I, at one point commanding a barricade on the Rue Saint-Jacques in Paris.

By 1861 William and his wife had returned to the States. In May 1861 he joined the U.S. Army, organized the 1st New Jersey Regiment, and was elected Captain. William Birney fought in the First and Second Battles of Bull Run, Chantilly, Fredericksburg and Chancellorsville, and eventually earned promotion to Major. His brothers, David, Dion, and Fitzhugh, also served in the Union Army. All three died of disease during the war.

In 1863 Birney was commissioned by the War Department to assist in recruiting black men to serve in United States Colored Infantry regiments. Promoted to Colonel, William Birney helped to recruit and organize eight regiments, and personally commanded the 2nd U.S. Colored Infantry. He was promoted to Brigadier General and led a brigade of black regiments.

During November 1863, hundreds of Accomack men enlisted, many of them from communities near their homes: Jenkins Bridge, Pungoteague, Horntown, Onancock, and Drummondtown. For most, Colonel William Birney was named as the enlisting officer.

The days were getting shorter, and the air was getting cooler. On November 4 the sun rose at 6:49 AM and set at 5:11 PM; the temperature at midday was in the mid-sixties. Twenty-three Accomack County men enlisted that day. Forty-four more enlisted on Saturday, November 7. On November 9 it was gloomy and cool; that Monday there were no enlistments, but twenty-three on Tuesday. Sunday the 15th the sun set at 5:00 PM and it rained all night. Enlistments gradually dropped off as the month went by and the weather changed. On November 30 the sky was sunny and cold; the temperature stayed in the low thirties.[5]

As they appeared before the enlisting officers to volunteer, the names the men gave would be familiar today to an Accomack native. Twenty-five men gave their last name as Bailey, Bayly, or the equivalent. Eighteen gave Sample as their last name, seventeen stated their last name was White. Eight gave their last name as Northern or Northam; seven gave their last name as Wise.

Almost all the enlistees marked their enlistment papers with an "X", as they had been prevented by law from learning to write. The men enlisted for three years, and were promised a $2 'recruiting premium' for the first months of their service. In July 1866 Congress voted to add a $100 enlistment bounty to their pay.

Through an error in interpretation of the law that created the U.S. Colored Troop units, soldiers enlisting in 1863 were initially paid $7 per month. Late in 1864 this was corrected, and they were paid the difference between $7 and $13 for each month they had been paid short.

Notations occasionally appear in soldiers' records indicating "Slave" or "Free on or before April 19 1861." When the first U.S.C.T. units were formed, the rules were interpreted to mean that men who had been slaves before the war were to be paid at a lower rate than men who had been free. The rules were later changed and clarified to pay former slaves the same wages as free blacks and as white soldiers of the same rank.[6]

As each man enlisted, information was collected that could be used to describe him, including his approximate age, height, complexion, eye color, and hair color. Without accurate birth records, many had to estimate their ages. The average age given was between twenty-four and twenty-five.

Private John Drummer was the youngest enlistee from Accomack County when he joined Company B of the 9th U.S. Colored Infantry on November 7, 1863 at age twelve. He had been free before the war. Private Drummer participated in the battles at John's Island, South Carolina, Deep Bottom, Virginia, and Chaffins Farm, Virginia.[7]

Private Isaac Floyd enlisted in Troop K of the 2nd U.S. Colored Cavalry on January 1, 1864 at Fort Monroe when he was fifty-one years old. He was assigned daily duty as a farrier but was discharged for disability September 8, 1864. Among older soldiers, health problems were common.[8]

Drummer Alfred Wallack was twenty-two years old and measured 4' 10" tall when he enlisted in Company I of the 19th U.S. Colored Infantry in June of 1864. Private Henry Rodgers was 6' 1 ¼" tall and twenty-six years old when he enlisted in Troop K of the 2nd U.S. Colored Cavalry in January 1864. Rodgers was discharged for disability in June 1865 with a hernia.[9]

Descriptions of soldiers' skin, eye, and hair color ranged widely. Black complexion, black eyes, and black hair was listed most often; soldiers with lighter features were harder to describe. Compiled Military Service Records for U.S. Colored troops include the following examples:

Complexion	Eyes	Hair
Black	Black	Chestnut
Griff	Black	Black
Copper	Brown	Black
Dark	Dark	Dark
Yellow	Black	Black
Mulatto	Blue	Black
Light	Blue	Light
Not Very Black	Black	Woolly

The newly enlisted men from Accomack County travelled ninety miles by ship across the Chesapeake Bay and up the Patuxent River to Charles County, Maryland. As many as 250 soldiers assigned to the 7th, 9th, and 10th U.S. Colored Infantry regiments met for their first roll call and inspection in late 1863 at Camp Stanton, on the west side of the Patuxent near the village of Benedict, Maryland. The Accomack men mustered along with troops born in and recruited from other counties.

Four men who had enlisted in the 9th Regiment were rejected by the mustering officer, likely for health reasons. The early winter weather may have been a factor, but a lot of men became sick during those first weeks at Camp Stanton.

During the first month nineteen Accomack County soldiers died of disease, most of them from 'congestive fever'. There were so many sick, Lieutenant Colonel Samuel C. Armstrong detailed men from the 9th U.S. Colored Infantry to serve as nurses in the post hospital. This was be the first of many bouts with illness the soldiers were to face. Inclement weather, inadequate food, filthy water and close quarters caused more death among these men over the next three years than Rebel muskets and artillery.

The men received uniforms, learned to march and drill, and got their first introduction to Army garrison life. They were issued weapons and taught how to load and fire them. They were armed, usually, with Springfield or Enfield rifle muskets. The Springfields were considered by soldiers to be more reliable.

The soldiers were issued basic equipment: Canteen, haversack, knapsack, bayonet with scabbard, belt, cartridge box, primer box, blanket, shelter tent. Certain accessories came with their muskets: The tampion kept dirt and water from getting into the barrel. A wiper could be attached to the ramrod to help with cleaning. A screwdriver was used to make adjustments. Sergeants and some corporals were issued a non-commissioned officers' sword with scabbard, and required to sew the insignia of their rank onto the sleeves of their uniform blouse.

At frequent intervals, especially before a march or battle, the men were inspected to make sure they had their complete kit, and to confirm that their uniforms, equipment and weapons were clean and serviceable. If any equipment was missing, the soldier was required to replace it, and a portion of his pay was withheld to cover the cost. A missing canteen cost sixty-five cents. At $7.00 per month, replacing that canteen cost about three days' pay; a missing haversack cost ninety-five cents, or about four days' pay.

Only twenty-two Accomack County men are shown as having served in Artillery units, most of them in Battery B of the 2nd U.S. Colored Light Artillery regiment.

In the 2nd U.S. Colored Cavalry, there were seventy troopers from Accomack County.

The majority of Accomack County's black soldiers enlisted in the Infantry. At least 179 enlisted in the 9th U.S. Colored Infantry. In the 10th U.S.C.I., 171 were enlisted; fifty-nine enlisted in the 7th U.S.C.I.

In several of these regiments, Accomack County men constituted a significant portion of their companies' strength. When initially organized, a company consisted of nearly 100 soldiers. A 'full' regiment consisted of ten companies, or around 1,000 soldiers. In the 9th U.S.C.I. there were forty-eight men in Company D and forty-one men in Company E born in Accomack County.

Company K of the 7th U.S. Colored Infantry included forty-eight Accomack men. Company I of the 10th U.S. Colored Infantry contained sixty-six men born in Accomack County. As the war progressed and the

194

regiments marched, disease and battle took a dramatic toll on the size of these formations.

As winter turned into spring in 1864, the regiments deployed to new duty stations. The 2nd U.S. Colored Cavalry Regiment was assigned to Camp Getty, four miles west of Portsmouth, Virginia. On a foraging expedition to the town of Suffolk in March 1864, a small detachment of soldiers from the 2nd Cavalry commanded by Lieutenant Colonel Nathan Pond was attacked by Rebels from the 49th North Carolina Infantry regiment commanded by Brigadier General Matthew W. Ransom. Another detachment, commanded by Colonel George Cole, was also attacked. Though outnumbered ten to one in bitter fighting, including some hand-to-hand combat, a majority of troopers from the 2nd U.S. Colored Cavalry were able to escape.[10] At least seven are known to have been killed in the fight. Private Jacob Parker, a 21-year-old from Accomack County who had enlisted in Company K in January, was killed in action at Suffolk.

The 10th U.S. Colored Infantry was stationed at Drummondtown until April, then moved to Yorktown, Virginia. Soldiers from the 10th were part of the garrison at Fort Powhatan on May 24, 1864 when the stronghold was attacked by more than 2,000 Confederate cavalry troopers commanded by Brigadier General Fitzhugh Lee, nephew of General Robert E. Lee. Although outnumbered by more than two to one, the all-black Union garrison at Fort Powhatan was able to repel the Rebel attack.[12]

Private Isaac West of Company D, however, died on June 4 in the General Hospital at Hampton of wounds received in the battle.[13] West was twenty years old, and had worked as a Sailor back on the Eastern Shore. Private Daniel Beach was hospitalized at Hampton on May 24, probably from wounds sustained at Fort Powhatan.[14] Beach was hospitalized again a year later, suffering from epilepsy, but survived the war and went home to his wife Sarah in Locust Mount, Virginia.

Levins Bloxam of Company E and Edmund Seymore of Company H was also hospitalized after the battle.[15] Sergeant Thomas Rue, only seventeen years old, survived the wounds he received that day and was promoted to First Sergeant of Company D in January 1865.[16] Private Daniel Ewell was sent to the Point of Rocks Hospital on May 24 but as nothing was heard from him afterwards he likely died as a result of his wounds.[17]

The 9th U.S. Colored Infantry was dispatched to South Carolina until early August. They fought in engagements at John's Island and James Island during July.

From April to October 1864, the 9th was commanded by Lieutenant Colonel Samuel Chapman Armstrong. Armstrong had been born in Hawaii, where his father was a missionary, and before the war had been attending college in Massachusetts. He was twenty-five years old. One of Armstrong's classmates was James A. Garfield. Like Garfield, he joined the Union Army when the war began. In a letter to a friend, Armstrong wrote that the war should be fought until *"every slave...can call himself his own, and his wife and children his own."*[18] Armstrong fought in the Battle of Gettysburg as a Captain, earned a promotion to Major, and was promoted again to Lieutenant Colonel when he accepted command of the 9th U.S. Colored Infantry regiment.

Armstrong survived the war and in 1868 helped found the Hampton Normal and Agricultural Institute, a school for training black teachers in Hampton, Virginia. One of Armstrong's most famous pupils was a former slave from Franklin County, Booker T. Washington, who came to Hampton in 1872. Washington was profoundly influenced by Armstrong's ideas on education and described the former soldier as *"the most perfect specimen of man, physically, mentally and spiritually the most Christ-like.*"[19] When he helped to found the Tuskegee Institute in Alabama, Washington incorporated many of Armstrong's ideas in the operation of the new school.

Many soldiers of the 9th contracted malaria during their stay in South Carolina. Private John Boggs[20] and Private Charles Culleny[21] of Accomack County died of malaria at the Beaufort, South Carolina hospital in July; both served in Company D. Private Charles Conquest of Company E died at sea on the journey back to Fort Monroe in August.[22]

Officers, too, were vulnerable to disease. Captain Douglas Risley of Company E was granted a thirty-day furlough in June 1864 to recover from chronic diarrhea.[23]

At least sixteen men from Accomack County served in the 23rd and 43rd U.S. Colored Infantry Regiments during the Battle of the Crater outside Petersburg on July 30, 1864. Privates Stephen Baines[24] of the 43rd U.S.C.I. was killed during the battle, as were Privates George Kellum[25] and Joseph West[26] of the 23rd U.S.C.I.

Private Charles H. Graham of the 23rd was wounded and captured during the battle, sent to the Confederate prisoner of war camp in Salisbury, North Carolina and then to Columbia, South Carolina for the rest of the war.[27] Private John W. T. Ashby of the 43rd was wounded in the right hip.[28] Private Jacob Grant of the 23rd was wounded in the left shoulder by a Minie ball.[29] Private William Jones of the 43rd received a gunshot wound in his left thigh.[30]

Private John R. Green of Company K, 23rd U.S. Colored Infantry, had joined the regiment less than a month before he was wounded in the lower right jaw during the Battle of the Crater. Green died on September 23, 1864 of his wounds at L'Overture Hospital in Alexandria and was buried in Grave #69 of the Freemans Cemetery.[31]

After their return from South Carolina to Virginia, the soldiers of the 7th and 9th U.S. Colored Infantry regiments were involved in the series of engagements at Deep Bottom. Among the soldiers born in Accomack County, Sergeant John Ayers of Company K, 7th U.S.C.I. was wounded in a successful attack on August 15 to retake some rifle pits from the Rebels.[32] Ayers recovered from his wounds in time to participate in the Battle of New Market Heights a few weeks later.

Sergeant Lewis Major of Company E, Corporal Henry A. Wise and Private Solomon Wise of Company C and Sergeant John Dennis of Company A were listed with other 9th U.S.C.I. soldiers in a news dispatch by Thomas Morris Chester to the Philadelphia Press as having been wounded at Deep Bottom on August 16.[33]

Sergeant Dennis's wounds were especially severe and painful. The regimental surgeon, E.M. Pease, wrote that Dennis suffered from a *"Gunshot wound in the right side. The ball entered the body near the short ribs and remaining imbedded probably in the wall of the chest has never been extracted. Breathing is difficult and other exertion impossible."*[34] This was *"A clear case for pension."* Dennis was discharged for disability in February 1865.

Corporal Henry A. Wise died at Summit Hospital in Philadelphia on August 25 of the wounds he received at Deep Bottom. A Minie ball had gone through his lower left jaw and right shoulder. Wise left a widow, Ann, back on the Eastern Shore.[35]

Private Solomon Wise, probably Henry's brother, survived and returned to duty with his regiment in January 1865. He travelled with his unit to Texas a few months later and was assigned to detached service with the Quartermaster Department in Brownsville.[36]

Corporal George Pruett of Company C, 9th U.S.C.I. received a particularly gruesome wound in his groin and right thigh at Deep Bottom. The only treatments listed while he was in the hospital at White Hall General Hospital in Bristol, Pennsylvania were "Cold Water Dressings". Pruett was discharged from the Army while he was a patient in the hospital.[37]

The brutal fighting September 28-30, 1864 at New Market Heights claimed the lives of several Accomack County men and changed the lives of many others. Company K of the 7th U.S. Colored Infantry was especially hard hit during the assault on Fort Gilmer.

The twenty-seven-foot earthwork in front of the fort proved to be a deathtrap. Private John Bailey was among the men killed as they attempted to climb out of the ditch to attack the fort.[38] Private Riley Pitts was captured in the attack and died a few months later in Salisbury as a prisoner of war.[39]

Private Isaiah Bull was captured and died in November at the Castle Thunder prison in Richmond.[40] Private Levin Wollop was missing in action after the assault on Fort Gilmer and was probably killed.[41] Private John Custus was wounded and likely died of his wounds; he never returned to his company.[42]

George Foskey had just been promoted to First Sergeant of Company K on September 27. Captured, he was confined in Richmond as a POW until the end of the war.[43]

Private Henry Massey received a "slight" wound during the fight at Fort Gilmer, but recovered from his wounds.[44] Private George Fletcher[45], Sergeant John Ayers[46], Corporal Abel Bagwell[47], and Sergeant James Bailey[48] also recovered. Private Isaac Coates survived, but his right leg was amputated when he contracted gangrene.[49]

Soldiers from the 9th U.S. Colored Infantry suffered grievously during the fighting at Chaffins Farm and Fort Gilmer.

From Company B, Corporal James Rogers[50] and Privates Henry Ashby[51], John Glenn[52], Walter Kellum[53] and Littleton Twinington[54] were all wounded during the battle. They recovered and were discharged with their regiment from New Orleans in November 1866. Private Suthy Chandler, however, ultimately died from his wounds.[55]

Private Levi Finney of Company B had been wounded in action at Deep Bottom on August 15. Finney was wounded a second time on September 29 at Chaffins Farm and survived to be discharged from New Orleans with the rest of his regiment.[56]

First Sergeant Henry P. Waters of Company C, who had been a Boatman in civilian life, was wounded at Chaffins Farm but survived.[57] Private James Lindsey, also of Company C, endured amputation of his right arm as the result of a gunshot wound received in that fight.[58] Many more Accomack County men's lives were forever changed as a result of the desperate fighting at New Market Heights, Fort Gilmer, Fort Harrison and Chaffins Farm at the end of September, 1864.

Private John Ames of Company G in the 2nd U.S. Colored Infantry was wounded in action at Natural Bridge, Florida on March 6, 1865.[59] He was hit in the back of the head by a shell fragment and shot with a Minie ball in his thigh. Because of his wounds, he was captured by the enemy and held as a POW until the war ended. He was discharged for disability from the Army while being treated at Hicks General Hospital in Baltimore, Maryland on September 21, 1865.

Throughout their enlistments, soldiers might be assigned to duty on "Detached Service" by special order. The most common special duty assignment among the Accomack men appears to have been that of teamster. In a time when almost all supplies and freight were hauled by wagons pulled by mule or horse teams, skilled teamsters were in high demand. Private John Roberts of Company K, 7th U.S.C.I., had been a farmer before the war. After he recuperated from the wounds he received in Deep Bottom in August of 1864, he was assigned to duty with the Quartermaster Department as a teamster, hauling supplies.[60] Corporal John Fletcher was reduced in rank to Private for disobeying an officer, refusing to drill when ordered to do so, then assigned to detached service as a teamster in the ambulance corps, transporting wounded men from the battlefield.[61]

Private Abel Savage of the 9th U.S.C.I. was assigned to serve as a teamster with the Quartermaster Department, then assigned to work as a boatman. Savage had been a boatman in civilian life.[62]

Privates Thomas Burden[63], Samuel Foreman[64], and Robert Phillips[65], all of the 9th U.S.C.I., were assigned by order of Brigadier General Rufus Saxon on June 17, 1864 to serve on the steamer *USS John Adams*, which was patrolling around Charleston. A year earlier, Harriet Tubman had led 150 troops on a raid up the Combahee River on the *John Adams*. Sergeant William Bourdon, assigned to the same detail, was described in his service record as *"Remarkable for neatness and soldierly bearing."*[66]

In every theater of the war, African American soldiers helped to win the war with their shovels. When Major General Benjamin Butler decided to dig a canal across a loop of the James River at Dutch Gap, soldiers from every black regiment in the area were assigned to 'fatigue duty' – digging and hauling dirt and rock building the canal. Confederate sharpshooters and artillerymen watching the work took frequent shots at them. The soldiers would take cover until the firing stopped, then resume digging.[67]

Strenuous activities like digging and heavy lifting also took a toll on the men. Private Moses Justice[68] of the 10th U.S. Colored Infantry, and Private Henry Rodgers[69] of the 2nd U.S. Colored Cavalry were both discharged for disability with hernias.

Private William Drummond, in Company K of the 7th U.S.C.I., was assigned to work as General William Birney's orderly; before that, he had been the company cook.[70] Private Franklin Wise of the 9th regiment worked as a recruiter, cook, provost guard and finally as a woodcutter during his three years of service.[71]

Privates Samuel Parker[72] and Peter Blockson[73], both of the 19th U.S. Colored Infantry, were discharged from the Army on April 17, 1864 and permanently transferred to the Navy. Parker had been a tanner in civilian life; Blockson had been a farmer back in Accomack County.

When his unit sailed from Virginia to Texas after Lee's surrender in 1865, Private Thomas Myers[74] along with Private Abner Conner[75] and Private Peter Custis[76]of the 10th U.S. Colored Infantry, were placed in charge of the regiment's horses on board the steamer *USS Empire* during the voyage.

Detached service and special duty assignments became more common as unit strength was diminished by battle casualties and sickness in the ranks. After companies lost so many men, they could no longer effectively fight. It made sense to assign the remaining men to support roles with other units.

In the course of their service, soldiers occasionally earned recognition from their officers for their service and professionalism. In the 9th U.S. Colored Infantry regiment, Private John Bell was described as '*A good soldier,*'[77] George Birch was promoted to Corporal for his '*soldierly qualities.*'[78] Harris Lewis was promoted for '*faithfulness in the discharge of his whole duty.*'[79]

Before sailing for Texas in 1865, several Accomack soldiers were allowed to take furloughs to visit with their families. A soldier requesting furlough had to have the approval of his commanding officer. Corporal Parker

Williams of Company I in the 10th U.S. Colored Infantry regiment was required to pass an equipment inspection before beginning his trip home to Onancock to visit his family.[80]

The many U.S. Colored Troop regiments assigned to Texas patrolled the border along the Rio Grande, partly to prevent incursion by the French forces then at war with Mexico, partly to prevent Confederate forces from crossing the border to regroup and resume fighting later. The duty was hot, mostly boring and often dangerous. Soldiers tempers flared; Private John Jines of the 23rd U.S.C.I. survived being wounded at the Battle of the Crater, tonly to be court martialed for manslaughter in Brownsville when he struck Private William Smith in the head with a stick of wood, killing him.[81] Private James Grey of the 9th was confined in the stockade and fined over a months' pay for *'maliciously destroying private property.'*[82]

Bored soldiers sometimes get drunk and go on a tear. Corporal William Griffin of Company E of the 9th had been promoted to Corporal for his *"promptness and soldierly bearing"* in January 1864, but was reduced to the ranks two years later for drunkenness.[83]

Soldiers died from accidents. Private John Drummer, who had enlisted at age 12 in Company B of the 9th U.S. Colored Infantry, died while swimming near Brownsville, Texas on August 12, 1865. Ironically, he had worked as a Boatman before joining the Army.[84] First Sergeant George Foskey accidentally drowned in Matagorda Bay, Texas on August 25, 1866.[85]

More often, soldiers died from disease. Between August and October, 1866, an outbreak of cholera killed at least six Accomack County soldiers stationed in Texas from the 7th and 9th U.S. Colored Infantry regiments. More than 100 of the 600 Union soldiers born in Accomack County died of disease or were killed in action, and would never return home to that "other shore" next to the Chesapeake.

The soldiers from Accomack County helped to win the war for freedom. Their story is representative of the other Virginia-born soldiers that fought in the United States Army during the Civil War.

In many Compiled Military Service Records for the Accomack County men, a note can be found stating that when the soldier was discharged, he retained 'his arms and accoutrements', 'one Springfield R.M.' or 'one Enfield rifle musket.' One soldier, Private Alexander Anderson of the 2nd U.S. Colored Cavalry, actually kept two repeating carbines when he completed his enlistment.

Just three years earlier, most of these men had been slaves. A slave found in possession of a firearm before the war would have been brutally punished and probably executed. Now, these soldiers were taking the weapons they had used to fight for their freedom with them as they headed home to begin their new lives. These dark-skinned soldiers from Virginia had helped to change the world.

Lincoln's Second Inauguration – March 4, 1865

For months leading up to Election Day in November 1864, it looked as if Abraham Lincoln might not be elected to a second term as President. The Democrats had a strong candidate in General George McClellan. Lincoln's own Republican party was split in factions. Casualties among Union soldiers were high.

By late August, however, General Ulysses S. Grant's Union army had advanced to within twenty miles of Richmond, the Confederate capital. Then, on September 2, General William Tecumseh Sherman captured the city

204

of Atlanta, a major supply and political center for the Rebels.

The good news changed everything. On November 8, Lincoln was reelected by a landslide, winning fifty-five percent of the popular vote and 212 electoral votes, against twenty-one electoral votes for McClellan. Lincoln was reinaugurated at the Capitol in Washington on March 4, 1865.[87]

The morning of the Inauguration, it rained. The weather had been poor for weeks. Most of the streets of Washington were still unpaved and covered with mud. Security measures included streets lined with soldiers and snipers posted on nearby rooftops. As many as 40,000 people crowded into the city for the event.

The new Vice President, Andrew Johnson, was ill and had been drinking that morning. Johnson's speech was barely coherent and even less memorable, as gloomy as the overcast sky.

Then, just as Lincoln stepped up to the podium to give his speech, the sun came out from behind the clouds.[88] The crowd was mostly silent as the President reaffirmed his commitment to winning the war, to ending slavery and to rebuilding the nation in peace:

"Fellow countrymen: at this second appearing to take the oath of the presidential office there is less occasion for an extended address than there was at the first. Then a statement somewhat in detail of a course to be pursued seemed fitting and proper. Now, at the expiration of four years during which public declarations have been constantly called forth on every point and phase of the great contest which still absorbs the attention and engrosses the energies of the nation little that is new could be presented. The progress of our arms, upon which all else chiefly depends is as well known to the public as to myself and it is I trust reasonably satisfactory and encouraging

to all. With high hope for the future no prediction in regard to it is ventured.

"On the occasion corresponding to this four years ago all thoughts were anxiously directed to an impending civil war. All dreaded it ~ all sought to avert it. While the inaugural address was being delivered from this place devoted altogether to saving the Union without war insurgent agents were in the city seeking to destroy it without war ~ seeking to dissolve the Union and divide effects by negotiation. Both parties deprecated war but one of them would make war rather than let the nation survive, and the other would accept war rather than let it perish. And the war came.

"One eighth of the whole population were colored slaves not distributed generally over the union but localized in the southern part of it. These slaves constituted a peculiar and powerful interest. All knew that this interest was somehow the cause of the war. To strengthen perpetuate and extend this interest was the object for which the insurgents would rend the Union even by war while the government claimed no right to do more than to restrict the territorial enlargement of it. Neither party expected for the war the magnitude or the duration which it has already attained. Neither anticipated that the cause of the conflict might cease with or even before the conflict itself should cease. Each looked for an easier triumph and a result less fundamental and astounding. Both read the same Bible and pray to the same God and each invokes His aid against the other. It may seem strange that any men should dare to ask a just God's assistance in wringing their bread from the sweat of other men's faces but let us judge not that we be not judged. The prayers of both could not be answered ~ that of neither has been answered fully. The Almighty has His own purposes. "Woe unto the world because of offenses for it must needs be that offenses come but woe to that man by whom the offense cometh." If we shall suppose that American slavery is one of those offenses which in the providence of God must needs come but which having continued through His appointed time He now wills to remove *and that He gives to both North and South this terrible war as the woe due to those by whom the offense came shall we discern therein any departure from those divine attributes which the believers in a living God always ascribe to Him. Fondly do we hope ~ fervently do we pray ~ that this mighty scourge of war may speedily pass away. Yet, if God wills that it continue until all the wealth piled by the bondsman's two hundred and fifty years of unrequited toil shall be sunk and until every drop of blood drawn with the lash shall be paid by another drawn with the sword as was said three thousand years ago so still it must be said 'the judgments of the Lord are true and righteous altogether.'*

"With malice toward none with charity for all with firmness in the right as God gives us to see the right let us strive on to finish the work we are in to bind up the nation's wounds, to care for him who shall have borne the battle and for his widow and his orphan ~ to do all which may achieve and cherish a just and lasting peace among ourselves and with all nations."[89]

Lincoln spoke for only seven minutes. After a brief interval, the crowd broke out into enthusiastic applause.

Chief Justice Salmon Chase marked the passages in the Bible that Lincoln kissed when he swore the oath of office[90]:

27 None shall be weary nor stumble among them; none shall slumber nor sleep; neither shall the girdle of their loins be loosed, nor the latchet of their shoes be broken:

28 Whose arrows are sharp, and all their bows bent, their horses' hoofs shall be counted like flint, and their wheels like a whirlwind: (Isaiah 5:27-28 KJV)

For the first time in history, a regiment of African American soldiers marched in the Presidential Inaugural Parade. Many of the men in the 45th U.S. Colored Infantry were former slaves. Soldiers from the 45th fought in the battles at New Market Heights and Fort Harrison in September 1864, and again on the Darbytown Road and at Fair Oaks in October 1864. A little over a month later, the 45th U.S. Colored Infantry was present at Appomattox when General Robert E. Lee surrendered his Confederate Army of Northern Virginia to General Ulysses S. Grant.[91]

Natural Bridge - March 4-6, 1865

In February 1865, Confederate raiders attacked Union outposts at Fort Myers and Cedar Key in Florida. Brigadier General John Newton, commander of the U.S. District of Key West and the Tortugas, believed the presence of Rebel raiders on the peninsula left Confederate defenses in the Florida Panhandle and southern Georgia vulnerable to attack.[92]

Working with Admiral C.K. Stribling of the U.S. Navy, Newton put together a force of almost 1,000 troops, including the 2nd and 99th U.S. Colored Infantry regiments, the 2nd Florida Union regiment, and a battery of two howitzers manned by sailors from the *USS Hendrick Hudson*. Newton's task force was to attack up the St. Marks River in the Florida Panhandle towards Tallahassee.

Having heard the Confederates were holding Union prisoners of war at Thomasville, Georgia, sixty miles from the coast, Newton hoped to cross into Georgia and liberate them. He was unaware the prisoners had already been moved by the Rebels.

The amphibious attack began in a dense fog on the night of March 4, at the lighthouse near the mouth of the St. Marks River. The U.S. Navy boats struggled to sail up the narrow, shallow channel. A group of soldiers and sailors rowed to East River, intending to seize the bridge there. They were attacked by a small detachment of Confederate cavalry commanded by Major William Milton. Under heavy fire, the Union landing force withdrew to the lighthouse.

The Confederates rapidly spread the alarm, contacting their headquarters and the Florida government in Tallahassee. Reinforcements were dispatched to the area by Brigadier General William Miller, including home guard soldiers and a group of teenaged cadets from the Florida Military and Collegiate Institute, which later became Florida State University.

On the morning of March 5, all the Federal troops had landed and were able to push the Rebels back from the East River Bridge. They were stopped by fierce resistance at the Newport Bridge. Realizing he could not take the Newport Bridge, Newton decided to make a night march up the east bank of the St. Marks that evening, and cross over at Natural Bridge, where the river flows underground for more than 1,300 feet.

The Confederates recognized that Natural Bridge was an obvious target, so they rushed to seize and fortify it before the Union troops could arrive. By 4:00 AM the next morning when the Federals attacked, the Rebels had dug trenches and set up artillery overlooking the bridge.

Newton's Union soldiers made three separate charges during a twelve-hour battle on March 6, but could not dislodge the Confederates from their strong positions guarding the bridge. The defenders continued to strengthen their fortifications as reinforcements continued to arrive during the day. After repelling a Rebel counterattack, Newton realized his exhausted troops were unable to capture Natural Bridge, and withdrew.

The Union lost twenty-one killed, eighty-nine wounded and thirty-eight taken prisoner. The

Confederates lost only three killed and twenty-two wounded. Tallahassee was the only state capital in the Confederacy not taken by Union forces during the war. The Battle of Natural Bridge, Florida had resulted in a Union defeat.[93]

Two Union Soldiers – Friends and Brothers in Arms. - *Photo: Library of Congress*

11. MORE VIRGINIA SOLDIER STORIES

Franklin Jasper was living in Somerset, Kentucky when he enlisted in the 5th U.S. Colored Cavalry at Camp Nelson on September 8, 1864. His enlistment papers note that his owner was named Thomas Jasper, of the 8th Kentucky District. Jasper was born in Charlotte County, Virginia.[1]

Wounded by Confederate guerillas at Simpsonville on January 25, 1865, Jasper was first reported missing in action. He was found and hospitalized in New Albany, Indiana in February, where he remained for at least two months. When he was hospitalized, he gave the name of Robert Jasper as his friend and emergency contact.

Private Jasper's service records show that he contracted smallpox, probably while hospitalized in New Albany, and was transferred to the military hospital in Louisville, where he died on May 25, 1865. Franklin Jasper was buried in the New Albany National Cemetery. On October 13, 1868 his widow, Patsy Jasper, was living in Dover, Virginia and working as a house servant when she filed an application for his service pension.

Virginia-born soldiers enlisted from all over the country. Private Peter White enlisted in the 54th Massachusetts Colored Infantry in February, 1864. He had been born in Buchanan County, but enlisted from Denver, in the Colorado Territory.[2]

Private John Parrish, born in Henry County, Virginia, also served in the 5th U.S. Colored Cavalry but was hospitalized with 'intermittent fever' on December 30, 1864 and remained in Bowling Green during early 1865. He was a company cook. Parrish was discharged with his regiment from Helena, Arkansas March 16, 1866.[3]

When Jorden Roberts enlisted in Company G of the 52nd U.S.C.I. on February 27, 1864 in Vicksburg, Mississippi, he gave his occupation as 'Distiller' – an appropriate trade for a man born in Franklin County, Virginia, a community known for its strong moonshining traditions. Roberts was forty years old when he enlisted, and was discharged with his regiment at Vicksburg in May 1866.[4]

A Contraband, wearing the clothes he had on when he arrived at the Union lines. -
Photo: Library of Congress

On April 26, 1865 – two and a half weeks after Lee's surrender – fifteen men from Bedford, Franklin, Henry and Patrick Counties enlisted in the 40th U.S. Colored Infantry Regiment in Greenville, Tennessee. Most were discharged from Chattanooga a year later. Among the Patrick County men were Privates Adam[5] and Allen Reynolds[6], who likely had been slaves at the Reynolds Homestead in Critz, Virginia. John H. Bogus of Henry County was discharged from Bridgeport, Alabama in March 1866. Bogus had contracted tuberculosis while in the service.[7]

When James Chafers enlisted in Company E of the 9th U.S. Colored Heavy Artillery on September 22, 1864, he was able to sign his name on his enlistment papers. Chafers had been born in Franklin County.[8]

Many soldiers were killed in action or died from their battle wounds. Joseph Lane of Surry County was wounded June 15, 1864 while serving in the 1st U.S.C.I. and died that evening.[9] Corporal Charles Teeters, a barber born in Rockingham County who had been free when he enlisted in the 5th U.S. Colored Infantry at Portsmouth, Ohio, was killed at New Market Heights on September 29, 1864.[10] Corporal Jefferson Carpenter, also from Rockingham County and also in the 5th regiment, was wounded at New Market Heights but survived for seven days before dying at Fort Monroe hospital.[11] Thousands more gave their lives in the fight for freedom and the Union.

Private John Anderson was born in Cabell County, West Virginia.[12] He joined Company G of the 8th U.S. Colored Infantry on June 14, 1863 at Cincinnati, Ohio. Anderson was wounded on May 18, 1864 near Petersburg, survived and was wounded again at New Market Heights on September 29, 1864.

Private Armistead Evans, born in Lunenburg County, was serving in Company K of the 55th

Massachusetts Infantry in September 1864, when Union troops finally captured Fort Wagner. Evans was injured in the side by falling timbers as he took cover in the fort's bombproof shelter during a Confederate bombardment, but survived the war.[13]

William H. Johnson of Nansemond County gave his occupation as 'Lumberman' when he enlisted in the 10th U.S.C.I. in December of 1863. He was promoted to Sergeant in May of 1864 and survived to be discharged with his regiment from Galveston on May 17, 1866.[14]

At fifty-seven years old, Benjamin Nimo was one of the oldest soldiers in his regiment when he joined Company I of the 1st Arkansas Infantry (African Descent) on April 10, 1863 at Helena, Arkansas, where he had been enslaved.[15] He had black skin, hazel eyes, and black hair, and was 5' 9 ½" tall. Private Benjamin Nimo had been born in Albemarle County, Virginia.

Nimo may have fought in the Battle of Goodrich's Landing in Louisiana on June 29 and 30, 1863. Likely because of his maturity, he was promoted to Sergeant soon after enlisting but was reduced to the ranks for disability in December of 1863 and discharged on June 30th 1864. Prior to his enlistment, he had broken his right knee and it had not properly healed; for a month before he was discharged, Nimo was hospitalized, no longer able to perform his duties.

When Private Richard Page joined the 1st Arkansas Infantry (AD) in Helena, Arkansas on May 5, 1863, he gave his age as forty-two years old, and his occupation as Farmer.[16] He remained with the regiment until he was discharged from Boca Chica, Texas on January 30, 1866. His regiment fought in the Battle of Goodrich's Landing. Page had been born in Augusta County.

Private Sprawles of the 1st Arkansas Infantry (AD) had been given the unlikely first name of "Colonel".[17] He was fifty years old when he joined the regiment on April

10, 1863. In December 1863 he was able to take a short furlough, so presumably he had family close by. Colonel Sprawles was born in Augusta County.

Private Jackson Minnis, born in Bedford County, Virginia, was thirty-five years old when he joined the 9th Louisiana Infantry (African Descent) in Milliken's Bend, Louisiana.[18] Minnis had most likely been transported to Louisiana as a slave. Minnis enlisted on May 1, 1863 and fought in the Battle of Milliken's Bend on June 7, 1863. Minnis died in the Post General Hospital at Vicksburg, Mississippi on April 28, 1865 of an unspecified illness. The 9th Louisiana Infantry was eventually redesignated and reorganized as the 5th U.S. Colored Heavy Artillery Regiment.

Private Albert Williams, also born in Bedford County joined the Company B of the 11th Louisiana Infantry (African Descent) in Grand Gulf, Mississippi on May 8, 1863.[19] His occupation was listed as a farmer; he was 5' 10" tall and thirty-two years old when he joined his regiment. The 11th Louisiana was later redesignated as the 49th U.S. Colored Infantry. Williams remained with the regiment until he was discharged March 22, 1866 from Vicksburg. He fought in the Battle of Milliken's Bend a month after he enlisted. A commander of Company B was 2nd Lieutenant Alembert G. Williams, a white officer who had been a private in the 10th New York Artillery Regiment was later promoted to sergeant, and agreed to command a company of Black troops in order to obtain an officer's commission.[20]

Private Alexander Patterson joined Company E of the 1st South Carolina Colored Infantry on November 20, 1862 at St. Simons Island. Patterson was born in Buckingham County. He likely participated in the March 1863 raid on Jacksonville. Patterson was listed as AWOL for three weeks during June 1864 but was not prosecuted when he returned to his unit. He remained with the regiment until he was discharged in January 1866.[21]

Corporal William Thompson enlisted in the 9th Louisiana Infantry (AD) on May 1, 1863 as a private. Born into slavery in Franklin County, Virginia, Thompson had been sold to an owner in the Mississippi, and was recruited at the Widow Tower's Plantation. Thompson was married; his wife lived in Natchez. He fought in the Battle of Milliken's Bend. After the war ended he was court martialed for going AWOL and sentenced to serve ten days hard labor in jail. He served out his sentence, and remained with his regiment until he was discharged April 30, 1866.[22]

Also born in Franklin County, Private John Lynn was a wagon driver assigned to Company H of the 17th United States Colored Infantry. Fellow soldiers said he had a happy disposition and frequently sang while driving his wagon. On December 15 he was wounded in the hand by a Confederate Minie ball as he looked out from behind a tree. This wound resulted in his disability, but he did not receive a full pension until 1890. While hospitalized for his wound, he caught smallpox, which partially blinded him. He settled in Indiana and married after the war.[23]

Private Edward Arrington served in Company F of the 17th US Colored Infantry.[24] Born in Franklin County, Arrington survived the battle to settle in Ohio and wed Mary J. Mitchell after the war, fathering a daughter named Dinah. In 1883 he applied for a pension as an invalid. He could read and write in 1900. Arrington died from pneumonia in 1905.

Private Jordan Hughes, a carpenter born in Franklin County, enlisted in Company H of the 18th US Colored Infantry on September 29, 1864, barely two months before the Battle of Nashville. Hughes survived the war and settled in Pike County, Missouri, where he served as a preacher.[25]

Private Josiah Taitt enlisted in Fulton, Missouri at the age of nineteen, served in Company H of the 18th US Colored Infantry, and like many other soldiers that fought at Nashville, died from pneumonia brought on by the bitter winter weather. His younger brother Granville signed a receipt on December 29, 1864 for Josiah's belongings – his uniform, two blankets, and $20 in banknotes.[26]

Private Granville Taitt served with his brother in Company H of the 18th US Colored Infantry and only survived him by a few months. Granville Taitt died of pneumonia on May 30, 1865 in Chattanooga, Tennessee, where he is buried in the National Cemetery. The Taitt brothers had been born in Franklin County.[27]

Peter Hooks, Andrew Jones, and John Jones were all born in Franklin County.

Private Peter Hooks served in Company L of the 12th US Colored Infantry. He participated in the assault on Overton Hill and survived the war to marry Cassie Hooks in Davidson County, Tennessee in 1866. The couple went on to have six children. Hooks applied for and began receiving a pension in 1890.[28]

Private Andrew Jones served in Company F of the 13th US Colored Infantry at Nashville but did not participate in the fighting as he was in the hospital, likely with an illness brought on by the weather. Andrew Jones survived the war and is believed to have returned to a wife and three children in Franklin Township, Missouri.[29]

Private John Jones also served in Company F of the 13th US Colored Infantry, participating in the charge at Overton Hill and the pursuit of Hood's retreating Confederates. John Jones became another casualty of the brutal winter weather. Hospitalized on January 12, 1865 he died of pneumonia on February 16, 1865. Private John Jones is buried in Nashville at the U.S. Burial Ground southwest of the city cemetery. His grave marker reads *"12087 J. Jones U.S.C.T."*[30]

William Noble was a free man, forty-three years old, working as a blacksmith when he joined the 1st South Carolina Colored Volunteers in Jacksonville, Florida on March 17, 1863. Private Noble had been born in Frederick County, Virginia. He was mustered in at Charleston, South Carolina. He remained with his regiment until he was discharged January 31, 1866 from Charleston. The 1st South Carolina was redesignated February 8, 1864 as the 33rd U.S. Colored Infantry Regiment and took part in the Battle of Honey Hill in November of 1864.[31]

Born in Henry County, Private Austin Bronson was thirty-five years old when he joined the 1st Arkansas Infantry Regiment (African Descent) on April 10, 1863. By November 1864 he was on daily duty as the Company Cook. In August of 1865 Bronson was charged $3.71 for a kettle and cooking utensils which had been lost – more than a week's pay for a private soldier. Private Bronson survived the war, and was discharged at Boca Chica, Texas on June 30, 1865.[32]

Levi Barer was born in Salem, Virginia. He was eighteen years old when he enlisted in the 1st Arkansas Infantry Regiment (AD) on April 15, 1863 at Helena. Private Barer was listed as missing in action on June 29, 1863 after the Battle of Mound Plantation, and only returned to his unit at Boca Chica, Texas in October of 1865.[33] Barer was likely captured during the battle.

David Freeman was thirty-five years old when he joined the 11th Louisiana Infantry (AD) at Jackson, Mississippi on May 16, 1863. He had been born a slave in Rockbridge County, Virginia, and sold to an owner in the west, where he had worked as a carpenter. Promoted to Corporal, Freeman was wounded in the right shoulder in the Battle of Milliken's Bend on June 7, 1863. He was discharged for disability a year later, unable to use his right arm; it was determined that he was unfit for duty in the Invalid Corps.[34]

Private Horace Lacy had been born in Lexington, Virginia as a slave and sold to an owner in the west. He joined the 11th Louisiana Infantry (AD) on May 25, 1863. Two weeks later he fought in the Battle of Milliken's Bend. He survived the battle and was promoted to Corporal in February 1865, but he was reduced to the ranks July 1, 1865 for "stealing peaches." He was later assigned to detached duty working for the military Telegraph Service, and remained with his regiment until he was discharged in March 1866.[35]

Born in Warren County, Kelly Walker joined Company G of the 11th Louisiana Infantry (AD) on May 25, 1863 and fight in the Battle of Milliken's Bend two weeks later. Twenty years old when he enlisted, Walker was promoted to Corporal. In early 1864 he was hospitalized at Vicksburg, where he died on April 4 of diarrhea.[36]

There were fewer African Americans living in West Virginia, as there had been fewer slaves in the counties that seceded from Virginia at the beginning of the war. However, many black West Virginians joined the Union armed forces during the war.

At 6' 3" tall, Private Mark Addison was one of the tallest men in his regiment. He had been born in Braxton County, West Virginia. Addison was eighteen years old when he enlisted in Company A of the 45th U.S. Colored Infantry at Weston, West Virginia on April 30, 1864. He was pulling guard duty at Camp Casey in Virginia when he was shot accidentally by another soldier in his regiment whose musket accidentally discharged.

Born in Calhoun County, West Virginia around 1836, Edmund Fox was likely sold to a slave owner in Arkansas. Fox joined Company B of the 54th U.S. Colored Infantry at Helena, Arkansas on June 17, 1863 and was discharged August 27, 1866 at Little Rock.[38]

The rate of desertion among U.S. Colored Troop ranks was comparable to that of other soldiers on both sides. As many as twelve percent of soldiers deserted or went AWOL (Absent Without Leave).

Some enlistees, like John Tyler[39] of Frederick County or James Woolridge[40] of Spotsylvania County, never showed up for muster after agreeing to join the service.

Deserters, if captured, were subject to stiff penalties. Private Dick Drummond of Accomack County was arrested in March 1865, after he had been absent without leave for six months. He was sentenced to six months hard labor in prison at Norfolk without pay, then discharged in October 1865.[41]

Other soldiers received light penalties or no penalties, possibly due to extenuating circumstances. Private Charles Lee of Frederick County was arrested as a deserter but later detailed as an orderly in Key West, Florida.[42] Private Oscar Irving was listed as having deserted from Orangeburg, South Carolina four months after the war ended. His record was amended to read *"The charge of desertion against this man has been removed and he is discharged to date 8/1/1865 under the provisions of the act of Congress approved 3/2/1889."*[43]

Some soldiers deserted after the war ended. Private Keymore Wynn of James City County was on board the steamer *USS Meteor* in the harbor at Hampton Roads, getting ready to ship out to Texas, when he deserted on June 13, 1865.[44] Wynn was likely homesick, and probably had no desire to go to Texas two months after the Confederates had surrendered.

12. VICTORY AND SORROW

Throughout early 1865 the Confederate defenders of Richmond and Petersburg fought off repeated Union attacks. Both sides suffered heavy casualties. The South had already sacrificed a generation of soldiers.

As early as January, Richmond's citizens had started shifting their accounts to banks in Danville.[1] During the last days of March, rained soaked the battlefield.

Appomattox – April 9, 1865

General Robert E. Lee's Army of Northern Virginia was down to 57,000 soldiers, divided into four corps of infantry, one of cavalry, and an assortment of militia units from the Department of Richmond and Department of North Carolina and Southern Virginia. The exhausted troops were running low on munitions and critically low on rations.[2]

Both armies were led by aggressive, brilliant commanders, but Union General Ulysses S. Grant had more than twice as many soldiers, organized into three well-led armies. The momentum was in the Federal's favor. The soldiers in blue were well armed, well fed and could taste victory.

On April 1, when Union cavalry under General Philip Sheridan attacked the Rebel breastworks at Five Forks near Petersburg, the Confederate commanders, Generals Pickett and Fitzhugh Lee, were literally out to lunch at a shad bake and had not informed their subordinate officers.[3] By the time they realized the Federals were attacking and got back to their commands, Union troops had breached their lines, and the defenders were withdrawing in confused disorder. Recognizing an opportunity, Grant ordered his commanders to keep the pressure on the Rebels and continue to attack the next day.

The morning of April 2 opened with a Federal artillery barrage of the Petersburg trenches and an attack by a Union army corps on a mile wide front. In quick, deadly fighting the Confederates were pushed back more than a mile. As General A.P. Hill and his aide were returning from a consultation with Lee, they encountered two Union soldiers, who shot and killed Hill, one of the most trusted Rebel corps commanders. An attack by another Union corps breached the outer Petersburg defenses. More than 4,000 Union soldiers overwhelmed the 350 Confederates defending Fort Gregg with repeated bayonet charges and hand to hand fighting. Other Rebel strongpoints fell as both sides suffered heavy casualties.

No longer able to defend Petersburg and Richmond, Lee advised the Confederate government to abandon both cities, and that evening began evacuating his soldiers towards the west. Lieutenant General Richard Ewell was ordered to have his men destroy anything of military value. Fires broke out in the city, possibly started by retreating soldiers, more likely by rioting civilians.

Lee planned to march to Amelia Court House to resupply. He intended to meet up with the Rebel government at Danville, march into North Carolina, combine with General Joseph Johnston's Army of the South, and continue the fight.

On April 3, Union forces marched into Petersburg and Richmond. Lee's army marched more than twenty miles. African American soldiers of the Army of the James occupied Richmond and helped to put out the widespread fires. That afternoon President Jefferson Davis and his cabinet reached the city of Danville, the last capital of the Confederacy.

When Lee's army arrived at Amelia Court House on April 4, they found that the expected trainload of rations had not arrived. The Rebel commander ordered his generals to leave behind the weaker horses and more than 300 wagons to allow the troops to move faster.

On April 5 Union cavalry captured two wagon trains of supplies destined for Lee's Confederates and blocked the route to the South. Lee was forced to march his force west towards Lynchburg, another principal city where he hoped to find rations for his starving men. Many soldiers wandered off to forage for food and never returned.

Three separate battles between Union and Confederate corps were fought near Sailor's Creek on April 6. The Rebels again sustained heavy casualties, and more than 7,700 were taken prisoner, including Lieutenant General Richard Ewell, a Confederate corps commander, and Major General George Washington Custis Lee, Robert E. Lee's oldest son.

Brutal fighting took place over two days at High Bridge, an Appomattox River crossing near Farmville, as the retreating Confederates tried to cross over.

On April 6 the Rebels prevented Union troops from burning the bridge. After Lee's army crossed the following day, Confederate rear guard soldiers attempted to set the bridge on fire to prevent the Federals from using it but were unsuccessful. Union troops continued in hot pursuit.

The night of the 7th, Lee received a letter from Grant recommending the Confederates surrender. He responded by asking Grant to specify terms.

Lee still thought it might be possible to evade the advancing Federals. On April 8 Union troops under Major General George Armstrong Custer captured another badly needed shipment of Confederate supplies and blocked Lee's approach to Appomattox Court

House. Grant sent a second letter to Lee, outlining the surrender terms, and proposing to meet.

On the morning of April 9, 1865, Lee's army was trapped, effectively surrounded on three sides. The Confederate commander told his staff that *"there is nothing left for me to do but to go and see General Grant and I would rather die a thousand deaths."*[4]

Accompanied by his aide, Colonel Charles Marshall, General Robert E. Lee rode his horse Traveler to the home of Wilmer McClean, arriving at 1:00 in the afternoon. General Ulysses S. Grant arrived at 1:30, and after a short conversation, offered Lee the following written terms:

Terms of Surrender
Headquarters Armies of the United States
Appomattox C H Va Apl 9th 1865.
Gen. R. E. Lee,
Comd'g C. S. A.

General,

In accordance with the substance of my letter to you of the 8th inst., I propose to receive the surrender of the Army of N. Va. on the following terms, to wit;

Rolls of all the officers and men to be made in duplicate, one copy to be given to an officer to be designated by me, the other to be retained by such officer or officers as you may designate. The officers to give their individual paroles not to take up arms against the Government of the United States until properly exchanged, and each company or regimental commander to sign a like parole for the men of their commands.

The arms, artillery, and public property to be parked and stacked and turned over to the officers appointed by me to receive them. This will not embrace the side-arms of the officers nor their private horses or baggage. This done officers and men will be allowed to return to their homes, not to be disturbed by the United States authority as long as they observe their parole and the laws in force where they may reside.

> *Very respectfully*
> *U. S. Grant*
> *Lt. Gen[5]*

Lee wrote a short letter, accepting Grant's terms with three sentences:

> *Headquarters Army N. Va.*
> *April 9th, 1865.*
> *Lt. Gen. U. S. Grant*
> *Com'dg Armies U. S.*
>
> *General:*
>
> *I have received your letter of this date containing the terms of the surrender of the Army of Northern Va, as proposed by you. As they are substantially the same as those expressed in your letter of the 8th inst, they are accepted. I will proceed to designate the proper officers to carry the stipulations into effect.*
>
> *Very Respectfully*
> *Your obt. Servt*
> *(Sgd) R. E. Lee*
> *General[6]*

Lee and his aide left the McClean House at around 3:00 PM that afternoon. On April 10, Lee addressed the following emotional farewell to his troops:

> *GENERAL ORDER*
> *No. 9*

After four years of arduous service marked by unsurpassed courage and fortitude, the Army of Northern Virginia has been compelled to yield to overwhelming numbers and resources.

I need not tell the brave survivors of so many hard fought battles, who have remained steadfast to the last, that I have consented to this result from no distrust of them.

But feeling that valor and devotion could accomplish nothing that would compensate for the loss that must have attended the continuance of the contest, I determined to avoid the useless sacrifice of those whose past services have endeared them to their countrymen.

By the terms of the agreement officers and men can return to their homes and remain until exchanged. You will take with you the satisfaction that proceeds from the consciousness of duty faithfully performed, and I earnestly pray that a merciful God will extend to you His blessing and protection.

With an increasing admiration of your constancy and devotion to your country, and a grateful remembrance of your kind and generous considerations for myself, I bid you all an affectionate farewell.

R.E. LEE
Genl.[7]

Anxious to end the fighting, Grant offered the Confederates generous terms of surrender. He allowed Lee's men to keep their horses and mules, as they were needed for spring planting, and he ordered his quartermasters to issue rations to the defeated soldiers.

The 8th, 29th, 31st, 41st, 45th, 116th and 127th U.S. Colored Infantry Regiments were present in Appomattox when Lee surrendered to Grant.

While the principal Confederate army had been defeated, Rebel resistance continued in the South for several more weeks. The war was won but it was not quite over.

Fort Blakeley – April 9-12, 1865

In late 1864, Mobile Bay, Alabama was one of the few Southern ports not yet captured by Union troops. U. S. Navy Admiral David Farragut led an amphibious attack against Mobile in August. During the battle, Farragut's men twice tied him to the rigging of his flagship when he climbed up for a better look at the enemy to keep him from falling. When his men tried to explain the slow progress of some of the Federal gunships due to underwater mines, then referred to as torpedoes, he is said to have exclaimed, "*Damn the torpedoes!*" and given orders to increase the ships speed in the attack. Farragut's task force was able to capture two forts guarding the entrance to the bay. Fort Gaines was armed with twenty-six guns; Fort Morgan was armed with forty-six guns. Union ground troops under Major General Edward Canby occupied the captured forts.[8]

Over the next few months Canby assembled a huge force along the eastern shore of the bay and planned another assault on the city of Mobile. As part of his plan to capture the city, Canby intended to overwhelm and capture Spanish Fort, actually a series of three connected forts, and Fort Blakeley, a large earthen fort guarding a fork of the Blakeley River about five miles farther north.[9]

The Confederate defenses were commanded by Major General Dabney H. Maury, an experienced war fighter from Virginia. Mobile was the most fortified city in the South, with a garrison of almost 10,000 Rebel soldiers. In addition to the torpedoes, underwater pilings had been driven into the sea floor to obstruct naval vessels. The city was circled by three lines of entrenchments and over 300 pieces of artillery. Confederate Navy ironclad gunboats patrolled the Bay.

Spanish Fort and Fort Blakeley completed the Rebel defenses on the eastern shore. Each was garrisoned by about 2,500 men. Spanish Fort, a series of earthen redoubts armed with forty-seven guns, stood on a bluff overlooking the river. Most of the artillery at Spanish Fort was actually aimed west over the Bay, to protect against approaching naval vessels.

Fort Blakeley consisted of a three-mile line of entrenchments with nine redoubts, and was armed with forty pieces of artillery. Trees and brush had been cut away for a distance of 800 yards east of the fortifications to provide a clear field of fire. Formidable barriers of abatis, telegraph wire strung between stumps and primitive land mines called "sub terra shells" blocked the landward approaches.[10]

Rebel soldiers were formidable fighters, but the South was running low on manpower. Many of the men in Mobile's defensive garrison had been part of the General John Bell Hood's Army of the Tennessee, routed at Nashville in December 1864. Fort Blakeley's garrison included hardened veterans from Missouri and Mississippi, but also teen-aged draftees from Alabama. Slave labor had been used to construct most of the defensive works around the city.

In March 1865 Canby's force attacked from the south, supported by Union navy ironclads in the Bay. After a siege lasting nearly two weeks, the Rebel garrison at Spanish Fort withdrew. Canby's soldiers took 500 prisoners. Many of the defenders escaped to Mobile; more than 500 were sent to reinforce Fort Blakeley.

A task force of 13,000 additional Union troops commanded by Major General Frederick Steele left Fort Barrancas near Pensacola in late March. The Union column on the march was seven miles long. First heading north towards Montgomery to mislead the Confederates as to the actual Union objective, Steele's force turned west about fifty miles north of Pensacola at Pollard, Alabama. Arriving at Fort Blakeley, they overran a Confederate outpost and began digging in. The Federals set up over ninety guns and aimed them towards the fort. For more than a week the two sides skirmished and continued to improve their own defenses.

After a Saturday artillery bombardment, an initial assault by two brigades of U.S. Colored troops began at 3:00 PM on Sunday against the Confederate left flank at the north end of Fort Blakeley. The main attack was launched at 5:30 PM as the rest of the Union force attacked westward along a three-mile front. Many of the Federal soldiers had to advance more than 1,000 yards through the tangled barrier of obstacles under heavy fire from the fort.

The Union troops overwhelmed the Confederate defenders at Fort Blakeley by sheer force of numbers. A little over thirty minutes after the Federals reached the fort, the fighting was finished. The Battle of Fort Blakeley had ended with a resounding Union victory.

Brigadier General John Liddell, the Confederate commander, surrendered at around 7:00 PM on April 9, 1865. Six hours earlier and seven hundred miles away, General Robert E. Lee had surrendered the Confederate Army of Northern Virginia to Union Lieutenant General Ulysses S. Grant at Appomattox.

The Union suffered at least 150 killed and 650 wounded during the battle. Seventy-five Rebels were killed in the defense of Fort Blakeley. There were accusations that U.S. Colored troops killed wounded Confederates who were trying to surrender, but no evidence has been found to suggest that this happened in more than a few isolated instances. Exact casualty figures are hard to pinpoint, as the buried mines continued to kill and inflict injuries for weeks after the battle.

On April 12 the mayor of Mobile surrendered the city without a fight. The remaining Confederates in the area surrendered on May 4.

About 5,000 African American soldiers participated in the Battle of Fort Blakeley, from the 47th, 48th, 50th, 51st, 68th, 73rd, 76th, 82nd, and 86th U.S. Colored Infantry Regiments.

Lincoln's Assassination - April 14, 1865

April 12, 1865 marked four years since the beginning of the Civil War, when the Union garrison at Fort Sumter surrendered to Rebel troops at Charleston, South Carolina. When Lee surrendered to Grant at Appomattox on April 9, the war appeared to be over. It seemed as if the long nightmare was coming to an end. The inhabitants of the nation's capital were in a celebratory mood, unaware that a new nightmare was about to begin.

On the night of April 14, 1865, Abraham Lincoln and his wife were attending a play at Ford's Theater in Washington when a fanatical Confederate sympathizer named John Wilkes Booth fired a single pistol shot into the back of the president's head.[11] Leaping from the president's booth to the stage and shouting, "*Sic Semper Tyrannis!*" the assassin ran out of the theater, mounted his horse and rode into the night, fleeing southeast. He managed to bluff his way past a sentry guarding the Navy Yard Bridge.

As a well-known stage actor, Booth was one of the most recognized men in Washington. He was readily identified by many of the people at Ford's Theater. As soon as he was notified, Edwin Dean Stanton, the Secretary of War, organized a manhunt.

Bystanders carried the president to a bedroom in Peterson's Boarding House, across the street from the theater; Lincoln was so tall they had to lay him diagonally across the bed. He lingered alive through the night but never regained consciousness. President Abraham Lincoln died on the morning of April 15, 1865, at 7:22 AM.

As he jumped from the stage, or as a result of a fall from his horse, Booth's leg was broken, and he was in a great deal of pain as he fled. That morning, Booth and a fellow conspirator arrived at the Maryland home of Dr. Samuel Mudd, fifteen miles away. They concealed their identities and convinced the doctor to set Booth's leg and let him rest for a few hours. When he woke up, Booth changed his appearance by shaving off his mustache. After leaving Mudd's home, Booth and his accomplice hid for a few hours out in a pine thicket. Booth complained in his diary about Rebel sympathizers who were afraid to help him.[12]

Lincoln's funeral procession carried the president's body on April 19th from the White House to the Capitol Rotunda, where the president's body lie in state on the 20th before being loaded onto a funeral train on the 21st for transport to Springfield, Illinois. The 22nd U.S. Colored Infantry Regiment was one of the U.S. Army units that marched in the procession. After the funeral, the 22nd was one of the units ordered to patrol along Maryland's eastern shore and search for the president's assassin.

Booth managed to cross the Potomac River on April 23rd into Virginia, where he expected a hero's welcome in the former Confederate state. Instead, he was humiliated when two Rebel sympathizers he encountered suggested he hide in the home of an African American family nearby.

By April 25th, Booth and his accomplice had made their way to the farm of Richard Garrett, who allowed them to spend that night in his tobacco barn. Garrett's sons, wary of the strangers' suspicious behavior, locked the fugitives inside the barn and spent the night in a corn crib close by.

President Abraham Lincoln's Funeral, Washington, D.C. The 22nd U.S. Colored Infantry marched in the funeral procession, and helped in the search for his assassin. - *Photo: Library of Congress*

Federal troops from the 16th New York Cavalry Regiment arrived at the Garrett house at 2:00 AM. Garrett's son told them where the men were hiding. The soldiers surrounded the barn and ordered the fugitives to surrender. The soldiers were accompanied by detective Everton Conger, who ordered them to set fire to the building.

Booth's accomplice David Herold gave up and was pulled from the flames by the soldiers. Against orders,

232

Sergeant Boston Corbett shot into the burning building and wounded Booth in the neck. Soldiers rushed into the building and pulled Booth out of the fire. The bullet had paralyzed him from the shoulders down. Booth was carried to the porch of the Garrett house, and a doctor was summoned. He would not live long.

Booth told the soldiers, *"Tell mother, I die for my country."* He asked that his hands be raised in front of his face so he could see them, and he spoke his last words: *"Useless; useless."* Abraham Lincoln's murderer, John Wilkes Booth, died at 7:15 AM on April 26, 1865 on Richard Garrett's porch, surrounded by the Union soldiers he so despised.[13]

President Lincoln was buried at Springfield, Illinois on May 4. Four people were quickly identified and confirmed to have participated with Booth in the conspiracy to kill the president. David Herold, Mary Surratt, George Atzerodt and Lewis Powell were executed by hanging on July 7, 1865.

Bennett's Place – April 26, 1865

The war continued. The Confederate government had fled Richmond a week earlier, first by train to Danville, Virginia and later to Greensboro, North Carolina. Jefferson Davis, president of the Confederacy, was determined to continue fighting and still believed the war might be won.[14]

Hero of the Battle of Buena Vista during the Mexican War, Davis had graduated from West Point a year before Confederate generals Robert E. Lee and Joseph Johnston. Elected to the U.S. Senate, he was appointed U.S. Secretary of War in 1853 by President Franklin Pierce. His first wife died of malaria just months after their marriage. He married his second wife, Varina Howell, in 1845. They lived at Brierfield Plantation near

Vicksburg, Mississippi. By 1860, Davis owned 113 slaves, most engaged in raising cotton.[15]

When the Rebellion began, Davis had expected to be appointed commander of the Southern armies. He was surprised to be elected President of the Confederate States of America by a majority of delegates at a constitutional convention in Montgomery, Alabama on February 9, 1861, when only six states had seceded from the Union: South Carolina, Mississippi, Florida, Georgia, Louisiana and Alabama. Five more states seceded later.

In mid-April 1865, the Confederacy was on the verge of collapse. Lee's surrender of the Army of Northern Virginia did not end hostilities. Rebel forces were still active in Texas, Oklahoma, Mississippi, the Carolinas, Georgia, and Florida.

When Jefferson Davis met with the Confederate cabinet in Greensboro on the 11th and 12th, he outlined an ambitious plan for continuing the war. Generals Joseph Johnston and George Pickett were at the meeting. Johnston recommended opening up surrender negotiations with Union General William Tecumseh Sherman, then in Raleigh. President Davis refused to permit Johnston to surrender but agreed to allow Johnston to negotiate with Sherman for a truce.

On April 12, North Carolina Governor Zebulon Vance sent commissioners to Sherman to discuss the state's surrender, but when Sherman's forces reached Raleigh, the state government had left the capital. The mayor of Raleigh surrendered the city to Sherman without a fight.

Davis ordered Johnston to disband his infantry and escape with his cavalry to continue the fight in the future. Not wanting to prolong the suffering of his soldiers or Southern civilians, Johnston ignored the president's order.

Johnson sent a message to the Union commander requesting a meeting. Escorted by sixty cavalrymen, he rode east toward Durham's Station in North Carolina, where he planned to meet Sherman. The Union general, escorted by 200 cavalry troopers, met Johnston's party near a farmhouse owned by James and Nancy Bennett. For the first time, Johnston learned of Lincoln's assassination when Sherman handed him a copy of the telegram he had received informing him of the tragedy. Gaining permission from the Bennetts, the two generals met privately for the first time in the Bennett farmhouse on April 17, where Sherman offered to give Johnston the same terms of surrender that Grant offered to Lee.[16]

They met again the next day, when Johnston proposed additional terms, including allowing the Confederate state governments to remain in place and allowing the Rebel states to retain a portion of their arms. Anxious to conclude a peace, Sherman accepted the revised terms, and Johnston agreed to surrender the remaining 90,000 Confederate soldiers under his command in North and South Carolina, Georgia, and Florida. On learning of the surrender, many men in Johnston's army started the long walk home.

On reviewing the terms, however, President Andrew Johnson and his Cabinet refused to accept the surrender and insisted on giving Johnston the same terms Grant had offered to Lee. Grant ordered Sherman to meet with Johnston again and renegotiate. In the meantime, Davis was meeting for the last time with members of the Confederate government in Charlotte, still planning to continue fighting the war. Johnston's army continued to shrink as more and more soldiers left the Confederate lines.

On April 26 Johnston and Sherman met again at Bennett's Farm, where Sherman offered Johnston the same terms Grant had extended to Lee. One of

Sherman's officers, Major General John Schofield, offered a few additional concessions on his authority as commander of the district including a few day's rations for the surrendering troops and transportation assistance to help the Rebels soldiers return to their homes. Johnston agreed, saying, *"I believe that is the best we can do,"*[17] and, for a second time, surrendered the forces under his command, contrary to the orders given him by President Davis.

The unrepentant Confederate president was captured by Union troops at Irwinville, Georgia on May 10, 1865. He would spend two years in jail but was never prosecuted. Amnestied by President Andrew Johnson, Davis died on December 6, 1889 at age eighty-one in New Orleans and was given a hero's funeral. On October 17, 1978, President Jimmy Carter signed into law a resolution by the 95th Congress to restore Jefferson's United States citizenship, rehabilitating the Rebel leader almost 100 years after his death.[18]

Military Justice

After Lee's surrender, many U.S. Colored Troop regiments were shipped from Virginia to Texas and assigned to guard against possible incursions across the southern border.

Discipline was difficult in the units guarding the Texas border after the war. Many of the soldiers were bored, homesick and anxious to finish their enlistments and go on with their lives. Those frustrations, in some instances, inevitably led to bad decisions.

William Johnson was twenty-two years old when he joined Company I of the 10th U.S. Colored Infantry on May 23, 1864. He was single and listed his nearest relative as Martha Johnson of Fredericksburg, possibly his mother or a sister.[19]

Johnson advanced rapidly through the ranks. He was promoted to Corporal on August 1, 1864, and to Sergeant a year later. On October 16 he was reduced to the ranks for reasons unknown; by then the 10th U.S. Colored Infantry had moved to Texas to guard the border with Mexico.

The following letter is retained in Johnson's service records:

> *Head Quarters Post of Galveston*
> *Galveston, Tex. Feby "22nd 1866*
> *Maj.*
> *I have the honor to send you the following statement, and respectfully ask that you cause an investigation to be made &c.*
>
> *Night before last Mrs. Baumgarten's Dry Goods & Grocery Store was broken open and pillaged. The City Marshall found a portion of the goods in the house of a colored person, near the foundery. Mrs. Baumgarten's Store is also near the foundery.*
>
> *The parties with whom the stolen goods were found represent that one William Johnson Co. I 10th U.S.C.T. brought the goods to their house & left them there.*
>
> *Mrs. Baumgarten can probably point out the persons had possession of the stolen goods-(which consisted of muslins, calicos, hoops, shawls &c.)- and who say that Wm Johnson of your Regt brought them there.*
>
> *The Mayor of the City – has reported the case to me, with the information above stated.*
> *I am Maj.*
> *Very Resptly*
> *Your obedient Servant*
> *Jar.N.Lynch*
> *G.dist?. Cmdg*
>
> *To_*
> *Maj W.F. Baker*
> *Cmdg 10th U.S.C. Troops*
> *Galveston, Tex*[20]

The request to convene a Court of Inquiry was approved by Major Baker and forwarded to the Department of Texas Headquarters on February 24, four days after the incident.

Johnson denied the charges and asked his company commander, Captain Foote, for assistance in defending himself. Foote wrote the following letter on Johnson's behalf and sent it to the regiment's legal officer, Lieutenant Duggan:

Camp 10 Regt U.S.C.T.
Galveston, Tex Feb 24"1866
1st Lieut. P.F. Duggan
Adjt 10" Regt U.S.C. Troops

Sir
I would respectfully request that a "Court of Inquiry" be convened at as early a date as practicable to examine into and report upon a charge of Larceny of which I am accused by a a Mrs. Baumgarten through the Civil authorities of this City.

Very respectfully
Your Obt Servt
His
William X Johnson
Mark
Private Co. I 10" Regt-USCT
Attest
H M Foote
Capt Comdg Co I 10" Regt USCT[21]

How Johnson planned to defend himself against these charges is unknown. There was another William Johnson in Company B of the 10th, but there is no evidence in the surviving documentation that anyone else was suspected in the case.

We may never know whether William Johnson made the bad decision on February 20, 1865 to rob Mrs. Baumgarten's Dry Goods store, but he did make one when he attempted to leave the post without permission and was shot by the guard.

Admitted to the Post Hospital at Galveston on March 1, Johnson's "Bed Card" indicates he received a pistol shot wound through his stomach; the bullet apparently lodged near his spine. The ball was extracted that afternoon, but Johnson died in the hospital on March 2, 1866.

Not all experiences U.S.C.T. soldiers had with military justice ended in tragedy. A black soldier was more likely to have a fair and impartial trial through a military court martial than with a civilian judge and jury.

George Thompson was born in Franklin County in 1844. By the time he was twenty-one years old, he had made his way to Lancaster, Pennsylvania, where he joined the United States Army as a substitute for a white man from Lancaster who had been drafted, George Nauman.[22] Many members of the Amish and Mennonite communities around Lancaster hired substitutes as their faith prohibited them from serving in the military.

Thompson enlisted on February 2, 1865 for three years, in Company L of the 2nd US Colored Cavalry Regiment. His enlistment records indicate he was 5' 9 ¾" tall, slightly above average height for the time. Thompson must have made a favorable impression on the regiment's officers, as he was promoted to First Sergeant on February 10, 1865, just a few days before the unit shipped out for Norfolk.

As the senior non-commissioned officer of an army company, the First Sergeant is responsible for communicating the orders of the commanding officer to the troops, and ensuring those orders are executed. In battle formation, the First Sergeant stood just behind the

Company Commander on the right side of the Company line, helping to maintain order in the ranks. If the Commander was killed or wounded and no other commissioned officers were present, the First Sergeant was expected to step forward and take command in his place. Routine duties of a First Sergeant included overseeing the distribution and care of any government property assigned to the unit, such as weapons, horses, and other equipment; making sure the enlisted soldiers were paid, armed, fed, and uniformed; and maintaining discipline.[23]

Not just any soldier could become a First Sergeant. Despite his youth, George Thompson had to have been a natural leader. With his heavy responsibilities, he had to maintain the respect of the other enlisted men in the company and of the officers that led it. African American regiments in the Union Army were commanded by white officers. The position of First Sergeant was one of the highest ranks that could be attained during the Civil War by an African American soldier.

By the time George Thompson joined the regiment, the war was nearing its end. The 2nd US Colored Cavalry was ordered February 18, 1865 to Norfolk, Virginia and then to City Point, Virginia a few weeks after the war ended in May, 1865.[24] In June 1865 they were ordered to Texas, where eventually they were posted to Brazos Santiago, a supply base on the southern end of Padre Island that had been hotly contested during the war.

As First Sergeant of a Union Cavalry Unit, Thompson would have worn an insignia on his coat sleeves consisting of three gold chevrons pointing downward, under a bugle. A leather strap across his chest supported a leather belt, on which he wore a standard Army issue pistol, cartridge box, and cap pouch. As a cavalry trooper, he was also authorized to carry a sword.

Thompson was accused by a soldier in his company, Private Jacob Wedlock, of stealing a watch and $280 in bonds. Court-martialed, he was tried by a military court consisting of three officers from the regiment. The prosecution presented testimony from five witnesses, one of whom was Private Wedlock, the accuser.

Thompson pled Not Guilty. The defense countered with testimony from another five witnesses. The proceedings and testimony were carefully recorded, handwritten on twelve pages by Lieutenant Enos B. Wood, the regiment's Adjutant. The trial began on a Saturday afternoon at 3:00 PM and lasted for five days, from September 9 to September 14, 1865. Thompson made a statement as the defense rested its case.

We don't have a picture of 1SGT George Thompson wearing his blue uniform and his First Sergeant's stripes, but we do have something just as rare - his own words, in testimony carefully recorded by Lieutenant Wood:

"I believe it is through prejudice that these men have made this accusation against me, because I have punished them for disobedience of orders, as I knew nothing whatever of the charge until the last day of July. I was told by my commanding officer that if Wedlock did not keep his arms and clothes clean, I should punish him without reporting it to him, which I did. Sergeant Tinsley on being ordered by me not to leave camp without permission, said that he would do so, taking men out with him. I reported it to Captain Herbert, who directed me to place him in arrest, when Sergeant Tinsley said he would work some way to reduce me to the ranks. George Scott also said so because I would not excuse him from duty. When I first heard that I was accused of taking Wedlock's bonds and watch, I asked him if he ever said so, and he replied that he never had. I think that he was made the tool of by men in the company to make this report and I heard Sergeant Tinsley tell Wedlock in his tent one day to "mind and tell these tales straight". This

is all I can say in regard to this affair, for I never saw his bonds, and only saw his watch once, when I gave it to him at the fairgrounds at Norfolk."[25]

First Sergeant Thompson's voice comes down to us as powerful and clear, confident of the justice that only a short time before would likely have been denied him because of the circumstances of his birth. George Thompson was acquitted, the court having determined that the only evidence against him was conflicting testimony from soldiers he had disciplined in the course of his duties as First Sergeant.

George Thompson mustered out with his unit on February 12, 1866 at Brazos Santiago. He settled in Fort Bend, Texas, a few miles southwest of Houston. On April 10, 1880 he married Phillis Kinchelow, where he was listed in the 1880 census as living with his wife and twelve-year-old stepdaughter, Lena Simmons, listed as "at school." Phillis had been born in South Carolina. The 1880 census lists a number of other Kinchelow family members, born in South Carolina, living nearby.[26]

First Sergeant George Thompson had a uniquely American experience. Born a slave or free black descendant of slaves, he had come a long way from Franklin County, enlisting as a substitute in the Army in Pennsylvania, being promoted to First Sergeant of a cavalry company, traveling through Virginia and Texas, being court martialed and exonerated, finally settling in a community where he could build a family and where his daughter could pursue an education.

The line between maintaining discipline and violating military regulations was sometimes unclear.

Private Frank Butts was sixteen years old and only 5' 4 ½" tall when he enlisted in Company C of the 1st U.S. Colored Cavalry Regiment. He gave his occupation as "Oysterman" and was described as having light skin, hazel eyes, and black hair. In Norfolk on February 16, 1865, Butts was charged with *"Conduct prejudicial to good order and military discipline in the careless use and discharge of fire arms."* Witnesses stated he *"discharged his revolver while attempting to make arrests and quell a drunken row"* on the corner of Little Water and Commerce Streets in Norfolk.[27]

Private Butts was arrested and must have been injured as he was later taken from the Norfolk City Jail to Balfour Hospital. He pled Not Guilty to the charges, was tried by General Court Martial, and was acquitted and returned to duty with his unit. He served as an orderly until his discharge from Brazos Santiago, Texas in February 1866.

A soldier might also find himself in attendance at another soldier's courts martial. Corporal Wesley Wades of Company E, 45th U.S.C.I. was assigned to serve as an orderly during a trial that took place on June 23, 1865.[28]

Palmito Ranch – May 12-13 1865

An estimated 3,000 Texans lost their lives during the Civil War, but most of the places where they died were far from the western state. Texas seceded from the Union on February 1, 1861, the seventh state to do so, and throughout the war provided men, horses, and cotton to the other Southern states to support the rebellion.

By May 1865, many Texans were aware of Lee's surrender to Grant in faraway Virginia, but for the Texas militia troops guarding the state, the war had yet to end. An informal truce existed between the Confederates remaining in Brownsville and the Union forces based in Brazos Santiago, near where the Rio Grande emptied into the Gulf.[29]

More than a century and a half after the end of the war, discussion continues on why the Confederates in

Texas still had not surrendered, and why the Union troops from Brazos Santiago chose to launch an attack after the war had ended.

In February 1865 Colonel Theodore Harvey Barrett, Union commander at Brazos Island, submitted a plan to his superiors to take the Rebel city and garrison at Brownsville, Texas. His plan was rejected. Instead, Major General Lewis Wallace got permission from General Grant to meet with the Confederate commanders in the area and conclude a separate peace, promising they would not be retaliated against if they agreed to take the oath of allegiance to the United States. While the Rebel leaders were considering Wallace's proposal, senior leaders of both sides agreed not to attack each other.

Contrary to the orders he had been given, Barrett decided to proceed with his plans. In May 1865 he ordered Lieutenant Colonel David Branson to launch the attack. Branson set out on May 11 with 250 soldiers from the 62nd U.S. Colored Infantry regiment and fifty men of the 2nd U.S. Texas Cavalry (Dismounted) towards Brownsville. The men were issued five days rations and 100 rounds of ammunition.

Marching through the night, the Union raiders arrived at White's Ranch at daybreak. Finding no one there, they proceeded to Palmito Ranch, where Branson ordered his men to hide in a thicket near the Rio Grande and get a few hours rest before continuing. However, they were spotted by Rebel sympathizers on the other side of the river, who alerted a company of Confederate cavalry nearby. After a brief skirmish, both sides withdrew. The Union troops made camp on a nearby hill. At 3:00 AM, the Confederates attacked again, and the Federals were forced to fall back to White's Ranch.

Branson sent a courier back to Brazos Santiago to request reinforcements. At 5:00 AM on May 13, Colonel

Barrett arrived, leading 200 men from the 34th Indiana Infantry Regiment. The larger Union force returned to Palmito Ranch and resumed the attack against the Confederates.

That afternoon, Confederate Colonel James "Rip" Ford arrived with 300 reinforcements and six pieces of artillery. Though still outnumbered, the Rebel infantry and cavalry with artillery were a lethal combination. The Confederates bombarded the Union lines and attacked both flanks; the Federals withdrew in disarray.

Barrett ordered forty-six men from the Indiana regiment left behind to delay the Rebel onslaught, and formed the men of the 62nd U.S. Colored Infantry in a line near the river to protect the Union right flank while the rest of the Federals ran back to Brazos Santiago. They were pursued all the way by Ford's Confederates, who only abandoned the chase when more Union reinforcements arrived.

The Union force suffered 101 men captured, twelve wounded and as many as thirty killed. The Confederates suffered five wounded and three captured. Private John J. Williams of the 34th Indiana Infantry Regiment, killed during the engagement, is generally recognized to have been the last soldier killed in battle during the Civil War.

The Rebel commander at Brownsville, former Texas Ranger and Indian fighter "Rip" Ford, had said that he would never surrender to "*a mongrel force of Abolitionists, negroes, plundering Mexicans, and perfidious renegades*".[30] His commander, Major General Edmund Kirby-Smith, had not yet been authorized by the Rebel governments of Texas, Louisiana and Missouri and Arkansas to disband his armies and end the war. Either or both reasons might justify the Confederate continuation of hostilities in Texas.

Barrett may have ordered the attack to capture cotton and cattle from the Rebels. It has also been speculated that Barrett wanted to boost his career by gaining combat experience before the war ended.

The Battle of Palmito Ranch was an unnecessary attack against an objective not worth defending that took place when the war should have been over. The battle was lost by the side that won the war.

On June 2, 1865, Major General Edmund Kirby-Smith officially surrendered all Confederate forces remaining in the Trans Mississippi Department, and on June 23, 1865, Brigadier General Stand Watie of the 1st Cherokee Mounted Rifles became the last Rebel general to surrender to the Union. Finally, the war was over. The Union could now be restored.

The American Civil War had resulted in almost 700,000 deaths. About two thirds of those deaths were the result of illness or disease. Many more had been wounded or captured. The total number of casualties may never be known. Battles had been fought in nineteen states all around the country. The price of freedom was high. Generations after the war, Americans struggle to deal with the complicated legacy that led to the war and the challenges of being a United States where all are free. We continue to strive to become *"a more perfect Union."*

At Galveston, Texas on June 19, U.S. Major General George Gordon Granger issued the following "General Order No. 3":

Head Quarters District of Texas
Galveston, Texas June 19th, 1865.
General Orders
No. 3

The people of Texas are informed that in accordance with a proclamation from the Executive of the United States, "all slaves are free". This involves an absolute equality of personal rights and rights of property between former masters and slaves and the connection heretofore existing between them becomes that between employer and hired labor.

The freedmen are advised to remain quietly at their present homes, and work for wages. They are informed that they will not be allowed to collect at military posts and that they will not be supported in idleness either there or elsewhere.

By order of Major General Granger.
F.W. Emery, [signed]
Major A.A. Genl.[31]

While in garrison during the winter of 1865 after the war, many soldiers of the 62nd U.S. Colored Infantry occupied their time by taking reading and writing lessons from 1st Lieutenant Richard Baxter Foster, an officer from the unit.

Foster worked with the men of the 62nd to gather support and raise funds, and on September 16, 1866, Lincoln Institute in St. Louis, which eventually was renamed Lincoln University and became the only institution of higher education in the United States established by the U.S. Colored Troops, financed by former slaves, and open to all men.[32]

13. RECONSTRUCTION

On March 3, 1865, Congress passed *"An Act to Establish a Bureau for the Relief of Freedmen and Refugees"*, creating what became known as the Freedmen's Bureau, a branch of the War Department. Initially created for a term of three years from the date of inception, the Act was renewed by Congress yearly until 1872. The Bureau was given authority to exercise *"control of all subjects relating to refugees and freedmen from rebel states"*. Through the Freedmen's Bureau, the Secretary of War was authorized to *"direct such issues of provisions, clothing, and fuel, as he may deem needful for the immediate and temporary shelter and supply of destitute and suffering refugees and freedmen and their wives and children"*.[1] A key provision of the Act allowed loyal refugees and freedmen to rent and eventually purchase forty acre tracts of land within the Rebel states that had been abandoned by former owners, confiscated, or purchased by the United States.

Beyond feeding and housing refugees and ex-slaves, the Freedmen's Bureau accomplished a great deal of good in a short time, helping reunite families broken up by slave sales, helping black families obtain medical care, and acting as agent for freedmen contracting their labor to white-owned farms and businesses. The Bureau organized initiatives to educate teachers and set up a free network of public schools; the Freedmen's schools became part of the Virginia public school system in 1870.[2] Not always, but sometimes, officers of the Freedmen's Bureau were able to intervene in legal cases and help African Americans obtain justice that was otherwise unavailable.

When Richmond fell on April 3, 1865, journalist Thomas Morris Chester was on hand to witness the event. The first Union troops to march into the former Confederate capital were soldiers of the 36th U.S.

Colored Infantry Regiment. Chester wrote his April 4, 1865 report on the fall of Richmond while sitting at the Speaker's desk of the former Rebel congress.[3]

Andrew Johnson had been Vice President for less than five weeks when he was catapulted into the presidency by the assassination of President Lincoln. An ambitious Tennessean, Johnson had been the only Southern senator to remain loyal to the Union when the Rebel states seceded. During the war, Lincoln had appointed him as military governor of Tennessee. In 1864, Lincoln selected Johnson as his running mate under the "National Union Party" ticket in a successful effort to gain Democrat votes and win re-election.

After taking office, Johnson hoped to consolidate power under the "National Union Party" brand by adopting a conciliatory approach toward the Southern states. Johnson did not believe African Americans should be allowed to vote. He sympathized with Southern elites and gave presidential pardons to many former leaders of the rebellion.[4] As a result, many decades passed before the freedoms the U.S. Colored troops helped to win could be experienced by their descendants.

Slavery had been abolished in the nation's capital when President Lincoln signed the District of Columbia Emancipation Act on April 16, 1862. Maryland abolished slavery on October 11, 1864. Two more Northern states abolished slavery before the end of the war: Missouri on January 11, 1865 and West Virginia on February 3, 1865.

Over the next few years, legislation was passed guaranteeing the rights of citizenship to black Americans. Ratified on December 9, 1865, the 13th Amendment to the U.S. Constitution outlawed slavery, with the following words: "*Neither slavery nor involuntary servitude, except as a punishment for crime whereof the party shall have been duly convicted, shall exist within the United States, or any place subject to their jurisdiction."*[5]

Finally, slavery was abolished in Delaware and Kentucky, as the two Northern states ratified the 13th Amendment in December of 1865. More than six months had passed since the "Juneteenth" reading of the order declaring emancipation in Texas.

On March 2, 1867, Congress passed the First Reconstruction Act, a law requiring the states formerly in rebellion to create new constitutions, *"framed by a convention of delegates elected by the male citizens of said State, twenty-one years old and upward, of whatever race, color, or previous condition"*.[6]

An election held on October 22, 1867 to elect delegates to a constitutional convention was the first in which black Virginians were allowed to vote. Of 105 delegates elected to participate in the convention, twenty-four were African American.

To be readmitted to the Union, Southern states had to pass new constitutions guaranteeing voting rights and equal protection under the law for African Americans. Ratified July 6, 1869, the new Virginia Constitution guaranteed the right to vote for all African American men.[7] The states formerly in rebellion were required to ratify the 14th Amendment to the U.S. Constitution, and to disenfranchise former Confederate officials from holding public office, although many were pardoned or amnestied.

Ratified in 1868, the 14th Amendment to the U.S. Constitution said that *"All persons born or naturalized in the United States, and subject to the jurisdiction thereof, are citizens of the United States and of the State wherein they reside. No State shall make or enforce any law which shall abridge the privileges or immunities of citizens of the United*

States; nor shall any State deprive any person of life, liberty, or property, without due process of law; nor deny to any person within its jurisdiction the equal protection of the laws."[8]

The 15th Amendment, ratified in 1870, stated that *"The right of citizens of the United States to vote shall not be denied or abridged by the United States or by any State on account of race, color, or previous condition of servitude."*[9]

In 1875, Blanche K. Bruce, who had been born in Prince Edward County, Virginia, was elected as U.S. Senator from Mississippi, and was the first African American senator to serve a full term in office.[10] (Hiram Revels had been *appointed* to serve a partial term in 1871-1872.)[11]

Among African American politicians in Virginia during the Reconstruction period there were several former Union soldiers:

James Taylor, born near Charlottesville, had served as a Sergeant in Company E of the 2nd U.S. Colored Infantry.[12] Taylor was a delegate to the Virginia Constitutional Convention of 1867-1868.[13]

Born free in Surry County in 1840, Goodman Brown served in the Navy on the *USS Maratanza* from 1862 to 1864 and was elected to the Virginia House of Delegates as a Republican and Readjuster in 1887.[14]

Robert Gilbert Griffin, born in Yorktown in 1847, enlisted in Company K of the 24th U.S. Colored Infantry in Philadelphia in March 1865. Griffin served in the Virginia House of Delegates from 1883 through 1885.[15]

Peter Jacob Carter, born in Northampton County, had served in Company B of the 10th U.S. Colored Infantry during the war. He attended Hampton Institute from 1869 through 1871 and was elected to the Virginia House of Delegates for four terms. Carter later served on the Board of Directors for the Virginia Normal and

Collegiate Institute which became Virginia State University.[16]

Littleton Owens, born in Princess Anne County, had been a Sergeant in Company C of the 2nd U.S. Colored Cavalry during the war. Owens served in the Virginia House of Delegates as a Republican and Readjuster.[17]

John Mercer Langston, who had recruited for the 54th and 55th Massachusetts Colored Infantry and the 5th Massachusetts Colored Cavalry, became President of Virginia State University and the first African American born in Virginia elected to the U.S. Congress.[18]

The soldiers who survived the war went back to their homes, and began new lives. They raised families; many bought land for the first time or started businesses. U.S. Colored troop veterans were leaders in their communities. They helped build churches, schools, and despite the many obstacles placed in their way, better lives for their families and for all Americans.

America was industrializing, settling the western frontier, and becoming a world economic power. Financial corruption and reckless investing led to an economic depression in 1873. Political corruption led to a lack of confidence in the Federal government. The hotly contested presidential election of 1876 was so close it had to be decided in the end by an electoral commission. A compromise decision was reached, with Democrats on the commission agreeing to declare Rutherford B. Hayes duly elected to the presidency if U.S. soldiers were withdrawn from the South.[19]

In 1877 troops were withdrawn from Louisiana and South Carolina, the last southern states to be occupied by Federal forces. The withdrawal of U.S. troops from the South effectively ended Reconstruction. The war to end slavery had been won, but equality under the law would only be realized after the passage of many more decades.

Remembering Those Who Served

African American soldiers who served during the Civil War have received some recognition through the years. In 1866 the Grand Army of the Republic was founded as a fraternal organization consisting of former Union soldiers, and permitted former black servicemen to become members.[20]

The remains of 249 U.S. Colored Troop veterans are buried at the National Cemetery in Alexandria, Virginia, which opened in 1862.[21] Another 1,500 are buried at Arlington, which became a national cemetery in 1864.[22] Thousands more are buried in public and private cemeteries around the United States; many are identified with tombstones memorializing their U.S.C.T. service.

Various monuments have been dedicated around the nation, honoring the heroism of the U.S.C.T. soldiers. One of the most well-known is the memorial to Colonel Robert Gould Shaw and the 54th Massachusetts Colored Infantry Regiment at the Boston National Historical Park, sculpted by Augustus Saint-Gaudens and dedicated in 1897.[23]

A memorial to African American veterans of the Civil War and Spanish American War, featuring a statue of Medal of Honor recipient William Harvey Carney, was dedicated at the West Point Cemetery in Norfolk in 1920.[24]

There is a memorial at Centennial Park in Fort Myers, Florida, dedicated in 1998 to the 2nd U.S. Colored Infantry Regiment. The monument is near 2101 Edwards Drive, Fort Myers, FL 33901.[25]

The African American Civil War Museum and Memorial opened in January 1999 in the nation's capital. Located at 1925 Vermont Avenue NW in Washington, the Museum offers exhibits, resources for teaching and research, and educational programs. The *"Spirit of*

Freedom", a bronze statue, depicts men from the Army, Navy and Marines on one side, and a family with a soldier leaving for the war on the other side. The names of 209,145 soldiers and sailors who served, taken from the Bureau of U.S. Colored Troops archives, are listed on a Wall of Honor.[26]

At the Vicksburg National Memorial Park there is a monument to members of the 1st and 3rd Mississippi Infantry Regiments (African Descent) and to civilian African Americans who served in the Vicksburg Campaign in 1863. The bronze monument shows a wounded soldier being supported by a soldier who looks forward to the future, and a civilian who looks back at the past.[27]

At the Unknown and Known Afro-Union Civil War Soldiers Memorial at 1001 Bells Mill Road in Chesapeake, Virginia, several U.S.C.T. soldiers are honored by a grouping of marble headstones in the Corprew family cemetery. The location was selected in the 1870s by Sergeant March Corprew of Company L, 2nd U.S. Colored Infantry regiment. The Memorial features a marker for Sergeant Miles James, Medal of Honor recipient born in Virginia, as well as a marker for Sergeant Littleton Owens, one of the first African Americans to serve in the Virginia House of Delegates after the war.[28]

A double row of tombstones on the Shelbyville Road east of Louisville, Kentucky, memorializes the twenty-two U.S. Colored Cavalry troopers massacred near Simpsonville in January 1865. The monument was dedicated in January 2009.[29]

At the site of a February 1865 battle near Wilmington, a statue was dedicated in 2021 called *"Boundless"* by North Carolina sculptor Stephen Hayes. The memorial features eleven life-sized bronze figures of soldiers from the 1st, 5th, 10th, 27th, and 37th U.S. Colored Infantry Regiments.[30]

The U.S.C.T. Monument at 21675 South Coral Drive, Lexington Park, Maryland honors soldiers from Saint Mary's County and features memorials to Medal of Honor recipients Private William H. Barnes, Sergeant James Harris, and Sailor Joseph Hayden. It was dedicated in 2012.[31]

Dedicated in 2021, a U.S.C.T. monument at 23144 Maddens Tavern Road, Lignum, Virginia honors three unknown African American soldiers executed near the spot by Confederate cavalry on May 8, 1864.[32]

The Fuller Story and March to Freedom U.S.C.T. Monument at the Public Square in Franklin, Tennessee was dedicated in 2021. More than 300 U.S.C.T. soldiers enlisted from Williamson County.[33]

There is a U.S.C.T. monument at the Fort Defiance Civil War Park and Interpretive Center at 120 Duncan Street in Clarksville, Tennessee that was dedicated in 2022.[34]

A monument was dedicated in 2025 at the Payne Chapel A.M.E. Cemetery at 23 Payne Place, Canonsburg, Pennsylvania, honoring eleven U.S.C.T. soldiers buried there. Eleven U.S.C.T. regiments were organized at Camp William Penn in Lamott, Pennsylvania, just north of Philadelphia. Today a museum located a block away from the site displays artifacts and hosts events associated with the history of the U.S. Colored Troops. The 3rd, 6th, 8th, 22nd, 24th, 25th, 32nd, 41st, 43rd, 45th & 127th U.S. Colored Infantry Regiments were formed at Camp William Penn. The Citizens for the Restoration of Historical La Mott hosts an excellent website with a database and archive great for conducting research on U.S.C.T. soldiers from these and other regiments.[35]

The Camp Nelson National Monument in Jessamine County, Kentucky is located at the site of an important supply, recruitment and training base, used by the Union Army during the Civil War. Eight U.S.C.T. regiments were organized at Camp Nelson, including the 5th and 6th U.S. Colored Cavalry and the 114th, 116th, 119th, 122nd, 123rd, and 124th U.S. Colored Infantry Regiments. Camp Nelson is located at 6614 Old Danville Loop 2 Road, Nicholasville, KY 40356.[36]

A small roadside marker placed by the Virginia Department of Historic Resources in 1993 identifies the location of the New Market Heights battlefield, on the New Market Road southeast of Richmond.[37] At a small park at Deep Bottom Landing, a modern-day boat ramp marks the location of a pontoon bridge that crossed the James River during the war. U.S.C.T. soldiers stepped onto the north shore of the James at Deep Bottom the night before the Battle of New Market Heights, the sound of their footsteps muffled by earth and straw laid on the planks of the bridge.

On January 18, 2026, a monument to seventy men born in Franklin County, Virginia who served in the Union armed forces was dedicated at the original location of the historic First Baptist Church in Rocky Mount. The former sanctuary is being renovated as a community and cultural center, and will feature an informational exhibit on Franklin County's U.S.C.T. soldiers and sailors.[38]

These monuments help tell the story of a painful part of American history.

14. GLORIOUS WORK TO DO

Most soldiers and sailors spend only a brief part of their lives in the military. USCT soldiers typically enlisted for three years, but towards the end of the war enlistments for one year became common.

For many of the men who had endured years of slavery, life in the military was a vast improvement over what they were used to. Soldiers were typically better fed than slaves; the hardships of garrison life bore no comparison to those of slavery. For most former slaves, their blue uniforms were the best set of clothes they had ever owned. Military discipline could be rigid but was far more tolerable than what former slaves had experienced. It was not uncommon for those who had escaped to die shortly after enlisting, their health already shattered by the hardships of slavery and flight.

War is traumatic. Some soldiers spent months on the front lines and in frequent combat; for others the horrors of battle might only last a few minutes or hours. Many would die. Others were horribly wounded, maimed for life. Those who were captured were re-enslaved, generally until the end of the war, under worse conditions than those of their prior enslavement. Soldiers who avoided becoming casualties in combat still risked debilitating sickness or injury; more died from disease than from wounds.

All were changed by their experiences, and the world had been changed by their efforts. When the war ended, those who survived had to figure out how to begin new lives.

Sergeant Hannibal Cox, a soldier born in Powhatan County and serving in Company B of the 14th U.S.C.I., enlisted at Gallatin, Tennessee in November 1863.[1]

Able to read and write, Cox composed the following poem and sent it to President Lincoln:

Hannibal Cox, Poem, March 30, 1864
From a man of no Education. And have been Doomed to Slavery —
During life, And was born In Powhatan Co. And was raised In
Richmond Virginia. And I am now a Soldier In U. S. Army.
And I will Speak these few words In Answer to all whom it
May Concern. Where Ever it may roam.
I. have left my wife And Children but —
Tho. I. have not yet for Saken them. and made one grasp —
at the Flag of the union and Declared it shall neaver fall —
For we love it like the Sunshine, and the Stars and azure air.
Ho for the flag of the union. the Stripes and the Stars of light. —
A million arms. Shall guard it. and may god defend the right. —
Ay, brothers let us love it, and let Every heart be true. —
And let Every arm be ready, for we have glorious work to do. —
Ho. for the Flag of the union. the Stripes and the Stars of Light.
a million arms shall guard it. and may. god defend the right. —
I. Hope we may meet again In the bonds of love to greet
fare well I. hope History may tell

Hannibal Cox
Co. B. 14th U. S. Cold Troop
Chattanooga Tenn march 30th 1864
I sends this for you to look at you must not laugh at it [2]

Pension applications sometimes provide vivid glimpses of the events soldiers experienced during and after the war. John Triplett, born in Franklin County,

258

was wounded in action near Petersburg while serving as a Private in Company G of the 22nd U.S.C.I.

The following eyewitness account from his commanding officer accompanied John Triplett's pension application:

Washington D.C.
February 10 1866

I hereby certify that John Triplett was a private in Co "G" 22nd Regt U.S. Col'd Troops when I was Colonel commdg said Regt. and I saw him wounded on the 28th day of June 1864. While in a Bomb Proof before Petersburg VA he was shot through his left wrist, causing him to lose the entire use of his left hand. He was discharged from the service of the U.S. on account of said wound.

J.D.B. Kiddoo
Late Col 22nd U.S. Col Troops
Bvt Maj Gen Vols [3]

Former soldiers and their families sought help from the Freedmen's Bureau in a variety of ways. Records maintained by the Bureau between 1865 and 1872 contain clues about their experiences in the years immediately following the war.

Born in Augusta County, Daniel Pompey and Stephen Blunt had served in Company G of the 37th U.S.C.I. and were discharged in 1867 from Raleigh, N.C. Daniel Pompey's father contacted the Freedmen's Bureau in 1868 to ask for their help in finding his son. Pompey had been living in North Carolina in mid-1867, and had not come back to Augusta County for a planned visit at Christmas.[4]

In 1868 Blunt received $50 through the Freedmen's Bureau, a payment on his enlistment bonus. He married a woman named Maggie in 1888; the Blunts had two daughters, Eva and Alice.[5]

Elam Washington of Amelia County was helped by the Bureau to receive $100 due on his enlistment bounty in 1867. Washington had served in Troop B of the 1st U.S. Colored Cavalry.[6]

Benjamin Whitfield, born in Fauquier County, was wounded in action at Petersburg while serving in Company E of the 4th U.S.C.I.[7] He was able to collect $131.06 of his bounty after paying a $10 attorney fee and $1.54 notary fee to D.W. Todd, a law firm specializing in helping former soldiers with bounty claims.[8] The same firm helped James Gail, born in Mathews County, collect his claim in 1868.[9] Gail had served in Company F of the 10th U.S.C.I.[10]

Using Wolf & Hart, a different claim agent, Private Jerome Newman was able to collect $86.50 of his enlistment bounty in December 1869.[11] Newman had been born in Frederick County, and had served in the 1st U.S.C.I.[12]

Cleburn Hill used still another agent, Chipman, Homer & Company of Washington D.C., to help with his bounty application in 1867.[13] Born in King William County, Hill served in Company C of the 2nd U.S.C.I.[14]

George Pleasant, born in Bath County, served in Troop H of the 5th Massachusetts Colored Cavalry, but died in October 1865 from a combination of asthma and scurvy at the Davids Island Hospital in New York Harbor.[15] In 1866, his brother John, who had also served in the 5th Massachusetts, applied for George's unpaid enlistment bounty when their mother, Catherine, passed away, on behalf of George's surviving heirs.[16]

William H. Almstead served in Company C of the 2nd U.S.C.I. and had been born in Gloucester County.[17] Shortly after mustering out in 1866, Almstead died of disease likely contracted while he was guarding prisoners in New York near the end of his enlistment. His mother, Mary Almstead, sought help from General S.C. Armstrong, then in charge of the 5th District Freedmen's Bureau office, in collecting his unpaid bounty.[18]

Born in Fluvanna County, Charles Dickenson had been a Private in Company K of the 16th U.S.C.I.[19] His 1870 bounty claim through the Bureau was denied, on the basis that he had already been paid all the bounty to which he was entitled.[20]

John King, born in King and Queen County, had his claim 'disallowed' because he had enlisted as a substitute and been paid by the man he replaced.[21] King had served in Company A of the 39th U.S.C.I.[22]

The Freedmen's Bureau helped with more than payment of outstanding enlistment bonuses.

Fleming Johnson of Appomattox County sought help from the Freedman's Bureau in recovering $20 and a pocketbook from a man named Edmund Reid who had obtained the money from Johnson under false pretenses.[23] Private Johnson had served in Battery H of the 14th U.S. Colored Heavy Artillery.[24]

The Bureau also helped with the disposition of abandoned properties. Private Edwin Williams, who had enlisted as a substitute in Company G of the 45th U.S.C.I. in 1864[25], was helped by the Bureau to rent a brick dwelling house at 4 Avon Street in Norfolk. His rent was $5 per month.[26]

Born in Hanover County, Henry Clay had served in Company H of the 5th U.S.C.I. until he was discharged for disability in 1864.[27] In 1867, his wife Laura asked the Bureau to help recover $27 that Clay had sent to her via his brother, who lived in Washington. The brother had failed to deliver the money – more than a month's pay.[28]

John H. Bogus had been born in Henry County, and served in Company H of the 40th U.S.C.I.[29] Living in

Wytheville after the war and suffering from tuberculosis, his doctor sought help from the Bureau in getting Bogus admitted to the Freedmen's Hospital in Lynchburg for treatment.[30]

Originally from Lancaster County, Thomas Monroe served in Company C of the 2nd U.S.C.I. until he was discharged from Key West in January 1866.[31] A few months after his discharge, the Bureau helped Monroe contract with a man named Edward Hawkins to work on his farm for a year, for $260 – better wages than he had been getting as a soldier.[32]

Nelson Wallace served in Company K of the 2nd U.S.C.I., fighting in the battle of Natural Bridge, Florida before returning home to Madison County, where he was born.[33] In August 1865, the Freedmen's Bureau helped Wallace contract with Fielding Carpenter to work on his farm as a 'Laborer' for seventeen months, at $5 per month. In January 1867, Wallace contracted with John Carpenter for Wallace's minor son, Jourdan, to work for Carpenter as a 'farm servant' for twelve months. In this case, Wallace was to be paid $65 for the year along with *"one calico dress"*. A condition of the contract for Jourdan's work stipulated *"and he is not to work out in wet weather or nights."*[34]

Civil and court records sometime reveal other details about the former soldier's lives after the war. John Polat, born in Allegheny County, had served in Company E of the 32nd U.S.C.I. until he was discharged in August 1865.[35] In November 1866 he bought land from a man named William Jones in Westmoreland County, Pennsylvania; Polat sold the property in April 1873.

Census records frequently contain details about surviving soldiers and their families.

Sonnie Brown was living in Ohio when the 1870 Census was taken. Born in Bedford County, Brown served in company I of the 5th U.S.C.I. during the war.

The Army paid for his transportation back to Gallipolis, Ohio, where he had enlisted.[36] He was still living in 1889 and was granted a pension.[37]

Born in Montgomery County, Private Othello Fraction served in Company H of the 40th U.S.C.I. during the war.[38] Both he and his brother, Sergeant Thomas Fraction were arrested and confined at Salem, Virginia in March 1866 without legitimate cause.[39] Army officials intervened to have them released. Othello Fraction was living in Maryland in 1900, and was awarded a pension.[40]

Private Clayborn Bazell served in Company B of the 27th U.S.C.I. as a cook.[41] After the war he returned to Ohio, where he had enlisted; in 1880 he was living in Washington Township, Miami County, Ohio. Bazell had been born in Charlotte County.[42]

Thomas Woldridge of Chesterfield County was wounded in action at New Market Heights on September 29, 1864 while serving in company H of the 5th U.S.C.I.[43] When the census was taken in 1880 he had a wife, Meilla, sons Abram, William, and Earnest, and daughters Lucy, Helen, and Mary.

In 1880, Joseph Valentine lived in Green Township, Gallia County, Ohio with his wife Belle, who was born in North Carolina.[44] Valentine had been born in Dinwiddie County and served in Company I of the 37th U.S.C.I. as a driver in the regimental ambulance train.[45]

Edward Logan, born in Patrick County, lived in Ross County, Ohio with his wife Polly after the war. Logan had served in Company K of the 55th Massachusetts Colored Infantry. He passed away in 1915.[46]

Living in Ohio in February 1892, Corporal Edward Calander, born in Rockbridge County, was awarded an invalid pension.[47] Calander had served in Company K of the 15th U.S.C.I.[48]

In May of the same year, Corporal Henry Mozee, born in Rockingham County, was awarded his pension.[49] Living in Tennessee, Mozee had served in Company F of the 1st U.S. Colored Heavy Artillery and worked as a cook during the last few months of his enlistment.[50]

Sergeant Walter Gilchrist of Prince George County was reissued his invalid pension in June 1895.[51] He had served in Company E of the 37th U.S.C.I.[52]

Applying for a widow's pension and keeping it up to date was a complicated process that frequently took years.

Private Edward Sorrell served in Company B of the 26th U.S.C.I. until he was killed in action in a skirmish at Graham's Neck, South Carolina on December 22, 1864.[53] Sorrell had been born in Northumberland County; before he enlisted, he lived with his wife in Dryden, New York. In March 1865, Sidney A. Sorrell began the process of applying for a widow's pension, by submitting a letter with her request via J.M. Ethery, the Clerk of Court for Tompkins County, where the couple had resided. To prove she was married to Edward Sorrell, she sent the original copy of their marriage certificate, dated December 18, 1845. They had been married at Zion Church in Baltimore by Reverend Jacob M. Moore. Sometime after marrying the Sorrells, Reverend Moore emigrated to Africa to work as a missionary – so Mrs. Sorrell was unable to obtain a letter from him verifying that he had married the couple in Baltimore in 1845 and that the marriage certificate was authentic. Instead, she had to submit depositions from multiple witnesses who had been present at their wedding and who could swear to that fact. She had to submit a statement from Sorrell's commanding officer, testifying that Sorrell had been killed in the line of duty, shot in the head *"by a ball from a short Enfield rifle."*[54] Page after page of deposition revealed more details; the Sorrells had a son who served in the same regiment with his father, but who survived the war. After many exchanges of letters and depositions, Sidney Sorrell's widow's pension application was approved. The lengthy and complicated correspondence appears to have been typical.

Typically a soldier might apply for an invalid pension, then his heir applied for a widow's pension after he passed away. Soldiers or their widows also occasionally applied for pension increases.

John Reed, a farmer from Scott County, served in Company F of the 10th U.S.C.I.[55] Reed's mother, Cecilia Alexander, applied for a pension in October of 1875 after Reed had passed away.

Private Mark Addison was killed in garrison when a comrade's musket accidentally fired in October 1864.[56] Addison had been born in Braxton County, West Virginia, and served with Company A of the 45th U.S.C.I. His mother applied for a pension soon after he was killed.

Born in Greenbrier County, West Virginia, Abraham Williams also served in Company A of the 45th.[57] He applied for a pension in 1888; his wife applied for a widow's pension in December 1913.[58]

Another soldier from Company A of the 45th was Julius Butler, born in Harrison County, West Virginia.[59] He was awarded an invalid pension in 1885.[60]

After serving in Company K of the 45th, Charles Augustus of Hampshire County applied for an invalid pension in 1891.[61] Jefferson Monroe, also of Company K of the 45th Infantry, was awarded his invalid pension in 1898; his wife applied for a widow's pension in 1918.[62]

Sailors and their wives applied for pensions, too. James Cannon, born in Greenville County, Virginia, served as a 1st Class Boy and Gunner on the *USS Linden* during the war.[63] He was discharged with asthma in October 1864 at Memphis. He and his wife Christiann lived at Box 125, Greenville, Mississippi until he died. They had been married on Christmas Day, 1851 at the Warfield Plantation. Christiann was awarded an update to her widow's pension in October 1891.[64]

Second Class Fireman Nick Jones served on the *USS Petrel*, the *USS General Price* and the *USS Great Western* during the war.[65] He and his wife Ida lived in a two-room house – "*not plastered, just a little shack*" at 2037 Allen Street, New Orleans.[66] Partly due to injuries he had incurred in the service, Jones had a number of health problems; he and Ida also had an eighteen-year-old son that was paralyzed – one of sixteen children. The others were all grown. Jones applied for an invalid pension in the 1890's; when he died in April 1905, Ida applied for and received a widow's pension, which she collected until her death in August 1926. When she applied, only five of the children were still living. Three of their sons, Nick, Henry, and Johnny, had fought in Company A of the 9th Volunteer Infantry in the Spanish American War.

Combinations of newspaper articles, burial records, census and Freedmen's Bureau records sometimes provide surprisingly detailed accounts of veteran's lives in the years after the war.

Private Henry Burden made his way from Virginia to Wisconsin to enlist in Company B of the 17th U.S.C.I. in early 1865 at Milwaukee.[67] After the war he made his way to Saline County, Nebraska, where he was for many years the only African American resident. He married and lived in Pleasant Hill, and became one of the county's leading citizens; the Burdens had eight children.[68] Henry Burden passed away in 1913.[69]

Born in Augusta County, John Ukkerd served in Company A of the 8th U.S.C.I. during the war.[70] He lived with his family in Chambersburg, Pennsylvania, where he worked as a porter at the National Hotel. Ukkerd testified for the prosecution in a bank robbery trial in

1876.[71] John Ukkerd was "Officer of the Guard" of Major Martin R. Delany Post #494 of the Grand Army of the Republic, which met weekly above a Chambersburg grocery store.[72] Ukkerd died in 1891 of consumption and was buried in the Lebanon Cemetery.

Roots Tibbs served as a Private in Company H of the 2nd U.S.C.I. and fought in several engagements, including the Battle of Natural Bridge, Florida.[73] Born in Caroline County, Tibbs married in 1874 and settled in Spotsylvania County, where he is listed as living with his life Maria, two daughters, a son and a grandson in the 1900 Census. He was a farmer, owned his farm, and the census taker noted that both he and his wife could read and write. Tibbs died of paralysis in January 1915 in Fredericksburg.[74]

Nathaniel Weaver was born in Carroll County and served as a Private in Company H of the 34th U.S.C.I.[75] He is listed in the 1880 Census as living in Washington, D.C. When Weaver died, a lawsuit was brought by two women claiming to be his wife and daughter by a slave marriage. The woman claiming to be his wife testified that during the war, Weaver had prevented some other black soldiers from burning the church where they were married – an event which the pastor of the church remembered. The pastor also remembered marrying the Weavers. His wife and daughter won the lawsuit.[76]

Born in Mecklenburg County, Cheeseman Hughs enlisted in the 2nd Mississippi Infantry, African Descent in October 1863.[77] His regiment was later redesignated as the 52nd U.S. Colored Infantry. In 1889 he applied for a pension. He suffered from rheumatism, and his hearing and sight were going bad. Hughs died in January 1915 and is buried in the Vicksburg National Cemetery.[78]

Beverly Harris of Middlesex County served in Company G of the 23rd U.S.C.I. and was discharged from Brazos Santiago, Texas in October 1865.[79] Returning to Virginia, he eventually became a pastor and a Mason; when he died in 1910 he was buried in the Antioch Baptist Church Cemetery at Saluda, Virginia.[80]

First Sergeant Henry E. Copeland signed his name when he enlisted in the Independent Battery of Light Artillery at Leavenworth, Kansas in 1864.[81] Born in Nansemond County, Copeland had been a carpenter. After the war he returned to Virginia and lived at 528 Walker Avenue, Norfolk. He died on March 3, 1909 and was buried in the Cedar Grove Cemetery.[82] His older brother James served in Troop H of the 2nd U.S. Colored Cavalry as a farrier.[83] James lived in Portsmouth after the war.

Elijah Roberts was born in Nelson County with one black and one grey eye. He could not see out of his left eye but was able to enlist in Company F of the 1st U.S.C.I. in June 1863.[84] After the war he lived in Baltimore with his wife Mary, and worked as a watchman for a local brickyard. On Christmas Day, 1891 he was found dead "from natural causes" at the brickyard.[85] He was buried in the Loudon Park Cemetery.[86]

Loyd Brickhouse enlisted in the 10th U.S.C.I. on October 30, 1863 when he was forty-four years old.[87] Enlisting on the same day were John[88], Nathan[89], Smyth[90], and West Brickhouse[91], possibly his sons. They lived in Northampton County. West Brickhouse died in 1866 at the City Point Hospital of disease. The other Brickhouse men were all discharged in May 1866. John Brickhouse lived until July 1907 and is buried in the Hampton National Cemetery.[92]

Born in 1812 as a slave in Lee County, Henry Bagby taught himself to read, bought his freedom and went into business with his former master as a business partner. He eventually sold his half of the business to his partner and emigrated to Indiana.[93]

Henry and his wife Charlotte had several sons. Robert Bruce Bagby enlisted in Company E of the 28th U.S.C.I. and was eventually promoted to First Sergeant.[94] After his service Robert returned to Indiana. After graduating from Oberlin College in 1874 he became an educator, school principal and publisher of the Indianapolis Leader. He went on to graduate from Columbia Law School and worked in the U.S. Treasury department, then returned to Indiana and became the first African American member of the Indianapolis City Council. Robert Bruce Bagby died of pneumonia in 1903 and is buried in the Crown Hill Cemetery.[95]

Robert's brother Edwin worked in the War Department, and later as a claims attorney. Another brother, Benjamin, assisted in publishing the newspaper and taught school; yet another brother, James Driff Bagby, became the first African American deputy sheriff of Marion County, Indiana.

Corporal Sawney Grimes, born in Orange County, served in Company E of the 45th U.S.C.I.[99] When the Frederick Douglass Post #21 of the G.A.R. conducted a Memorial Day service at Harmony Cemetery in Washington in May 1917, Chaplain Sawney Grimes gave the invocation.[100]

When Elijah Hines joined Company H of the 18th U.S.C.I. in August 1864, he was fifteen years old.[101] His former slaveholder, Elizabeth Hines of Pulaski County, submitted a compensation claim. Elijah Hines emigrated to Grand Junction, Colorado after the war where he and his wife Nicey had two daughters and a son. He became a well-known fruit grower. Elijah Hines was a member of John A. Logan Post #21 of the G.A.R., a Mason, and attended the 1st A.M.E. church in Grand Junction. When he died of pneumonia in 1925, he was buried in the Richard Mesa Cemetery.[102]

Born in Roanoke County, Ellis Kile enlisted in Company K of the 45th U.S.C.I. during the war.[103] His father was Nelson Kile. He and his wife Vina lived at 314 Alabama Street. Ellis Kile died of chronic nephritis in 1936; he was ninety-three years old. Kile is buried at the East Hill Cemetery in Salem, Virginia.[104]

Silas Lightfoot, born in Southampton County, served in Company A of the 2nd U.S.C.I. during the war as a Private.[105] He was only thirty-nine years old when he died in 1884, and was buried in the Page Jackson Cemetery in Sanford, Florida.[106]

Sergeant Stanley Ward served in Company K of the 34th U.S.C.I.[107] Ward lived with his wife Leatha in Oklahoma after the war; when he died in 1931 he was buried at the Eudora Cemetery in Greenfield, Oklahoma.[108] Sergeant Ward had been born in Stafford County.

Born in Sussex County, Private Charles Dillard served in Troop K of the 2nd U.S. Colored Cavalry.[109] The life of a cavalryman must have suited him; Dillard joined Troop K of the 9th Cavalry Regiment after the war and became a Buffalo Soldier. Charles Dillard died in 1891 and is buried at the Forest Lawn Memorial Park in Omaha, Nebraska.[110]

Harrison Shipe served in the 45th U.S.C.I. as a teamster during the war.[111] He had been born in Warren County. After the war, he lived in Greencastle, Pennsylvania and built a produce business; Shipe died in 1913 and is buried at the Cedar Hill Cemetery.[112]

When Corporal Isaiah Fassett died in 1946, his obituary stated he was born in Maryland, but when he enlisted in Company D of the 9th U.S. Colored Infantry in November 1863, Fassett stated he was born in Accomack County, Virginia.[113] He was the head of his G.A.R. post in Berlin, Maryland; amazingly, he lived to be 102 years old. Isaiah Fassett is buried in the St. Paul United Methodist Church Cemetery.[114]

The words of Samuel H. Smothers, soldier and educator born in Franklin County, express a hope shared by so many of these Americans:

"For my own part all I ask of any man is an equal chance, and then if he can outstrip me in the race of life let him do it."[115]

The enduring legacy of these men, and of all those Americans who fought for freedom, is that equal chance that rightfully belongs to all of us.

15. RESEARCH ON SOLDIERS AND SAILORS

Information about African American soldiers and sailors that served in the Civil War can be accessed through a variety of methods, and most of these sources can be accessed at little or no cost. The Internet is a good place to start. Numerous websites offer access to information about individuals who served, the units they served in, and the battles in which those units fought.

Books about the war, specific units and specific battles can be found in public libraries; local historical societies and museums can also be helpful. In fact, there is so much information, the first challenge is figuring out the best place to start.

Begin with a vision of the end result in mind. What exactly are you looking for? When you have finished your research, what do you hope to have accomplished?

Are you looking for general information, details about a particular individual, maybe an ancestor? Do you know anything about that soldier or sailor, or about his descendants? Do you know where he lived before he enlisted? Was he enslaved, or free before the war?

Keep a notebook handy, and take lots of notes as you search. Use a pencil. History should be written with a pencil. As you learn and validate details, you will likely need to make corrections.

In your notebook, write down everything you know about the person you're looking for: Name, date of birth, place of birth or residence, family members names. What did he do for a living? When did he die, and where is he buried?

Company Descriptive Book and Muster Rolls

When a man enlisted in the Army during the Civil War his personal details were entered in a document called a 'Descriptive List', which was usually recorded in a bound volume called the 'Company Descriptive Book'. The information collected in the Descriptive List included his name, estimated age, height in feet and inches, and place of birth. If the soldier was an African American, information was included on his skin complexion, the color of his eyes, and the color of his hair. (Sometimes, these descriptions said more about the perceptions of the person entering the data than they did about the man being described.) The date and place of enlistment was recorded.

If the new recruit was unable to sign his name, an orderly or officer signed on his behalf and the enlisting man put a mark, usually an "X", where his name appeared on the document. Multiple copies of his enlistment papers were prepared: One for the enlisting soldier, one for his regiment, and at least one to be forwarded up the chain of command. At least one copy would ultimately wind up in the War Department.

After enlisting, the new recruit was handed off to a non-commissioned officer, usually a corporal or sergeant, who would show him his accommodations, usually a tent in camp or a barracks in garrison, and begin introducing him to Army life. He would be ordered to appear at a particular place on a specified date to 'muster' with his unit. The muster might be immediate and take place nearby, or it might be weeks later and take place miles away.

At muster a complete roll was called of everyone belonging to that regiment. Another document was completed, called a 'Muster In Roll', with the name of the regiment, the name and rank of each soldier, the company to which he was assigned, and the identifying information about him that appeared on the Descriptive List. The object of the muster was to associate the soldier with his unit and his specific place in that organization. He might be 'detailed' to perform specific duties, such as assisting in the preparation of food, fetching water, tending livestock, gathering firewood, or preparing and cleaning latrines in the camp.

When the soldier enlisted, he met the Sergeant or Corporal immediately responsible for him, and began to receive training on what was expected of him. After attending muster his training began in earnest. If he had not received one already, he would be issued a uniform, along with his weapon and kit.

Sometimes the Descriptive List included other details, such as the name of the state and district to which his enlistment was credited. If the soldier had been a slave the name of his former slaveholder might appear. The enlisting officer or clerk sometimes wrote the name of the soldier's next of kin or place of residence.

Similar information was collected for men joining the Navy but documented differently. More about that later.

Most of the information available to us on individual soldiers is derived from the details recorded in the Descriptive List and Muster in Rolls.

During the war, these documents, along with copies of the soldier's enlistment contract and other paperwork collected along the way constituted the soldier's personnel file. They were used to keep track of the pay he was due, of money he might owe the government for lost equipment, and records of actions pertaining to the soldier such as promotions, courts martial, or furlough. If the soldier was sick and sent to hospital, wounded, missing in action or taken prisoner, killed in action, deserted or died of disease, the event was recorded either on his descriptive list, the muster rolls, or both.

274

After the war, these documents were kept on file in the War Department and used to research information about the soldier's service for back pay claims and eventually for pension applications. Government clerks soon realized that while the descriptive lists and muster rolls were convenient documents for gathering the soldier's information and tracking his service, they were not well suited for researching that information years after the fact.

Compiled Military Service Records

In the 1870s, details from hundreds of thousands of descriptive lists and muster rolls were transcribed onto a new, standard set of documents called "Compiled Military Service Records". The work was done by hand, by an army of copyists, hired by the War Department. The standardized system made it easier to look up a soldier's records when researching his pension eligibility, back pay due, or general details about his service.

Any information you are likely to find about an individual Civil War soldier will be found in his Compiled Military Service Records (CMSR).

These records follow a consistent format. The first page is similar to a table of contents, and will include the soldiers first and last name, the company and regiment to which he was assigned, his rank when he enlisted, his final rank, and a list of card numbers. The card numbers were used by the copyists that transcribed the CMSR and no longer have any consistent association. However, a short list of numbers on the cover page is an indicator that the soldier's service was brief; a longer list of numbers indicates that there are more documents in the file, and the soldier likely served for a longer time.

The second page is usually, but not always, blank. Occasionally there might be notes on the blank page from a copyist or from a clerk looking up the soldier's data decades after the war, but most of the time there might be one or two long sequences of numbers, that no longer have any identifiable association with the remainder of the file.

The third page is usually labelled *"Appears on Company Descriptive Book of the organization named above"*. The soldier's name, company, and regiment are listed at the top of the page. His age and height are listed, as are his complexion, eye and hair color. His place of birth is listed in the 'Where born' field, followed by his occupation. His enlistment date and location are listed: 'When' and 'Where'. In the 'By Whom' field, the name of the enlisting officer is given. The 'term' field lists the number of years for which the soldier enlisted. Most USCT soldiers enlisted for three years, but towards the end of the war, many enlistments were for one year only. There are several lines for 'Remarks'; the information on these lines can be very revealing.

The information is all handwritten. If you are not familiar with cursive, you might find it challenging to read these records, but it gets easier as you look at more examples.

At the bottom of the page, there is a space for the signature of the 'Copyist' that transcribed the soldier's information from the Company Descriptive Book. When you have looked at hundreds of these, you will begin to recognize the names of specific copyists, and their handwriting. Some were better at transcribing this information than others. Others were casual spellers, or had handwriting so poor (or elaborate) that it is hard to read. The work must have been tedious.

Suggestion: If your intention is to find out all you can about a specific soldier, write down all the information from his CMSR into your notebook. Every note was put there for a reason, and every note can tell you something useful. For example, the name of the enlisting officer might be inconsequential, or it might be the name of a famous commander, whose signature might appear on a set of orders or a commendation for your soldier, or who might approve his furlough, or who might sit in judgement if he is court martialed. Every detail is significant.

It is a good idea to get in the habit of looking up details on the notes written on the CMSR. Find the place of birth (usually a county, but not always) on a map. Do an Internet search on the enlisting officer's name, or on the soldier's regiment. You might find that something significant happened at the place where the soldier enlisted.

Usually the next page will feature the soldier's name, company and regiment, followed by the label *"Appears on Company Muster-In and Descriptive Roll of the organization named above."* This page will show the location and date in which the regiment mustered. The muster is usually the first time the entire regiment meets.

Descriptive information follows: Where born, Age, Occupation, When enlisted, Where enlisted, For what period enlisted, Complexion, Hair, Eyes, When mustered in, Where mustered in. Much of the information on the muster in page is a duplicate of information from the descriptive roll. The following fields are often blank: Bounty paid, due, where credited, Company to which assigned, Remarks. There might be a 'Book mark' field near the bottom of the page, but the significance of the book marks have generally been lost. Finally, the last line of this page contains the signature of the copyist. The copyist on this page and the following pages may or may not be the same as the copyist on the first page; again, the copyists were War Department clerks transcribing the soldier's information onto these standardized forms years after the war.

The next few pages are usually labelled "*Appears on Company Muster Roll*" and normally included information on the soldier's status for two months at a time. In the field labelled 'Present or Absent', if the soldier is on hand when the roll is called, he will be marked Present. If a soldier is marked Absent, there will usally be an explanation for his absence in the Remarks section at the bottom of the page. There is a field labelled 'Stoppage' and a field labelled 'Due Gov't'. A dollar amount entered in the Stoppage field indicates the soldier was issued a piece of clothing or equipment and that part of his pay will be withheld to cover the cost. A dollar amount in the Due Gov't field usually indicates that the soldier was overpaid, or has had an advance on his pay, or owes money for transportation costs he incurred while on furlough. At the bottom of the page there is a 'Remarks' section, the 'Book Mark' field, and the 'Copyist' signature.

There should be an "Appears on Company Muster Roll" page similar to this one in the soldier's Compiled Military Service Record for each two months of his enlistment. It is important to note that, even if the soldier dies, is killed in action, or deserts, there may be pages like this one for several months after the date the soldier is no longer present. His discharge paperwork may not be completed until his regiment is mustered out of service.

Near the end of the Compiled Military Service Record, there will be a page labelled "*Appears on Co. Muster Out Roll*". When the soldier leaves the Army, when his regiment is disbanded, or if he dies or is killed, the soldier is 'mustered out' of the service and his paperwork is updated to reflect that fact.

The soldier's name, rank, company and regiment appear at the top of the Muster Out page. Below the heading, the name of a place and date will be written in, indicating where and when the muster out roll was prepared. There will be a second date below that, indicating when the muster out is effective. The next entry indicates that the soldier has been paid in full, as of the date in the 'Last paid to' field.

The next few fields show whether or not the soldier owes any outstanding amount for clothing or equipment to be deducted from his final pay and the status of his bounty payments. Not all soldiers were eligible for bounties; not all soldiers were able to collect the same bounty. Bounties were usually paid in increments. Below the 'Remarks' section there is another 'Book mark' field, and the 'Copyist' signature at the very bottom of the page.

On some soldier's records, the Muster Out Roll page is the last page of their file. However, many CMSR's include other documents. A checklist of 'Inclosures' might be included. The checklist is actually the cover of an envelope for holding other documents associated with the soldier. A wide variety of document types are listed, with a space beside the document type for the number of pages included. These "extra" documents often reveal the most moving details of the soldier's story.

The Compiled Military Service Record may not be the only source of information pertaining to an individual soldier, but it is often the most important and the most informative, and can usually be accessed for free – if you know where to look.

There are multiple ways to get at a soldier's Compiled Military Service Records. We'll look at two different methods.

Method 1: CMSR's on the National Archives Website

In the Old Lick Cemetery in Roanoke, Virginia, there is a tombstone marking the burial place of a U.S. Colored Troop soldier named John W. Leftridge, who served in Company F of the 100th U.S. Colored Infantry Regiment. We know a name, and we know a company and regiment in which a soldier served – that is a good start.

Navigate to the National Archives website at *www.archives.gov*. Click on the "Research Our Records" tab, then scroll down and click on the "Research Military Records" link. On the "Military Records" page, scroll down until you see "Research by War or Conflict", then click on "Civil War (1861-1865)". On the "Military Records – Civil War page", scroll down until you see the link "+ Compiled Service Records" and click it to expand the selection. You will see a list of links; click on the one that says "Compiled Military Service Records". Scroll down until you see the heading "Accessing CMSRs", and expand the "+Available CMSRs" link. A list of options will appear. Click on the "300398" link next to 'Carded Service Records of Volunteer Organizations: Civil War (Union), 1861-1865 (NAID: 300398)'.

You will see a page titled "Carded Records Showing Military Service of Soldiers Who Fought in Volunteer Organizations During the American Civil War, 1890–1912". Scroll down until you see the heading "Subjects and References", and below that, a short list of "Topics". Click on the link that says "Soldiers". On the Soldiers topic page, scroll down until you see a list of "Narrower Terms". Click on the "African American Soldiers" link. When you reach the African American soldiers topic page, save this page to your favorites.

In the Search field at the top of the screen, type the name of the soldier you are searching for. In this example, search for "John Leftridge". On this site, it works best if you enclose the soldier's name in quotation marks.

You should now see a list of results. As you scroll down the page, you will actually see records for two different soldiers named John Leftridge. The first is for a twenty-year-old John Leftridge who enlisted in the 16th U.S. Colored Infantry in 1865. However, the information from the grave marker at the Old Lick Cemetery that the John Leftridge we are looking for served in the 100th U.S. Colored Infantry. The second John Leftridge listed is our soldier. If you click on the link, you will see the "Military Service Record of John Leftridge, United States Colored Troops: 100th US Colored Infantry". You can click on the thumbnail menu on at the right side of the screen to view different pages of Private Leftridge's Compiled Military Service Records. The images are in color; red ink appears on some of the pages. These scanned images were provided to the National Archives by *Fold3.com*, a subscription military history database created by *Ancestry.com* .

Not all soldier's records are available on the National Archives, but the ones that are may be viewed for free, and the National Archives website has links to many other great record collections.

Method 2: CMSR's on www.Ancestry.com

Ancestry.com is a premier genealogy website with great resources for looking up military history, and is an ideal site for researching U.S. Colored Troops. In addition to finding service records for soldiers and sailors, you may be able to find relevant Freedmen's Bureau records pertaining to your search. Subscriptions to *Ancestry.com* are inexpensive; they offer a free trial to new subscribers; affordable bundles are also offered that feature subscriptions to *Fold3.com* and *Newspapers.com*, other great resources for researching history. You may also be able to access *Ancestry.com* at no cost through your school or public library.

In the National Cemetery at Dayton, Ohio, there is a grave marker for a soldier named Herod Beverly, who served in Company D of the 5th U.S. Colored Infantry.

Follow the instructions on the Ancestry website to set up an account, then log in at *www.Ancestry.com* .

On the Menu at the top of the screen, select "Search", then "Military".

On the Military search page, scroll down a bit until you see the heading, "Featured data collections". Click the "View all in Card Catalog" button. A page will appear with the heading "Card Catalog".

In the "Title" field at the left of the screen, enter "U.S., Colored", then click the "Search" button. This will filter the choices in the Card Catalog to just a few selections. Click on the link to "U.S., Colored Troops Military Service Records, 1863-1865". A Search form will appear; this is where you will enter information about the USCT soldier you wish to find.

For our example, enter "Herod" in the 'First & Middle Name(s)' field, and "Beverly" in the 'Last Name' field. A page will appear titled 'All U.S., Colored Troops Military Service Records, 1863-1865 results for Herod Beverly' with three records. Hover over the first "View Record" link, and you should see that this record is for Private Herod Beverly, who enlisted in the 5th U.S. Colored Infantry Regiment on August 4, 1863 in Summit County, Ohio.

The soldier's Compiled Military Service Record should be visible in the Image field. Click the 'View Image' button (or click on the image). In this case, you will see a slightly larger image of Private Herod

Beverly's CMSR. You can pan or zoom the image to focus on particular details. Private Herod Beverly was thirty-five years old when he enlisted in Company D of the 5th U.S.C.I. regiment. He was 5′ 2″ tall. His skin was dark, his hair and eyes were black. Private Beverly was born in Franklin County, Virginia and gave his occupation as Teamster.

You can scroll through the CMSR by clicking on the arrows on the side of the screen. Scrolling through Private Beverly's record, you will see that he mustered in at Camp Delaware, Ohio on August 21, 1863 – seventeen days after he enlisted. Keep scrolling. On the record taken from the Company Muster Roll for July and August, 1864, you will see a note in the Remarks section that states, "Free Apl 19, 1861". Herod Beverly was a free person of color, not a slave, before the beginning of the war. On the page with information from the Co. Muster-out Roll, you will see that Private Beverly was discharged from Carolina City, N.C. on September 20, 1865. He had been paid through April 30, 1865. He had drawn $13.30 on his clothing account since June 30, 1864; in the Remarks section, the note indicates he owes the Sutler, R.D. Kuhn, $5.00.

If you are unsure of the name of your soldier, or if you search for a soldier with a common name, you can change the parameters of your search to home in on the correct soldier.

You can also change the parameters to search for lists of groups of soldiers. For example, to list all the soldiers born in Virginia, in the Birth – Location field, start typing the word "Virginia", then click on the drop-down menu selection labelled "Virginia, USA". Then click on the "Search" button.

Wow! You will see the first page of a list of 17,247 soldiers, appearing in no particular order. It's a little overwhelming.

You can refine your search parameters by clicking the "Edit your search" link or clicking on the Pencil icon above and to the left of the list. Change the Birth Location to "Carroll County", then click "Carroll County, Virginia, USA" from the drop-down menu that appears when you start typing. In the Military Year field, change the date to 1864, check the 'Exact to' box, and select '+/- 2 years' from the drop-down option menu. Then click Search…and you should see a list with the names of six soldiers who gave their birthplace as Carroll County, Virginia. You can browse through the list by clicking on the "View Record" link for each one, then clicking the 'View Image' button to read through the CMSR for that soldier.

Experiment. With a little practice you can easily access CMSR's for almost any soldier, born anywhere, who served in any Army regiment during the war.

Once you have the soldier's service dates, regiment number and company, you can find out more about where he served and the battles in which he may have participated.

Use your Internet browser to search for the regiment in which your soldier served. For example, type "23rd U.S. Colored Infantry" in your Search bar and press Enter. You will get page after page of results. A good, short summary of "Battle Unit Details" can be found on the *National Park Service* website, including a list of places where the regiment served and engagements in which the regiment fought.

Browse through the links; a surprising amount of information is available. The more you research, the more proficient you can become at researching information about the soldiers, their regiments, and the engagements in which their regiments fought.

Searching for Sailors

Information on sailors was not recorded the same way as it was for soldiers and was not transcribed in the Compiled Military Service Records format. To research African American sailors who served in the Civil War, you will need to look in a different type of record.

One of the best ways to access information on African American Civil War sailors is to use *www.Ancestry.com* . Naval records are found in a different Collection than the records for soldiers.

From the *www.Ancestry.com* home page, click "Search" on the Menu bar, then "Military". Scroll down to the "Featured data collections" and click the "View all in Card Catalog" button.

In the "Title" field, begin typing "Web: US, African", then click the "Search" button. A link will appear for "Web: US, African American Civil War Sailor Index, 1861-1865". Click that link.

A page will appear titled, "Web: US, African American Civil War Sailor Index, 1861-1865" with a Search form.

James Mifflin earned the Congressional Medal of Honor for his actions during the Battle of Mobile Bay on September 5, 1864 while he served on the USS Brooklyn.

On the Search form, in the 'First and Middle Name(s)' field, enter "James". In the Last Name field, enter "Mifflin", then click the 'Search' button.

Four records will appear on the "…results for James Mifflin" page. You will notice all of them list the same Birth Date of "abt 1839". All list the same Birth Place as Richmond, Virginia. All have the same Enlistment Date, 1 Apr 1864. However, all the Muster Dates listed are different. This is because these records are all for the same man, Landsman James Mifflin. Each time he was present for a ship's muster, a new record was created for him. Landsman Mifflin mustered on the *USS Brooklyn* on 10 May 1864, then again on 7 Jun 1864. On 30 September 1864, Mifflin mustered on the *USS Ossipee*, but he returned to the *USS Brooklyn* by 1 October 1864.

Each sailor will have multiple records – a different one for each date he attended muster. Some sailors attended several musters on the same ship for their entire naval career; others mustered on different ships regularly throughout their careers.

Again: Experiment and practice. Change your search. Clear the First and Last Name fields, and enter "*Hartford*" in the 'Vessel' field. You should see a list of 526 records. If you browse through them, you will find five records for Landsman Charles Dennis, born on the Eastern Shore in Virginia, who enlisted on December 2, 1863 and served for most of his career on the *USS Hartford*.

Where did they serve?

Once you find the service dates, company and regiment for a soldier, or the muster dates and ship assignments for a sailor, you can work out where they were assigned, and what battles they may have been involved in.

By looking up the history of your soldier's regiment, and comparing his service dates with the dates of that regiment's organization, movements, and the battles in which they fought, you will be able to get a pretty good idea of where they were at different times during the war.

For example, Private Herod Beverly joined the 5th U.S. Colored Infantry regiment on August 4, 1863. On the Battle Unit Details page of the National Park Service website for his regiment, the 5th U.S. Colored Infantry, you can see that after his enlistment the 5th moved to

286

Norfolk, Virginia, where they remained until they moved to North Carolina in early 1865. As he mustered out with the rest of his regiment in North Carolina on September 20, 1865, and was not absent sick in hospital, on detached duty or on furlough during any of that time, it is reasonable to conclude that Private Herod Beverly was present during all the battles in which the 5th U.S.C.I. fought.

You can do the same with sailors, by comparing their muster dates and ship assignments with the dates of engagements in which those ships fought. You can usually find ship histories and often a photograph or sketch of the ship with a quick Internet search. By comparing Landsman Charles Dennis's muster dates with the history of the *USS Hartford*, one can work out that Landsman Dennis was probably serving on the *Hartford* during the Battle of Mobile Bay on August 5, 1864, when Admiral Farragut gave his famous order, *"Damn the torpedoes! Full speed ahead!"*, led the ship through a minefield and forcing the surrender of the Confederate ship Tennessee a few hours later. Today, we are impressed when we reflect on the boldness of Admiral Farragut's order. One has to wonder at how the crewmen of the *Hartford* felt when they heard Farragut give the command to sail through that minefield. It took courage to obey that order!

Once you determine which engagements your soldier or sailor may have fought in, you can look up details on that engagement on the web, often with maps and timelines that show where and when the events of that battle transpired.

Many websites contain information on specific battles.

The *American Battlefield Trust* is a non-profit organization that raises funds to preserve battleground sites around the United States and educate members of the public about the battles that were fought here. Originally founded in Fredericksburg, Virginia in 1987 by a group of historians, the Trust works to protect battleground sites from the Civil War and the American Revolution. Some of the best and most comprehensive details of battles fought within the United States can be found on the *American Battlefield Trust* web pages.

Private Herod Beverly of the 5th U.S. Colored Infantry served during the Battle of New Market Heights on September 29, 1864. His brother, Private Samuel Beverly, was wounded and captured during that battle, and later died of his wounds in a prisoner of war camp. On the *American Battlefield Trust* website, there is an excellent map that shows the position of the opposing regiments during various phases of the battle. The 5th U.S. Colored Infantry was right in the thick of the attack, leading the assault on the Rebel lines north of the New Market Road.

With a little detective work you can find more details about your soldier, the conditions in which he served, and what happened to the soldiers and sailors that managed to survive the war.

There is a certain, unique thrill that comes from revealing the lost role these men played in our nation's history. While there are many stories in this book of individual soldiers and sailors, there are thousands more, yet to be rediscovered and shared. You can participate in those discoveries.

We need to remember these men, the circumstances that made it necessary for them to fight, and the sacrifices they made. We need to learn from what they endured. These soldiers and sailors played an active role in obtaining their freedom, not a passive one, and helped to build a 'more perfect union' for all Americans. Keeping their story alive is one way we can express our gratitude and respect.

ACKNOWLEDGEMENTS

A lot of thoughtful, kind people have helped in the preparation of this book.

Thank you, Glenna and Larry Moore, for making me aware of the United States Colored Troops from Franklin County, Virginia, inviting me to help with the Raising the Shade research, introducing me to so many nice people that share our interest in history, and offering so much encouragement along the way.

Many thanks to Dr. Sarah Plummer, Appalachian Studies professor at Virginia Tech, who has provided so much support for the Raising the Shade project. She took an interest in my research and encouraged me to keep digging.

Thank you, Cathie Cummins, Research Director for Raising the Shade, who has done and continues to do such an artful job of coordinating the efforts of a diverse group of researchers, encouraging all of us and providing a reality check as needed.

Melissa Powell Gay, author and friend, thank you for your insight on writing and suggestions for publishing my research.

I am very grateful to Karl Edwards, author, retired educator and friend, for his excellent advice on how to present this history in a clear and orderly way and prepare it for publication.

David and Dabney Tucker, thanks for your interest in the project and for lending me a copy of Henry Hopkins' notes on slaves from Franklin County conscripted to work on the Richmond breastworks during the war.

I am especially grateful to my sister Pat Wood, who shares my interest in history, got me interested in genealogy, and who is always discovering cool information about both subjects. We have fun. We tend to lose track of the time when we speak of these things.

My daughter, Emily Wood Hylton, contributed her journalistic expertise to help me clean up my manuscript and delighted me with her enthusiasm for the project.

Finally, I am most grateful to my wife Dixie Wood, who has cheered me on every step of the way, helps me keep things in perspective, patiently supports me more than I deserve, and who remains the love of my life after all these years. I am blessed and highly favored.

NOTE ON SOURCES

A wide variety of sources were used in the preparation of this history, including books from the author's personal collection, from the Franklin County Public Library and others. Details about battlefields, engagements and some of the individuals involved were gleaned from a host of websites.

Most, but not all, newspaper articles were accessed through *Newspapers.com* and are cited accordingly. Much of the pension information cited is from *Fold3.com*. Both *Ancestry.com* and *FamilySearch.com* are great places to access Freedman's Bureau records on servicemen and their families.

Information on where many of the soldiers and sailors lived and died after the war was accessed through *FindAGrave.com*. State libraries, historical societies, and tourism websites are frequently cited. Readers are encouraged to visit these websites; many make for fascinating reading on places and events associated with the history of these soldiers and sailors and are great tools for historical and genealogical research.

Unless otherwise specified, individual soldier records were accessed through *Ancestry.com* from the collection "*U.S., Colored Troops Military Service Records, 1863-1865*" and individual sailor records were accessed through *Ancestry.com* from the collection "*Web: US, African American Civil War Sailor Index, 1861-1865.*"

In the NOTES on the following pages, citations for individual soldier and sailor records have been abbreviated for brevity and clarity. Detailed instructions for looking up records using the serviceman's name on *Ancestry.com* and through the *National Archives* are provided in Chapter 15.

NOTES

Preface: History We Should Know

1. "We Honor Those Who Served: The Shenandoah Valley African American Men Who Served With the United States Colored Troops, the U.S. Navy and the Confederacy During the Civil War." *Shenandoah Valley Black Heritage Project [SVBHP]*. 2018. Harrisonburg, Virginia, United States of America, Campbell Print Company.

2. Price, James S. "The Battle of New Market Heights: Freedom Will be Theirs by the Sword." *The History Press*, 2011. 53-95

3. Fleche, Andre. "The United States Colored Troops - Encyclopedia Virginia." *Encyclopedia Virginia*, 18 Feb. 2025, encyclopediavirginia.org/entries/united-states-colored-troops-the.

4. "All U.S., Colored Troops Military Service Records, 1863-1865 Results - U.S., Colored Troops Military Service Records, 1863-1865." *Ancestry.com*. www.ancestry.com/search/collections/1107/?birth=_Virginia &birth_x=_1-0&count=50.

5. "All Web: US, African American Civil War Sailor Index, 1861-1865 Results - Web: US, African American Civil War Sailor Index, 1861-1865." *Ancestry.com*. www.ancestry.com/search/collections/9748/?birth=_virginia-usa_49&birth_x=_1-0&count=50.

6. "1860 US Population | Statistics and Facts" *World Data*. 13 Oct. 2025, theworlddata.com/1860-us-population-statistics.

7. "Raising the Shade | USCT Monument | Rocky Mount, VA." *Raising the Shade*, www.raisingtheshade.org.

8. "Slaves to Soldiers." *www.SlavesToSoldiers.org*. www.slavestosoldiers.org.

9. "Black Virginians in Blue." *University of Virginia - John L. Nau III Center for Civil War History*. community.village.virginia.edu/usct/node/1.

10. "Civil War Bluejackets" *Zooniverse - People-powered Research*. www.zooniverse.org/projects/bluejackets/civil-war-bluejackets.

Chapter 1: A Peculiar and Powerful Interest

1. "The Evolution of Slavery: From Ancient Civilizations to the Modern Era - History Collection." *History Collection,*

historycollection.com/the-evolution-of-slavery-from-ancient-civilizations-to-the-modern-era.

2. "Code of Hammurabi." *The Avalon Project.* Retrieved 25 Jan. 2026, avalon.law.yale.edu/ancient/hamcode.asp.

3. "What Is Modern Slavery?." *Anti-Slavery International,* 25 Nov. 2025, www.antislavery.org/slavery-today/modern-slavery.

4. "History Timeline." *Historic Jamestowne Part of Colonial National Historical Park (U.S. National Park Service).* historicjamestowne.org/history/jamestown-timeline.

5. Mark, Joshua J., and Eyre Crowe. "Virginia Slave Laws and Development of Colonial American Slavery." *World History Encyclopedia,* Jan. 2026, www.worldhistory.org/article/1740/virginia-slave-laws-and-development-of-colonial-am.

6. "Bacon's Rebellion" *Historic Jamestowne Part of Colonial National Historical Park (U.S. National Park Service).* www.nps.gov/jame/learn/historyculture/bacons-rebellion.htm.

7. Mark, Joshua J., and Eyre Crowe. "Virginia Slave Laws and Development of Colonial American Slavery." *World History Encyclopedia,* Jan. 2026, www.worldhistory.org/article/1740/virginia-slave-laws-and-development-of-colonial-am.

8. Mark, Harrison W., and William L. Champney and J. H. Bufford. "African Americans in the American Revolution." *World History Encyclopedia,* 09 May 2024, www.worldhistory.org/article/2449/african-americans-in-the-american-revolution.

9. James, C. L. R. *The Black Jacobins: Toussaint L'Ouverture and the San Domingo Revolution.* Vintage, 1989.

10. "Chatham Slave Revolt." *Fredericksburg and Spotsylvania National Military Park (U.S. National Park Service).* www.nps.gov/frsp/learn/historyculture/chatham-slave-revolt.htm.

11. "'an ACT to Amend the Several Laws Concerning Slaves' (1806)." *Encyclopedia Virginia,* 7 Dec. 2020, encyclopediavirginia.org/primary-documents/an-act-to-amend-the-several-laws-concerning-slaves-1806.

12. Mark, Joshua J. "Clotilda, the Last Slave Ship: Greed, Rebellion, and Ultimate Triumph." *World History Encyclopedia,* Sept. 2025, www.worldhistory.org/article/2787/clotilda-the-last-slave-ship.

13. Little, Becky. "How a Movement to Send Formerly Enslaved People to Africa Created Liberia." *HISTORY,* 31 Jan. 2025,

www.history.com/articles/slavery-american-colonization-society-liberia.

14. Mark, Joshua J., and William Henry Shelton. "Nat Turner's Rebellion." *World History Encyclopedia*, Apr. 2025, www.worldhistory.org/Nat_Turner's_Rebellion.

15. "William Lloyd Garrison, Biography, Facts, Significance." *American History Central*, 15 July 2024, www.americanhistorycentral.com/entries/william-lloyd-garrison.

16. "Illustrated List of Abolitionists and Activists." *americanabolitionists.com*. americanabolitionists.com/illustrated-list-of-abolitionists-and-activists.html.

17. "The Uncomfortable Truth: How Christianity Both Supported and Fought Against Slavery - History Collection." *History Collection*, historycollection.com/the-uncomfortable-truth-how-christianity-both-supported-and-fought-against-slavery.

18. "Lincoln's Second Inaugural Address." *Lincoln Memorial (U.S. National Park Service)*. www.nps.gov/linc/learn/historyculture/lincoln-second-inaugural.htm.

19. "Fugitive Slave Acts - Definition, 1793 and 1850." *HISTORY*, 28 May 2025, www.history.com/articles/fugitive-slave-acts.

20. "1850 to 1900 - Books That Shaped America." *Library of Congress*. www.loc.gov/exhibits/books-that-shaped-america/1850-to-1900.html.

21. Hurmence, Belinda. "My Folks Don't Want Me to Talk About Slavery: Twenty-one Oral Histories of Former North Carolina Slaves." *Blair*, 1984. 55

22. "Industry and Economy During the Civil War." *(U.S. National Park Service)*. www.nps.gov/articles/industry-and-economy-during-the-civil-war.htm.

23. "1860 US Population | Statistics and Facts." *The World Data*, 13 Oct. 2025, theworlddata.com/1860-us-population-statistics.

24. "Bleeding Kansas." *(U.S. National Park Service)*. www.nps.gov/articles/bleeding-kansas.htm.

25. "The Caning of Senator Charles Sumner." *U.S. Senate*. 8 Sept. 2023, www.senate.gov/artandhistory/history/minute/The_Caning_of_Senator_Charles_Sumner.htm.

26. "Dred Scott V. Sandford (1857)." *National Archives*, 21 Apr. 2025, www.archives.gov/milestone-documents/dred-scott-v-sandford.

27. "John Brown's Harpers Ferry Raid." *American Battlefield Trust*, www.battlefields.org/learn/topics/john-browns-harpers-ferry-raid.

28. "Election of 1860 - Summary, Lincoln and Significance." *HISTORY*, 27 May 2025, www.history.com/articles/election-of-1860.

29. "Abraham Lincoln's First Inaugural Address." *abrahamlincolnonline.org.* www.abrahamlincolnonline.org/lincoln/speeches/1inaug.htm.

30. "Fort Sumter." *American Battlefield Trust*, www.battlefields.org/learn/civil-war/battles/fort-sumter.

31. "The Civil War: The Senate's Story." *U.S. Senate.* 8 Aug. 2023, www.senate.gov/artandhistory/history/common/civil_war/LincolnEmergencySession_FeaturedDoc.htm.

32. Zeller, Bob. "How Many Died in the American Civil War?." *HISTORY*, 31 Jan. 2025, www.history.com/articles/american-civil-war-deaths.

33. Long, McKenzie. "Whatever Happened to Virginia's Black Patriots?" *The UncommonWealth*, 7 Aug. 2024, uncommonwealth.lva.virginia.gov/blog/2024/08/07/virginias-black-patriots.

34. "All U.S., Colored Troops Military Service Records, 1863-1865 Results - U.S., Colored Troops Military Service Records, 1863-1865." *Ancestry.com.* www.ancestry.com/search/collections/1107/?birth=_Virginia&birth_x=_1-0&count=50.

35. "All Web: US, African American Civil War Sailor Index, 1861-1865 Results - Web: US, African American Civil War Sailor Index, 1861-1865." *Ancestry.com.* www.ancestry.com/search/collections/9748/?birth=_virginia-usa_49&birth_x=_1-0&count=50.

Chapter 2: The Divided House

1. "The Civil War's Black Soldiers." *National Park Civil War Series* www.npshistory.com/publications/civil_war_series/2/sec6.htm.

2. "Robert E. Lee - Biographies - the Civil War in America." *Library of Congress.* www.loc.gov/exhibits/civil-war-in-america/biographies/robert-e-lee.html.

3. Stark, Chandler. "Southern Generals and Admirals Who Chose to Fight for the Union." *Grunge*, 5 July 2023, www.grunge.com/1266759/southern-generals-admirals-chose-fight-for-union.

4.   Fox, John. *Hang George H. Thomas.*
      www.anglevalleypress.com/hang-george-h-thomas.
5.   Grant, Ulysses S. "Personal Memoirs". *Penguin*, 1999. 552
6.   Sherman, W.T. "Grant, Thomas, Lee.". *North American Review*.
      (366). May 1887. 445
7.   Bearss, Edwin C. "Philip St. George Cooke (1809–1895) -
      Encyclopedia Virginia." *Encyclopedia Virginia*, 22 Dec. 2021,
      encyclopediavirginia.org/entries/cooke-philip-st-george-1809-
      1895.
8.   Clemens, Thomas G. "Winfield Scott (1786–1866) -
      Encyclopedia Virginia." *Encyclopedia Virginia*, 18 Feb. 2025,
      encyclopediavirginia.org/entries/scott-winfield-1786-1866.
9.   "John Wynn Davidson (D. 26 June 1881)" *Library of Virginia*.
      old.lva.virginia.gov/public/dvb/bio.asp?b=Davidson_John_
      Wynn.
10.   "SGT Toliver Pharoh Vest (1834-1902)" - *Find a Grave*,
      www.findagrave.com/memorial/49775453/toliver_pharoh-
      vest. [On his Combined Military Service Record, Vest gave his
      birthplace as Patrick County, Virginia.]
11.   Curtis, Matthew and Lindert, Peter H. "GPIH - American
      Incomes." *University of California – Davis*. 30 Jan. 2026.
      gpih.ucdavis.edu/tables.htm.
12.   "Inflation Rate Between 1860-2026" *Inflation Calculator*.
      www.in2013dollars.com/us/inflation/1860?amount=1
13.   "How Much Did a House Cost in 1860?" *Answers*, 13 Sept.
      2023, www.answers.com/us-
      history/How_much_did_a_house_cost_in_1860.
14.   Zaborney, John J. "The Domestic Slave Trade in Virginia -
      Encyclopedia Virginia." *Encyclopedia Virginia*, 26 Aug. 2024,
      encyclopediavirginia.org/entries/slave-sales.
15.   "Prices and Wages by Decade: 1860-1869." *University of
      Missouri Library*. 2025,
      libraryguides.missouri.edu/pricesandwages/1860-1869.
16.   "Industry and Economy During the Civil War." *(U.S. National
      Park Service)*. www.nps.gov/articles/industry-and-economy-
      during-the-civil-war.htm.
17.   Barnard, Charles H. and Jones, John. "Farm real estate values
      in the United States by counties, 1850-1982." *United States
      Department of Agriculture*. Statistical Bulletin No. 751. 1987.
      https://babel.hathitrust.org/cgi/pt?id=uiug.30112046854219&
      seq=3
18.   (SVBHP). We Honor Those Who Served: The Shenandoah
      Valley African American Men Who Served With the United

States Colored Troops, the U.S. Navy and the Confederacy During the Civil War. 223

19. "Robert E. Lee and Slavery." *Arlington House, the Robert E. Lee Memorial (U.S. National Park Service).* www.nps.gov/arho/learn/historyculture/robert-e-lee-and-slavery.htm.

20. Hayes, Diane and Dudley, Audrey. "Oh Master...Researchers Guide to Slavery in Franklin County, Virginia - Pension application for Charles James." *Hayes and Dudley.* 2002. [This collection includes copies of pension applications for African Americans from Franklin County, Virginia who worked as servants for the Confederate Army during the Civil War, with related correspondence.]

21. Hayes and Dudley. *Oh Master...* Pension application for John Lemons.

22. Hayes and Dudley. *Oh Master...* Valuation made the 1st day of January 1863 of slaves sent from Franklin County, Virginia.

23. Hayes and Dudley. *Oh Master...* Valuation made the 6th day of October 1863 of slaves sent from Franklin County, Virginia.

24. "Rose O'Neal Greenhow." *American Battlefield Trust,* www.battlefields.org/learn/biographies/rose-oneal-greenhow.

25. "A Brief Account of the Battle of Wilson's Creek." *Wilson's Creek National Battlefield (U.S. National Park Service).* www.nps.gov/wicr/learn/historyculture/brief-account-of-the-battle.htm.

26. "Ball's Bluff." *American Battlefield Trust,* www.battlefields.org/learn/civil-war/battles/balls-bluff.

27. "The Forgotten: The Contraband of America and the Road to Freedom" *National Trust for Historic Preservation.* savingplaces.org/stories/the-forgotten-the-contraband-of-america-and-the-road-to-freedom.

28. Manning, Chandra. "Civil War "Contraband Camps." *Underground Railroad Online Handbook.* housedivided.dickinson.edu/sites/ugrr/thematic-essays/civil-war-contraband-camps-manning.

29. "Living Contraband - Former Slaves in the Nation's Capital During the Civil War." *(U.S. National Park Service).* www.nps.gov/articles/living-contraband-former-slaves-in-the-nation-s-capital-during-the-civil-war.htm.

30. "The Revolutionary Summer of 1862." *National Archives,* 13 July 2023, www.archives.gov/publications/prologue/2017/winter/summer-of-1862.

31. Masters, Dan and Mingus, Scott. "Give the Devil All He Wants: The 1862 Rebel Raid on Chambersburg." *Emerging Civil War*, 10 Oct. 2020, emergingcivilwar.com/2020/10/10/give-the-devil-all-he-wants.

32. "The Revolutionary Summer of 1862." *National Archives*, 13 July 2023, www.archives.gov/publications/prologue/2017/winter/summer-of-1862.

33. "The 1st South Carolina Volunteers." *(U.S. National Park Service)*. www.nps.gov/articles/000/the-1st-south-carolina-volunteers.htm.

34. Ghost, John. "The First Kansas Colored Infantry, America's Pioneering Black Regiment." *When in Your State*, 14 Aug. 2025, wheninyourstate.com/kansas/the-first-kansas-colored-infantry-americas-pioneering-black-regiment.

35. African American Registry. *"The First Louisiana Native Guard Is Formed - African American Registry."* African American Registry, 27 Sept. 2025, aaregistry.org/story/the-first-louisiana-native-guard-is-formed.

Chapter 3: Fighting for Freedom
1. "William Chalk." Civil War Sailor Records, *National Archives* - Ancestry.com.

2. "Greet Jonston." Compiled Military Service Records, *National Archives* - Ancestry.com.

3. "Century Magazine 1897 Vol. 32☐: VictorianVoices.net☐: Free Download, Borrow, and Streaming☐: Internet Archive." *Internet Archive*, 1897, archive.org/details/century-1897-v-32/page/194/mode/2up.

4. Taylor, Susie King. "Reminiscences of My Life in Camp With the 33d United States Colored Troops Late 1st S.C. Volunteers." 22-23. docsouth.unc.edu/neh/taylorsu/taylorsu.html.

5. Taylor, Susie King. "Reminiscences of My Life in Camp With the 33d United States Colored Troops Late 1st S.C. Volunteers." 30.

6. "Susie King Taylor." *(U.S. National Park Service)*. www.nps.gov/people/susie-king-taylor.htm.

7. "The Sack of Lawrence." *ushistory.org*. www.ushistory.org/us/31c.asp.

8. "Pottawatomie Massacre – Kansapedia." *Kansas Historical Society*. www.kansashistory.gov/kansapedia/pottawatomie-massacre/16699.

9. "James H. Lane – Grim Leader in the Free-State Fight." *Legends of America*. www.legendsofamerica.com/ks-jameslane.

10. Ghost, John. "The First Kansas Colored Infantry, America's Pioneering Black Regiment." *When in Your State*, 14 Aug. 2025, wheninyourstate.com/kansas/the-first-kansas-colored-infantry-americas-pioneering-black-regiment.

11. "Affairs in the West." The New York Times, 19 November 1862, retrieved 27 January 2026. www.nytimes.com/1862/11/19/archives/affairs-in-the-west-a-negro-regiment-in-actionthe-battle-of-island.html.

Chapter 4: Black Sailors In Blue

1. "Black Men in Navy Blue During the Civil War." *National Archives*, 16 Oct. 2023, www.archives.gov/publications/prologue/2001/fall/black-sailors.

2. "A Brief List of Old, Obscure and Obsolete U.S. Navy Jobs." *USNI News*, 25 Jan. 2026, news.usni.org/2014/12/03/brief-list-old-obscure-obsolete-u-s-navy-jobs

3. "REGULATIONS FOR THE GOVERNMENT THE UNITED STATES NAVY. 1865." 1865, civilwarnavy.com/wp-content/uploads/2021/08/Regulations-of-the-US-Navy-1865.pdf.

4. "George Diggs." Civil War Sailor Records, *National Archives* - Ancestry.com.

5. "Archey Lane." Civil War Sailor Records, *National Archives* - Ancestry.com.

6. "Walter Garner." Civil War Sailor Records, *National Archives* - Ancestry.com.

7. "Charles Cooper." Civil War Sailor Records, *National Archives* - Ancestry.com.

8. "James Smother." Civil War Sailor Records, *National Archives* - Ancestry.com.

9. "York Gayton." Civil War Sailor Records, *National Archives* - Ancestry.com.

10. "Virgin Williams." Civil War Sailor Records, *National Archives* - Ancestry.com.

11. "Samuel Robinson." Civil War Sailor Records, *National Archives* - Ancestry.com.

12. "George Dandridge." Civil War Sailor Records, *National Archives* - Ancestry.com.

13. "Benjamin Haywood." Civil War Sailor Records, *National Archives* - Ancestry.com.

14. "Robert Jackson." Civil War Sailor Records, *National Archives -* Ancestry.com.

15. "Daniel Mack." Civil War Sailor Records, *National Archives -* Ancestry.com.

16. "Washington Johnson." Civil War Sailor Records, *National Archives - Ancestry.com.*

17. "Perry Bowles." Civil War Sailor Records, *National Archives -* Ancestry.com.

18. "Washington Brown." Civil War Sailor Records, *National Archives - Ancestry.com.*

19. "Joseph Stocks." Civil War Sailor Records, *National Archives -* Ancestry.com.

20. "John Tatson." Civil War Sailor Records, *National Archives -* Ancestry.com.

21. "George Mathews." Civil War Sailor Records, *National Archives - Ancestry.com.*

22. "Gilbert Dawson." Civil War Sailor Records, *National Archives -* Ancestry.com.

23. "Jacob Ludwick." Civil War Sailor Records, *National Archives -* Ancestry.com.

24. "Billy Jones." Civil War Sailor Records, *National Archives -* Ancestry.com.

25. "Fayette Jones." Civil War Sailor Records, *National Archives -* Ancestry.com.

26. "Lewis Jones." Civil War Sailor Records, *National Archives -* Ancestry.com.

27. "Siah Carter." Civil War Sailor Records, *National Archives -* Ancestry.com.

28. "Robert H. Cook." Civil War Sailor Records, *National Archives -* Ancestry.com.

29. "William Scott." Civil War Sailor Records, *National Archives -* Ancestry.com.

30. "Hampton Roads." *American Battlefield Trust,* www.battlefields.org/learn/civil-war/battles/hampton-roads.

31. "Henderson Cruiser." Civil War Sailor Records, *National Archives -* Ancestry.com.

32. "Sabine I (Frigate)." *Naval History and Heritage Command.* 1 September 2015. https://www.history.navy.mil/research/histories/ship-histories/danfs/s/sabine-i.html.

33. "Robert J. Hern." Civil War Sailor Records, *National Archives -* Ancestry.com.

34. "Daniel Jones." Civil War Sailor Records, *National Archives -* Ancestry.com.

35. "Battle of Port Royal, 1861, Civil War." *American History Central*, 6 Jan. 2025, www.americanhistorycentral.com/entries/battle-of-port-royal.

36. "William Davis." Civil War Sailor Records, *National Archives - Ancestry.com*.

37. "Cornelius Richardson." Civil War Sailor Records, *National Archives - Ancestry.com*.

38. "The Battle of Fort Jackson and Fort St. Philip." *MyCivilWar.com*. Retrieved 27 January 2026. www.mycivilwar.com/battles/620416.html.

39. "James Cromell." Civil War Sailor Records, *National Archives - Ancestry.com*.

40. "George W. Tynes." Civil War Sailor Records, *National Archives - Ancestry.com*.

41. "Elias E. Thomas." Civil War Sailor Records, *National Archives - Ancestry.com*.

42. "Alexander Caine." Civil War Sailor Records, *National Archives - Ancestry.com*.

43. "USS St. Louis | Civil War Track." *Civil War Track*, www.civilwartrack.com/uss-st-louis.

44. "Squire Henderson." Civil War Sailor Records, *National Archives - Ancestry.com*.

45. "Campbell Ligan." Civil War Sailor Records, *National Archives - Ancestry.com*.

46. "Joseph Ligan." Civil War Sailor Records, *National Archives - Ancestry.com*.

47. "John Stuart." Civil War Sailor Records, *National Archives - Ancestry.com*.

48. "USS Benton (1862) Ironclad River Gunboat." *www.MilitaryFactory.com*, www.militaryfactory.com/ships/detail.php?ship_id=USS-Benton-1862.

49. "Wilson Armistead." Civil War Sailor Records, *National Archives - Ancestry.com*.

50. Bocquelet, David. "USS New Ironsides (1862)". *Naval Encyclopedia*. naval-encyclopedia.com/industrial-era/american-civil-war/uss-new-ironsides.php#google_vignette.

51. "James Williams." Civil War Sailor Records, *National Archives - Ancestry.com*.

52. "The Sinking of the USS Housatonic by the Submarine CSS H.L. Hunley, off Charleston, South Carolina, 17 February 1864Original U.S. Navy Documents." Naval History and

Heritage Command. 31 October 2017.
https://www.history.navy.mil/research/library/online-reading-room/title-list-alphabetically/s/the-sinking-of-the-uss-housatonic-by-the-submarine-css-h-l-hunley.html

53. Cole, Steve. "Battle of Ft Pillow - Overview." *Custermen.com*. 2 October 2015
www.custermen.com/DixieBoys/FtPillow.htm#RiverFleet.

54. "Boyce Prince." Civil War Sailor Records, *National Archives - Ancestry.com*.

55. "Charles Dennis." Civil War Sailor Records, *National Archives - Ancestry.com*.

56. "Mobile Bay." *American Battlefield Trust*,
www.battlefields.org/learn/civil-war/battles/mobile-bay.

57. "Lawson, John Henry." *National Medal of Honor Museum.* 2025.
mohmuseum.org/recipient/lawson-john-henry.

58. Lane, Walter. "Second Attack upon Fort Fisher, showing the positions of the vessels, and the lines of fire, 13-15 January 1865." *Wikimedia Commons.*
commons.wikimedia.org/wiki/File:Fort_Fisher_vessels.jpg.
[Chart published in "The Soldier in our Civil War", Volume II - showing positions of Union vessels during the Second Battle of Fort Fisher]

59. "George Watson." Civil War Sailor Records, *National Archives - Ancestry.com*.

60. "John T. Weaver." Civil War Sailor Records, *National Archives - Ancestry.com*.

61. "Beaddy Carter." Civil War Sailor Records, *National Archives - Ancestry.com*.

62. "Iveson Robinson." Civil War Sailor Records, *National Archives - Ancestry.com*.

63. "Henry C. Bailey." Civil War Sailor Records, *National Archives - Ancestry.com*.

64. "Thornton Puller." Civil War Sailor Records, *National Archives - Ancestry.com*.

65. "Stephen Jasper." Civil War Sailor Records, *National Archives - Ancestry.com*.

66. "Civil War Naval Operations and Engagements: Trent's Reach, Virginia. 23-24 January 1865. *Naval History and Heritage Command.* https://www.history.navy.mil/browse-by-topic/wars-conflicts-and-operations/civil-war/cw-operations-and-engagements/1865-civil-war/trents-reach.html

67. "Port Royal Davis." Civil War Sailor Records, *National Archives - Ancestry.com*.

302

68. "Thornton Smith." Civil War Sailor Records, *National Archives - Ancestry.com*.

69. "Mosel Carey." Civil War Sailor Records, *National Archives - Ancestry.com*.

70. "James Roots." Civil War Sailor Records, *National Archives - Ancestry.com*.

71. "Blake, Robert." *National Medal of Honor Museum*. 2025. mohmuseum.org/recipient/blake-robert.

72. "US People--Mifflin, James, Engineer's Cook, USN." *www.ibiblio.org*. 28 April 2006. www.ibiblio.org/hyperwar//OnlineLibrary/photos/pers-us/uspers-m/j-miflin.htm.

Chapter 5: Emancipation

1. "Emancipation Proclamation (1863)." *National Archives*, 10 May 2022, www.archives.gov/milestone-documents/emancipation-proclamation.

2. Parr, Jessica. "The Compensated Emancipation Act of 1862." *We're History*, 15 Apr. 2018, werehistory.org/the-compensated-emancipation-act-of-1862.

3. "West Virginia Statehood, June 20, 1863." *National Archives*, 22 Apr. 2024, www.archives.gov/legislative/features/west-virginia.

4. "Slavery and Emancipation in Sharpsburg - Antietam National Battlefield." *U.S. National Park Service*. 2025. www.nps.gov/anti/learn/historyculture/slavery-and-emancipation-in-sharpsburg.htm.

5. "Emancipation Day in the Ozarks" *State Historical Society of Missouri*. 2023. shsmo.org/interactives/emancipation-day-ozarks.

6. "13th Amendment to the U.S. Constitution: Abolition of Slavery (1865)." *National Archives*, 10 May 2022, www.archives.gov/milestone-documents/13th-amendment.

7. Hemmings, Jay. "The Louisiana Native Guards – the First African-American Civil War Unit to Go Into Battle." *Warhistoryonline*, 13 Feb. 2019, www.warhistoryonline.com/instant-articles/the-louisiana-native-guards.html.

8. Wexler, Charles J. "The Capture of New Orleans." *Essential Civil War Curriculum*. June 2020. www.essentialcivilwarcurriculum.com/the-capture-of-new-orleans.html.

9. *Second Louisiana Native Guard (U.S. National Park Service)*. www.nps.gov/articles/2la-guard.htm.

10. Hewitt, Lawrence Lee. "An ironic route to glory: Louisiana's native guards at Port Hudson." as printed in "Black Soldiers In Blue: Let Us All Be Grateful – African American Troops in the Civil War Era" – (Anthology) - John David Smith. *University of North Carolina Press.* 2002. 78-106.

11. "Harriet Tubman." *National Women's History Museum,* www.womenshistory.org/education-resources/biographies/harriet-tubman.

12. "Beaufort History: Harriet Tubman and the Combahee Ferry Raid." *Explore Beaufort SC,* 10 Mar. 2025, explorebeaufortsc.com/beaufort-history-harriet-tubman-and-the-combahee-ferry-raid.

13. "Jun 04, 1863, Page 1 - the Charleston Mercury at Newspapers.com™." *Newspapers.com,* www.newspapers.com/image/605431302/?match=1&terms=Charleston%20mercury.

14. Lowe, Richard. "Battle on the Levee: The Fight at Milliken's Bend." as printed in "Black Soldiers In Blue: Let Us All Be Grateful – African American Troops in the Civil War Era" – (Anthology) - John David Smith. *University of North Carolina Press.* 2002. 107-135.

15. *Goodrich's Landing, June 29-30, 1863 - Vicksburg National Military Park (U.S. National Park Service).* www.nps.gov/vick/learn/historyculture/goodrichs-landing-june-29-30-1863.htm.

16. "First Arkansas Volunteer Infantry Regiment (African Descent) (US)." *Encyclopedia of Arkansas,* 3 Oct. 2025, encyclopediaofarkansas.net/entries/first-arkansas-volunteer-infantry-regiment-5904.

17. "Brigadier General Stand Watie of the Confederate Army." *MyCivilWar.com.* 28 January 2026. www.mycivilwar.com/leaders/watie_stand.html.

18. "Cabin Creek Battlefield | Oklahoma Historical Society." *Oklahoma Historical Society,* 28 January 2026. www.okhistory.org/sites/cabincreek.

19. "Military History of the First Kansas (Colored) Volunteer Infantry." *KSGenWeb.org.* 2001. www.ksgenweb.org/archives/statewide/military/civilwar/adjutant/1col/history

20. Green, Hilary N. "Unforgettable Sacrifice: How Black Communities Remembered the Civil War." *Fordham University Press.* 2025.

21. Blacknall, Charles. "Letter to brother George Blacknall, June 18, 1863." *Carolina Watchman.* July 13, 1863.

22. "The Foray on Chambersburg." *Daily Alta California*. July 15, 1863.

23. Dickinson, Jack L. "Albert Gallatin Jenkins." e-WV: *The West Virginia Encyclopedia*. 08 February 2024. https://www.wvencyclopedia.org/entries/967

24. Green, Hilary N. "Unforgettable Sacrifice: How Black Communities Remembered the Civil War." *Fordham University Press*. 2025.

25. Brown, O. "Letter to Priscilla Marshall, March 14 1866."

26. "New York Draft Riots: 1863, Civil War and Causes | HISTORY." *HISTORY*, 27 May 2025, www.history.com/articles/draft-riots.

27. Smith, Jacqueline. "What Happened During the New York City Draft Riots?" *The New York Historical Society*. 10 July 2018. www.nyhistory.org/blogs/new-york-city-draft-riots.

28. "Honey Springs." American Battlefield Trust, www.battlefields.org/learn/civil-war/battles/honey-springs.

29. "The Battle of Honey Springs | Oklahoma Historical Society." Oklahoma Historical Society, www.okhistory.org/sites/hsbattle.

30. *Stories - African American Civil War Memorial (U.S. National Park Service).* www.nps.gov/afam/learn/historyculture/stories.htm

31. Avalon Project. "Confederate States of America - Declaration of the Immediate Causes Which Induce and Justify the Secession of South Carolina From the Federal Union. Adopted December 24, 1860" *Yale Law School, Lillian Goldman Law Library*. 2008. avalon.law.yale.edu/19th_century/csa_scarsec.asp.

32. Cox, Clinton. "Undying Glory: The Story of the Massachusetts 54th Regiment." *Scholastic, Inc.*, 1991.

33. "The Pretty Little Place Was Burnt to the Ground": The Destruction of Darien, Georgia | *Beehive*. 25 Oct. 2017, www.masshist.org/beehiveblog/2017/10/the-pretty-little-place-was-burnt-to-the-ground-the-destruction-of-darien-georgia.

34. Cox, Clinton. "Undying Glory: The Story of the Massachusetts 54th Regiment." *Scholastic, Inc.*, 1991

35. "William H. Carney, Jr. - New Bedford Whaling National Historical Park." (U.S. National Park Service). www.nps.gov/nebe/learn/historyculture/williamcarney.htm.

Chapter 6: Come and Join Us Brothers
1.   "An Act to Further Regulate and Provide for the Enrolling and Calling Out the National Forces..." *MacMillan Center for International and Area Studies at Yale.* 2026. macmillan.yale.edu/glc/act-further-regulate-and-provide-enrolling-and-calling-out-national-forces.
2.   "Spencer Northern." Compiled Military Service Records, *National Archives* - Ancestry.com.
3.   "Esaw Northern." Compiled Military Service Records, *National Archives* - Ancestry.com.
4.   "Erastus Northern." Compiled Military Service Records, *National Archives* - Ancestry.com.
5.   "Levi Northern." Compiled Military Service Records, *National Archives* - Ancestry.com.
6.   "George T. Northern." Compiled Military Service Records, *National Archives* - Ancestry.com.
7.   "Raymond Northern." Compiled Military Service Records, *National Archives* - Ancestry.com.
8.   "Jackson Haddox." Compiled Military Service Records, *National Archives* - Ancestry.com.
9.   "James Arnold." Compiled Military Service Records, *National Archives* - Ancestry.com.
10.   "Payton Tinsley." Compiled Military Service Records, *National Archives* - Ancestry.com.
11.   "William Bourdon." Compiled Military Service Records, *National Archives* - Ancestry.com.
12.   "James Marshall." Compiled Military Service Records, *National Archives* - Ancestry.com.
13.   "13th Amendment to the U.S. Constitution: Abolition of Slavery (1865)." *National Archives,* 10 May 2022, www.archives.gov/milestone-documents/13th-amendment.
14.   "Slave Compensation Claims." *St. Louis County Library.* 19 May 2023, www.slcl.org/research-learn/genealogy/north-american-genealogy/african-american/slave-compensation-claims.
15.   Bergeron, Arthur W., Jr. "The Battle of Olustee." as printed in "Black Soldiers In Blue: Let Us All Be Grateful – African American Troops in the Civil War Era" – (Anthology) - John David Smith. *University of North Carolina Press.* 2002. 136-149.
16.   "American Civil War." *Suffolk, VA African American Heritage.* www.suffolkafricanamericanheritage.com/american-civil-war.html.
17.   "History of the 2nd United States Colored Cavalry in the Civil War." *The Civil War in the East,* 19 Oct. 2022,

civilwarintheeast.com/us-regiments-batteries/us-colored-troops/2nd-united-states-colored-cavalry/#google_vignette.

18. "Black Cavalry Troopers Burn in Grim Civil War Clash Near Suffolk." *The Virginian-Pilot,* 13 Aug. 2019, www.pilotonline.com/2014/02/12/black-cavalry-troopers-burn-in-grim-civil-war-clash-near-suffolk.

19. "English Buffkin." Compiled Military Service Records, *National Archives* - Ancestry.com.

20. "Thomas Washington." Compiled Military Service Records, *National Archives* - Ancestry.com.

21. "Charles Stopher." Compiled Military Service Records, *National Archives* - Ancestry.com.

22. "Lincoln, Grant, and the 1864 Election - Lincoln Home National Historic Site" (*U.S. National Park Service*). www.nps.gov/liho/learn/historyculture/lincolngrant.htm.

23. Jlbworks. "Civil War Tennessee - Tennessee Politics - Tennessee Historical Society." *Tennessee Historical Society*, 14 Nov. 2020, tennesseehistory.org/civil-war-2.

24. Cimprich, John. "The Fort Pillow Massacre: Assessing the Evidence." as printed in "Black Soldiers In Blue: Let Us All Be Grateful – African American Troops in the Civil War Era" – (Anthology) - John David Smith. *University of North Carolina Press*. 2002. 150-168.

25. "May 1863: Confederates Declare Black US Soldiers Insurrectionists - New York Almanack." *New York Almanack*, 3 May 2024, www.newyorkalmanack.com/2024/05/confederates-declare-black-soldiers-insurrectionists.

26. "Dark Shadows: Nathan Bedford Forrest; Fort Pillow, 1864." *The Past,* 9 Nov. 2023, the-past.com/feature/dark-shadows-nathan-bedford-forrest-fort-pillow-1864.

27. "Battle of Fort Pillow - Alchetron, the Free Social Encyclopedia." *Alchetron.com,* 8 Oct. 2024, alchetron.com/Battle-of-Fort-Pillow.

28. "The Second Fall of Fort Pillow." The Civil War Months, 30 Mar. 2024, civilwarmonths.com/2024/04/12/the-second-fall-of-fort-pillow.

29. "Dark Shadows: Nathan Bedford Forrest; Fort Pillow, 1864." *The Past,* 9 Nov. 2023, the-past.com/feature/dark-shadows-nathan-bedford-forrest-fort-pillow-1864.

30. Leaming, Mack J. "The Fort Pillow Massacre, 1864. " *Gilder Lehrman Institute of American History.* www.gilderlehrman.org/history-resources/spotlight-primary-source/fort-pillow-massacre-1864.

31. Forrest, Nathan Bedford. "Major-General Nathan Bedford Forrest on the 'massacre at Fort Pillow.'" *OR*, Apr. 1864, sharetngov.tnsosfiles.com/tsla/cwsb/1864-04-Article-142-Page181.pdf.

32. "Fort Pillow Massacre, by the Joint Committee on the Conduct and Expenditures of the War." *Project Gutenberg.org.* www.gutenberg.org/files/41787/41787-h/41787-h.htm.

33. "Engagement At Poison Spring." *Encyclopedia of Arkansas*, 29 Jan. 2024, encyclopediaofarkansas.net/entries/engagement-at-poison-spring-37.

34. Cox, Dale. "Battle of Poison Spring, Arkansas - in Depth." *ExploreSouthernHistory.com.* www.exploresouthernhistory.com/poisonspring3.html.

35. "Action At Marks' Mills." *Encyclopedia of Arkansas*, 31 Jan. 2025, encyclopediaofarkansas.net/entries/action-at-marks-mills-1135.

36. "Engagement At Jenkins' Ferry." *Encyclopedia of Arkansas*, 13 Nov. 2025, encyclopediaofarkansas.net/entries/engagement-at-jenkins-ferry-1136.

37. "First and Second Kansas Colored Volunteer Infantry Regiments." *Encyclopedia of Arkansas*, 19 Mar. 2025, encyclopediaofarkansas.net/entries/first-and-second-kansas-colored-volunteer-infantry-15144.

38. "Enrollment Act (1863) (the Conscription Act)" *Encyclopedia.com.* www.encyclopedia.com/history/encyclopedias-almanacs-transcripts-and-maps/enrollment-act-1863-conscription-act.

39. "James Henry Carter." Compiled Military Service Records, *National Archives* - Ancestry.com.

40. "Peter Chisley." Compiled Military Service Records, *National Archives* - Ancestry.com.

41. "Littleton Creath." Compiled Military Service Records, *National Archives* - Ancestry.com.

42. "Samuel Wallace." Compiled Military Service Records, *National Archives* - Ancestry.com.

43. "James Saddler." Compiled Military Service Records, *National Archives* - Ancestry.com.

44. "George Thompson." Compiled Military Service Records, *National Archives* - Ancestry.com.

45. "Carey Phillips." Compiled Military Service Records, *National Archives* - Ancestry.com.

46. "Charles M. Ward." Compiled Military Service Records, *National Archives* - Ancestry.com.

47. "George Wilson." Compiled Military Service Records, *National Archives* - Ancestry.com.

48. "Benjamin Allen." Compiled Military Service Records, *National Archives* - Ancestry.com.

49. "William Anderson." Compiled Military Service Records, *National Archives* - Ancestry.com.

50. "William Ray." Compiled Military Service Records, *National Archives* - Ancestry.com.

51. "Magnes Henderson." Compiled Military Service Records, *National Archives* - Ancestry.com.

52. "William Robinson." Compiled Military Service Records, *National Archives* - Ancestry.com.

53. "John Peck." Compiled Military Service Records, *National Archives* - Ancestry.com.

54. "William Taylor." Compiled Military Service Records, *National Archives* - Ancestry.com.

55. "William Gordon." Compiled Military Service Records, *National Archives* - Ancestry.com.

56. "Joseph Marshall." Compiled Military Service Records, *National Archives* - Ancestry.com.

57. "John R. Green." Compiled Military Service Records, *National Archives* - Ancestry.com.

58. Mark, Harrison W., and Timothy H. O'Sullivan. "Overland Campaign: Throwing Men Into the Meat Grinder of the US Civil War." *World History Encyclopedia*, Dec. 2025, www.worldhistory.org/Overland_Campaign.

59. Searles, Harry. "Battle of Port Walthall Junction, 1864, Civil War." *American History Central*, 17 Mar. 2024, www.americanhistorycentral.com/entries/battle-of-port-walthall-junction.

60. Searles, Harry. "Battle of Swift Creek, 1864, Civil War." *American History Central*, 17 Mar. 2024, www.americanhistorycentral.com/entries/battle-of-swift-creek.

61. Searles, Harry. "Battle of Chester Station, 1864, Civil War." *American History Central*, 17 Mar. 2024, www.americanhistorycentral.com/entries/battle-of-chester-station.

62. Searles, Harry. "Battle of Drewry's Bluff, 1862, Civil War." American History Central, 6 Jan. 2025, www.americanhistorycentral.com/entries/battle-of-drewrys-bluff.

63. Searles, Harry. "Battle of Ware Bottom Church, 1864, Civil War." *American History Central*, 17 Mar. 2024,

www.americanhistorycentral.com/entries/battle-of-ware-bottom-church.

64. "Battle - Fort Pocahontas." *Fort Pocahontas*, 15 Nov. 2018, www.fortpocahontas.org/battle.

65. Edward Wild (*U.S. National Park Service*). www.nps.gov/people/edward-wild.htm.

66. "Battle - Fort Pocahontas." *Fort Pocahontas*, 15 Nov. 2018, www.fortpocahontas.org/battle.

67. Ibid.

68. "May 24, 1864 – This Day During the American Civil War – the Battle of Wilson's Wharf." *U S Military History*, 24 May 2019, mwh52.wordpress.com/2019/05/24/may-24-1864-this-day-during-the-american-civil-war-the-battle-of-wilsons-wharf.

Chapter 7: No Power On Earth

1. "Joseph Diggs." Civil War Compiled Military Service Records, *National Archives*

2. "Mechlin Smith." Civil War Compiled Military Service Records, *National Archives*

3. "Zachariah Taylor." Civil War Compiled Military Service Records, *National Archives*

4. "Henry Washington." Civil War Compiled Military Service Records, *National Archives*

5. "Alfred Wallack." Civil War Compiled Military Service Records, *National Archives*

6. "George Jones." Civil War Compiled Military Service Records, *National Archives*

7. "Edmund West." Civil War Compiled Military Service Records, *National Archives*

8. "Oscar Terry." Civil War Compiled Military Service Records, *National Archives*

9. "Carry Malone." Civil War Compiled Military Service Records, *National Archives*

10. "Willis Moore." Civil War Compiled Military Service Records, *National Archives*

11. "John Baily." Civil War Compiled Military Service Records, *National Archives*

12. "George Carter." Civil War Compiled Military Service Records, *National Archives*

13. "John Edward Pine." Civil War Compiled Military Service Records, *National Archives*

14. "Calvin Cooper." Civil War Compiled Military Service Records, *National Archives*

15. "Richard Stamps." Civil War Compiled Military Service Records, *National Archives*

16. "Thomas Kinney." Civil War Compiled Military Service Records, *National Archives*

17. "Jorden Roberts." Civil War Compiled Military Service Records, *National Archives*

18. "Grayson Jones." Civil War Compiled Military Service Records, *National Archives*

19. "Payton Wilkes." Civil War Compiled Military Service Records, *National Archives*

20. "Edward Arrington." Civil War Compiled Military Service Records, *National Archives*

21. "Aaron Calloway." Civil War Compiled Military Service Records, *National Archives*

22. "William Elliott." Civil War Compiled Military Service Records, *National Archives*

23. "Edward C. Grant." Civil War Compiled Military Service Records, *National Archives*

24. "George H. Smith." Civil War Compiled Military Service Records, *National Archives*

25. "Thomas Gaskins." Civil War Compiled Military Service Records, *National Archives*

26. "Josephus Miller." Civil War Compiled Military Service Records, *National Archives*

27. "Dawson Wright." Civil War Compiled Military Service Records, *National Archives*

28. "Stephen Cox." Civil War Compiled Military Service Records, *National Archives*

29. "Joseph Anderson." Civil War Compiled Military Service Records, *National Archives*

30. Wolfe, Brendan. "Battle of the Crater." *Encyclopedia Virginia*, 18 Feb. 2025, encyclopediavirginia.org/entries/crater-battle-of-the.

31. "Battle of the Crater - Petersburg National Battlefield" *(U.S. National Park Service)*. www.nps.gov/pete/learn/historyculture/battle-of-the-crater.htm.

32. Luebke, Peter C. "William Mahone (1826–1895)." *Encyclopedia Virginia*, 22 Dec. 2021, encyclopediavirginia.org/entries/mahone-william-1826-1895.

33. Johnston, Terry. "Battle at the Crater." *Civil War Monitor*, 28 July 2025, www.civilwarmonitor.com/battle-at-the-crater.

34. "Robert Stokes." Civil War Compiled Military Service Records, *National Archives*

35.   "Enos Stokes." Civil War Compiled Military Service Records, *National Archives*

36.   "George Polson." Civil War Compiled Military Service Records, *National Archives*

37.   "William Polson." Civil War Compiled Military Service Records, *National Archives*

38.   "William Jubilee." Civil War Compiled Military Service Records, *National Archives*

39.   "Samuel Jubilee." Civil War Compiled Military Service Records, *National Archives*

40.   "First Deep Bottom." *American Battlefield Trust*, www.battlefields.org/learn/articles/first-deep-bottom.

41.   O'Connell, Dan. "The First Battle of Deep Bottom: July 27-29." *The Siege of Petersburg Online*, 2 Feb. 2015, www.beyondthecrater.com/news-and-notes/research/battles/the-first-battle-of-deep-bottom-july-27-29-by-dan-oconnell.

42.   Searles, Harry. "Second Battle of Deep Bottom, 1864, Civil War." *American History Central*, 6 Jan. 2025, www.americanhistorycentral.com/entries/second-battle-of-deep-bottom.

43.   Ress, Thomas V. "Battle of Sulphur Creek Trestle." *Encyclopedia of Alabama*, Jan. 2026, encyclopediaofalabama.org/article/battle-of-sulphur-creek-trestle.

44.   "We Honor Those Who Served: The Shenandoah Valley African American Men Who Served With the United States Colored Troops, the U.S. Navy and the Confederacy During the Civil War." *Shenandoah Valley Black Heritage Project [SVBHP]*. 2018. Harrisonburg, Virginia, United States of America, Campbell Print Company.

45.   "Lewis Gill." Civil War Compiled Military Service Records, *National Archives*

46.   Curnutt, Autumn, Plummer, Sarah and Wood, John. "Lewis Gill." *Raising the Shade*, www.raisingtheshade.org/lgill.

47.   "Dutch Gap Canal." 8 Sept. 2025, *Virginia Places*. www.virginiaplaces.org/transportation/dutchgap.html.

48.   Crenshaw, Douglas. "Fort Harrison and the Battle of Chaffin's Farm: To Surprise and Capture Richmond." *Civil War*, 2013.

49.   Price, James S. "The Battle of New Market Heights: Freedom Will be Theirs by the Sword." *The History Press*, 2011. 43

50.   Price, Jimmy. "History of the Battle." *Battle of New Market Heights*, 26 Feb. 2021, battleofnewmarketheights.org/history-of-the-battle.

312

51. "Fort Harrison - Richmond National Battlefield Park." (*U.S. National Park Service*). www.nps.gov/rich/learn/historyculture/fort-harrison.htm.

52. Crenshaw, Doug. "African American Soldiers at Fort Gilmer." *Emerging Civil War*, 25 Feb. 2019, emergingcivilwar.com/2019/02/25/african-american-soldiers-at-fort-gilmer.

53. "Clara Barton Chronology 1861-1869 - Clara Barton National Historic Site" (*U.S. National Park Service*). www.nps.gov/clba/learn/kidsyouth/chron2.htm.

54. "Butler Medal - U.S. Colored Troops." *Military Wives Network*, www.militarywives.com/index.php/1939-descriptions/1401-butler-medal-u-s-colored-troops.

55. "Saltville Battle and Massacre - Camp Nelson National Monument" (*U.S. National Park Service*). www.nps.gov/cane/battle-of-saltville-and-massacre.htm.

56. Brown, David. "The Saltville Massacre." *5thuscc.net*. 5thuscc.net/massacr.htm.

57. "Saltville Battle and Massacre - Camp Nelson National Monument" (*U.S. National Park Service*). www.nps.gov/cane/battle-of-saltville-and-massacre.htm.

58. Fermin, Margaret. "How This Union General Who Executed Guerrillas and Imprisoned Political Foes Became the Most Hated Man in Kentucky." *History*, 25 Aug. 2023, www.historyonthenet.com/how-this-union-general-who-executed-guerrillas-and-imprisoned-political-foes-became-the-most-hated-man-in-kentucky.

59. Hall, Alex. "Saltville 1864: Battle for the Saltworks and a Massacre That Followed." *Appalachianhistorian.org*, 29 Sept. 2025, appalachianhistorian.org/saltville-1864-battle-for-the-saltworks-and-a-massacre-that-followed.

60. "Saltville Battle and Massacre - Camp Nelson National Monument" (*U.S. National Park Service*). www.nps.gov/cane/battle-of-saltville-and-massacre.htm.

61. Ibid.

62. Rust, Randal. "Ferguson, Samuel." *Tennessee Encyclopedia*, 1 Mar. 2018, tennesseeencyclopedia.net/entries/samuel-ferguson.

63. "Saltville." *Virginia Center for Civil War Studies | Virginia Tech*, civilwar.vt.edu/programs/drivingtour/saltville.html.

64. Searles, Harry. "Battle of Darbytown Road, 1864, Civil War." *American History Central*, 23 Oct. 2025, www.americanhistorycentral.com/entries/battle-of-darbytown-road.

65. "Battle of Darbytown (New Market) Road, One Last Advance□." *Henrico County, Virginia,* henrico.gov/locations/one-last-advance-battle-darbytown-new-market-road.

66. Suderow, Bryce. "'An Ugly Looking Chance for a Charge': The Battle of Darbytown Road, October 13, 1864." *The Siege of Petersburg Online,* 13 Feb. 2024, www.beyondthecrater.com/news-and-notes/research/battles/an-ugly-looking-chance-for-a-charge-the-battle-of-darbytown-road-october-13-1864-by-bryce-suderow.

67. "Battle of Burgess Mill - Petersburg National Battlefield." *(U.S. National Park Service).* www.nps.gov/pete/learn/historyculture/battle-of-burgess-mill.htm.

68. Suderow, Bryce. "The Battle of Burgess Mill: October 27, 1864 (First Day of Battle of Boydton Plank Road)." *The Siege of Petersburg Online,* 2 Feb. 2015, www.beyondthecrater.com/news-and-notes/research/battles/the-battle-of-burgess-mill-october-27-1864-first-day-of-battle-of-boydton-plank-road-by-bryce-suderow.

69. Coffey, Walter. "Go As You Propose." *The Civil War Months,* 31 Oct. 2024, civilwarmonths.com/2024/11/02/go-as-you-propose.

70. Wise, Stephen R. "Honey Hill, Battle Of - South Carolina Encyclopedia." *South Carolina Encyclopedia,* 8 Aug. 2022, www.scencyclopedia.org/sce/entries/honey-hill-battle-of.

71. Ridgeland, Town Of. *Town of Ridgeland.* www.ridgelandsc.gov/battle-of-honey-hill.

72. McWhirter, Christian. "Andrew Jackson Smith Earns Medal of Honor." *Abraham Lincoln Presidential Museum,* presidentlincoln.illinois.gov/Blog/Posts/13/Civil-War/2020/7/Andrew-Jackson-Smith/blog-post.

73. Bak, Luca. "Battle of Deveaux's Neck, South Carolina." *Today's Flashback,* 6 Dec. 1864, www.todaysflashback.com/battle-of-deveauxs-neck-south-carolina/#google_vignette.

74. Hodan, Marty. "December 6, 1864 – This Day During the American Civil War – the Battle of Tulifinny." *U S Military History,* 6 Dec. 2018, mwh52.wordpress.com/2018/12/06/december-6-1864-this-day-during-the-american-civil-war-the-battle-of-tulifinny.

75.　McTernan, Walter and Kullberg, Andrew. "U.S. Marines Face Citadel Cadets At Tulifinny Crossroads." *Leatherneck Magazine*, March 2013. 47.

Chapter 8: Stories of Soldiers and Sailors
1.　Connolly, Maire et al. "Deadly comrades: war and infectious diseases." *The Lancet*, Volume 360, s23 – s24.
2.　"Jeremiah Sanders." Civil War Compiled Military Service Records, *National Archives*
3.　"John James." Civil War Compiled Military Service Records, *National Archives*
4.　"Henry Pulliman." Civil War Compiled Military Service Records, *National Archives*
5.　"Richard Giles." Civil War Compiled Military Service Records, *National Archives*
6.　"Richard Vons." Civil War Compiled Military Service Records, *National Archives*
7.　"Paul Pearson." Civil War Compiled Military Service Records, *National Archives*
8.　"Smith Holloway." Civil War Compiled Military Service Records, *National Archives*
9.　"Josiah Taitt." Civil War Compiled Military Service Records, *National Archives*
10.　"Granville Taitt." Civil War Compiled Military Service Records, *National Archives*
11.　"John Mason." Civil War Compiled Military Service Records, *National Archives*
12.　"Richard Smith." Civil War Compiled Military Service Records, *National Archives*
13.　"General Scott." Civil War Compiled Military Service Records, *National Archives*
14.　"William Moore." Civil War Compiled Military Service Records, *National Archives*
15.　"Washington Ray." Civil War Compiled Military Service Records, *National Archives*
16.　"Elisha Boggess." Civil War Compiled Military Service Records, *National Archives*
17.　"John Q. Adams." Civil War Compiled Military Service Records, *National Archives*
18.　"Henry Lee." Civil War Compiled Military Service Records, *National Archives*
19.　"Robert Ardis." Civil War Compiled Military Service Records, *National Archives*

20. "Joseph Anderson." Civil War Compiled Military Service Records, *National Archives*

21. "John Green." Civil War Compiled Military Service Records, *National Archives*

22. "George Foskey." Civil War Compiled Military Service Records, *National Archives*

23. "Thomas Drummer." Civil War Compiled Military Service Records, *National Archives*

24. "James Tatman." Civil War Compiled Military Service Records, *National Archives*

25. "William Williams." Civil War Compiled Military Service Records, *National Archives*

26. "Benjamin Jones." Civil War Compiled Military Service Records, *National Archives*

27. "Samuel Parker." Civil War Compiled Military Service Records, *National Archives*

28. "Napoleon Bonaparte." Civil War Compiled Military Service Records, *National Archives*

29. "Joseph Lacy." Civil War Compiled Military Service Records, *National Archives*

30. Gonaver, W. "The Peculiar Institution and the Making of Modern Psychiatry 1840-1880." *University of North Carolina*, 2018. 256.

31. "Our History." *Central State Hospital*, 10 Feb. 2023, dbhds.virginia.gov/facilities/csh/our-history.

32. "The Union Literary Institute Preservation Society." *The Union Literary Institute Preservation Society*, unionliterary.org.

33. "Samuel Smothers." Civil War Compiled Military Service Records, *National Archives*

34. "Samuel Smothers | Raising the Shade." Raising the Shade, www.raisingtheshade.org/ssmothers.

35. "The Students' Repository□." *Internet Archive*, 1863, archive.org/details/studentsreposito00spar/page/n5/mode/2up.

36. "History - the Union Literary Institute Preservation Society." *The Union Literary Institute Preservation Society*, unionliterary.org/history.

37. "The Students' Repository□." *Internet Archive*, 1863, archive.org/details/studentsreposito00spar/page/n5/mode/2up.

38. "45th Regiment, United States Colored Infantry." *(U.S. National Park Service)*. www.nps.gov/civilwar/search-battle-units-detail.htm?battleUnitCode=UUS0045RI00C.

39.   "Robert Atkins." Civil War Compiled Military Service Records, *National Archives*

40.   "Wesley Wades." Civil War Compiled Military Service Records, *National Archives*

41.   "James Monroe." Civil War Compiled Military Service Records, *National Archives*

42.   "Feb 17, 1880, Page 2 - St. Louis Globe-Democrat at Newspapers.comTM." *Newspapers.com,* www.newspapers.com/image/571033926.

43.   "Dalton." *Georgia Civil War Commission,* 12 Jan. 2025, georgiacivilwar.org/track-georgias-civil-war-heritage/historic-high-country/dalton.

44.   Bevens, William E. "Reminiscences of a Private : William E. Bevens of the First Arkansas Infantry, C.S.A." *University of Arkansas Press.* 1992. 199.

45.   "Charles Lawrence." Civil War Compiled Military Service Records, *National Archives*

46.   Mark, Harrison W. "John Bell Hood: The Most Aggressive Confederate General." *World History Encyclopedia,* Oct. 2025, www.worldhistory.org/John_Bell_Hood.

47.   "The Promotion of Hood (July–August 1864) - War History." *War History,* 13 Dec. 2024, warhistory.org/@msw/article/the-promotion-of-hood-july-august-1864.

48.   "The 1864 Nashville Campaign." *Essential Civil War Curriculum.* www.essentialcivilwarcurriculum.com/the-1864-nashville-campaign.html.

49.   Searles, Harry. "George Henry Thomas, Soldier, Rock of Chickamauga." *American History Central,* 2 Apr. 2025, www.americanhistorycentral.com/entries/george-h-thomas.

50.   Einolf, Christopher J. "George H. Thomas (1816–1870)." *Encyclopedia Virginia,* 3 May 2024, encyclopediavirginia.org/entries/thomas-george-h-1816-1870.

51.   "Battle of Spring Hill." *Spring Hill, TN - Official Website.* www.springhilltn.org/426/Battle-of-Spring-Hill.

52.   Searles, Harry. "Battle of Nashville, 1864, Civil War." *American History Central,* 17 Mar. 2024, www.americanhistorycentral.com/entries/battle-of-nashville.

53.   Cooling, B. Franklin. "The Decisive Battle of Nashville." *American Battlefield Trust,* www.battlefields.org/learn/articles/decisive-battle-nashville.

54.   Chan, Amy, and Noah Andre Trudeau. "Blood Proof: USCT and the Battle of Nashville." *HistoryNet,* 1 Feb. 2024, www.historynet.com/blood-proof-usct-and-the-battle-of-nashville.

55. Mark, Harrison W. "Battle of Nashville: The Bitter End of the Army of Tennessee." *World History Encyclopedia*, Oct. 2025, www.worldhistory.org/article/2816/battle-of-nashville.

56. Ibid.

57. "The Question Is Settled — Negroes Will Fight: Albemarle County's USCT Soldiers at the Battle of Nashville." *John L. Nau III Center for Civil War History*, 3 July 2020, naucenter.as.virginia.edu/blog-page/question-settled-negroes-will-fight-albemarle-countys-usct-soldiers-battle-nashville.

58. "Henry Helm." Civil War Compiled Military Service Records, *National Archives*

59. Schiller, Lawrence D. "The Evolution of Union Cavalry 1861-1865" *Essential Civil War Curriculum.* www.essentialcivilwarcurriculum.com/the-evolution-of-union-cavalry-1861-1865.html.

60. Heiser, John. "Cavalry." *Civilwar.com.* www.civilwar.com/overview/315-weapons/148532-cavalry-62478.html.

61. Main, Edward M. "The Story of the Marches, Battles, and Incidents of the Third United States Colored Cavalry." *Globe Printing Company, Louisville, KY.* 1908. 92-123

62. Ibid. 217-235.

63. Faulkner, Ronnie W. "Battle of Fort Fisher." *NCpedia*, www.ncpedia.org/fort-fisher-battle.

64. "1st Attack: The Christmas Battle." *NC Historic Sites.* historicsites.nc.gov/all-sites/fort-fisher/history/civil-war-ft-fisher/1st-attack.

65. "First Battle of Fort Fisher." *Civil War Era NC.* cwnc.omeka.chass.ncsu.edu/exhibits/show/fall-fort-fisher/first-battle/first-battle.

66. "Donovan, Alex. "Honor and Duty: The Life of Alfred Howe Terry." *Connecticut History | a CTHumanities Project - Stories about the people, traditions, innovations, and events that make up Connecticut's rich history.*, 1 Sept. 2023, connecticuthistory.org/honor-and-duty-the-life-of-alfred-howe-terry.

67. Lewis, J.D. "2nd Fort Fisher - January 13-15, 1865." *Carolana.com.* 2013. www.carolana.com/NC/Civil_War/1865_01_13-15_2nd_fort_fisher.html.

68. Bennington, Michelle. "Remembering the Simpsonville Massacre." *Michelle Bennington*, 28 Dec. 2021,

www.michellebennington.com/post/remembering-the-simpsonville-massacre.

69. Jones, Tina C. "5th US Colored Cavalry." *SlavesToSoldiers.org* 2021. www.slavestosoldiers.org/us-colored-troop-veterans/cavalry-regiments/5th-us-colored-cavalry.

70. Craig, Berry. "Old Time Kentucky: Simpsonville Slaughter, Not in Most History Books, Should Be Remembered." *NKyTribune*, 18 Sept. 2016, nkytribune.com/2016/08/old-time-kentucky-simpsonville-slaughter-not-in-most-history-books-should-be-remembered.

71. "Horrible Massacre by Guerrillas — Thirty-five Colored Soldiers Murdered — Eight More Dangerously Wounded." *Cincinnati Daily Gazette*, Vol. 76 No. 183., 28 January 1865. Retrieved from: 5thuscc.net/simpson.htm

72. "John Henry." Civil War Compiled Military Service Records, *National Archives*

73. "Artillery Civil War Facts." *MyCivilWar.com.* www.mycivilwar.com/facts/info-artillery.html.

74. Christ, Mark K. "Little Rock to Mount Elba, Expedition From." *Encyclopedia of Arkansas*, 14 June 2023, encyclopediaofarkansas.net/entries/expedition-from-little-rock-to-mount-elba-17961.

75. Smith, Toni, Cummins, Cathie, and Wood, John. "John Henry." *Raising the Shade*, www.raisingtheshade.org/jhenry.

Chapter 9: Medals of Honor
1. "William Harvey Carney."*National Medal of Honor Museum.* mohmuseum.org/recipient/carney-william-harvey.

2. "William Carney." Civil War Compiled Military Service Records, *National Archives*

3. "William H. Carney." *(U.S. National Park Service).* www.nps.gov/articles/william-h-carney.htm.

4. "West Point Monument at West Point Cemetery." *VisitNorfolk,* 6 June 2022, www.visitnorfolk.com/attraction/west-point-monument-at-west-point-cemetery.

5. "Robert Blake." *National Medal of Honor Museum.* mohmuseum.org/recipient/blake-robert.

6. "Robert Blake (Medal of Honor) Explained." *Everything Explained.* everything.explained.today/Robert_Blake_(Medal_of_Honor).

7. "James Mifflin. - Hall of Valor: Medal of Honor, Silver Star, U.S. Military Awards." *Military Times,* 5 Nov. 2024, valor.militarytimes.com/recipient/recipient-1495.

8.   "James Mifflin." Civil War Sailor Records, *National Archives -* Ancestry.com.

9.   "Beaty, Powhatan." *(U.S. National Park Service).* www.nps.gov/rich/learn/historyculture/beaty.htm.

10.   "Powhatan Beaty." Civil War Compiled Military Service Records, *National Archives*

11.   Menegay, Chad. "Ohio Medal of Honor Recipient: From Slavery to Freedom." *www.army.mil,* 28 Feb. 2019, www.army.mil/article/217886/ohio_medal_of_honor_recipient_from_slavery_to_freedom.

12.   "Powhatan Beaty — Badass of the Week." *Badass of the Week,* www.badassoftheweek.com/beaty.

13.   "James Gardiner."*National Medal of Honor Museum.* mohmuseum.org/recipient/gardiner-james.

14.   "James Gardiner." Civil War Compiled Military Service Records, *National Archives*

15.   "Miles James." *National Medal of Honor Museum.* mohmuseum.org/recipient/james-miles.

16.   "Miles James." Civil War Compiled Military Service Records, *National Archives*

17.   "Miles James." *(U.S. National Park Service).* home.nps.gov/rich/learn/historyculture/james.htm.

18.   "Edward Ratcliff." *Medal of Honor Valor Trail,* www.valortrail.org/stories/edward-ratcliff.

19.   "Edward Ratcliff." Civil War Compiled Military Service Records, *National Archives*

20.   "Charles Veal." *(U.S. National Park Service).* www.nps.gov/rich/learn/historyculture/veal.htm.

21.   "Charles Veal." Civil War Compiled Military Service Records, *National Archives*

22.   "Medal of Honor: Heroes of the Battle of Chaffin's Farm." *VA National Cemetery Administration.* www.cem.va.gov/docs/wcag/history/Medal-of-Honor-Heroes-of-Battle-of-Chaffins-Farm.pdf.

Chapter 10: The Other Shore

1.   Krogh, Matthew. "A Community Gone: the Eastern Shore Natives." *Genealogy and History of the Eastern Shore of Virginia.* www.esva.net/ghotes/Matthew/ES%20Indians.htm#google_vignette.

2.   "About the County." *Accomack County, Virginia.* https://www.co.accomack.va.us/about-us/about-the-county

3.   Kurlansky, Mark. "The Big Oyster: History on the Half Shell." *Random House Trade Paperbacks,* 2007. 200.

320

4.   Roberts, Matthew. "William Birney." *Encyclopedia of Alabama*, Nov. 2025, encyclopediaofalabama.org/article/birney-william.

5.   Krick, Robert K. "Civil War Weather in Virginia." *University of Alabama Press*, 2007. 112.

6.   Beard, Rick. "Black Union Soldiers Fought a Costly Battle for Equal Pay." *Military Times*, 19 Aug. 2022, www.militarytimes.com/military-honor/black-military-history/2018/02/12/black-union-soldiers-fought-a-costly-battle-for-equal-pay.

7.   "John Drummer." Civil War Compiled Military Service Records, *National Archives*

8.   "Isaac Floyd." Civil War Compiled Military Service Records, *National Archives*

9.   "Alfred Wallack." Civil War Compiled Military Service Records, *National Archives*

10.   "History of the 2nd United States Colored Cavalry in the Civil War." *The Civil War in the East*, 19 Oct. 2022, civilwarintheeast.com/us-regiments-batteries/us-colored-troops/2nd-united-states-colored-cavalry/#google_vignette.

11.   "Jacob Parker." Civil War Compiled Military Service Records, *National Archives*

12.   "Battle - Fort Pocahontas." *Fort Pocahontas*, 15 Nov. 2018, www.fortpocahontas.org/battle.

13.   "Isaac West." Compiled Military Service Records, *National Archives* - Ancestry.com.

14.   "Daniel Beach." Compiled Military Service Records, *National Archives* - Ancestry.com.

15.   "Levins Bloxam." Compiled Military Service Records, *National Archives* - Ancestry.com.

16.   "Thomas Rue." Compiled Military Service Records, *National Archives* - Ancestry.com.

17.   "Daniel Ewell." Compiled Military Service Records, *National Archives* - Ancestry.com.

18.   Engs, Robert Francis. "Samuel Chapman Armstrong (1839–1893)." *Encyclopedia Virginia*, 22 Dec. 2021, encyclopediavirginia.org/entries/armstrong-samuel-chapman-1839-1893.

19.   Washington, Booker T. "Up From Slavery." Doubleday, Page, & Co., 1907. 54.

20.   "John Boggs." Compiled Military Service Records, *National Archives* - Ancestry.com.

21.   "Charles Culleny." Compiled Military Service Records, *National Archives* - Ancestry.com.

22. "Charles Conquest." Compiled Military Service Records, *National Archives* - Ancestry.com.
23. "Douglas Risley." Compiled Military Service Records, *National Archives* - Ancestry.com.
24. "Stephen Baines." Compiled Military Service Records, *National Archives* - Ancestry.com.
25. "George Kellum." Compiled Military Service Records, *National Archives* - Ancestry.com.
26. "Joseph West." Compiled Military Service Records, *National Archives* - Ancestry.com.
27. "Charles H. Graham." Compiled Military Service Records, *National Archives* - Ancestry.com.
28. "John W. T. Ashby." Compiled Military Service Records, *National Archives* - Ancestry.com.
29. "Jacob Grant." Compiled Military Service Records, *National Archives* - Ancestry.com.
30. "William Jones." Compiled Military Service Records, *National Archives* - Ancestry.com.
31. "John R. Green." Compiled Military Service Records, *National Archives* - Ancestry.com.
32. "John Ayers." Compiled Military Service Records, *National Archives* - Ancestry.com.
33. Blackett, R. J. M. "Thomas Morris Chester, Black Civil War Correspondent." *Da Capo Press*, 1991.
34. "John Dennis." Compiled Military Service Records, *National Archives* - Ancestry.com.
35. "Henry A. Wise." Compiled Military Service Records, *National Archives* - Ancestry.com.
36. "Solomon Wise." Compiled Military Service Records, *National Archives* - Ancestry.com.
37. "George Pruett." Compiled Military Service Records, *National Archives* - Ancestry.com.
38. "John Bailey." Compiled Military Service Records, *National Archives* - Ancestry.com.
39. "Riley Pitts." Compiled Military Service Records, *National Archives* - Ancestry.com.
40. "Isaiah Bull." Compiled Military Service Records, *National Archives* - Ancestry.com.
41. "Levin Wollop." Compiled Military Service Records, *National Archives* - Ancestry.com.
42. "John Custus." Compiled Military Service Records, *National Archives* - Ancestry.com.
43. "George Foskey." Compiled Military Service Records, *National Archives* - Ancestry.com.

44. "Henry Massey." Compiled Military Service Records, *National Archives* - Ancestry.com.

45. "George Fletcher." Compiled Military Service Records, *National Archives* - Ancestry.com.

46. "John Ayers." Compiled Military Service Records, *National Archives* - Ancestry.com.

47. "Abel Bagwell." Compiled Military Service Records, *National Archives* - Ancestry.com.

48. "James Bailey." Compiled Military Service Records, *National Archives* - Ancestry.com.

49. "Isaac Coates." Compiled Military Service Records, *National Archives* - Ancestry.com.

50. "James Rogers." Compiled Military Service Records, *National Archives* - Ancestry.com.

51. "Henry Ashby." Compiled Military Service Records, *National Archives* - Ancestry.com.

52. "John Glenn." Compiled Military Service Records, *National Archives* - Ancestry.com.

53. "Walter Kellum." Compiled Military Service Records, *National Archives* - Ancestry.com.

54. "Littleton Twinington." Compiled Military Service Records, *National Archives* - Ancestry.com.

55. "Suthy Chandler." Compiled Military Service Records, *National Archives* - Ancestry.com.

56. "Levi Finney." Compiled Military Service Records, *National Archives* - Ancestry.com.

57. "Henry P. Waters." Compiled Military Service Records, *National Archives* - Ancestry.com.

58. "James Lindsey." Compiled Military Service Records, *National Archives* - Ancestry.com.

59. "John Ames." Compiled Military Service Records, *National Archives* - Ancestry.com.

60. "John Roberts." Compiled Military Service Records, *National Archives* - Ancestry.com.

61. "John Fletcher." Compiled Military Service Records, *National Archives* - Ancestry.com.

62. "Abel Savage." Compiled Military Service Records, *National Archives* - Ancestry.com.

63. "Thomas Burden." Compiled Military Service Records, *National Archives* - Ancestry.com.

64. "Samuel Foreman." Compiled Military Service Records, *National Archives* - Ancestry.com.

65. "Robert Phillips." Compiled Military Service Records, *National Archives* - Ancestry.com.

66. "William Bourdon." Compiled Military Service Records, *National Archives* - Ancestry.com.

67. "Dutch Gap Canal." *Virginia Places.* 8 Sept. 2025. www.virginiaplaces.org/transportation/dutchgap.html.

68. "Moses Justice." Compiled Military Service Records, *National Archives* - Ancestry.com.

69. "Henry Rodgers." Compiled Military Service Records, *National Archives* - Ancestry.com.

70. "William Drummond." Compiled Military Service Records, *National Archives* - Ancestry.com.

71. "Franklin Wise." Compiled Military Service Records, *National Archives* - Ancestry.com.

72. "Samuel Parker." Compiled Military Service Records, *National Archives* - Ancestry.com.

73. "Peter Blockson." Compiled Military Service Records, *National Archives* - Ancestry.com.

74. "Thomas Myers." Compiled Military Service Records, *National Archives* - Ancestry.com.

75. "Abner Conner." Compiled Military Service Records, *National Archives* - Ancestry.com.

76. "Peter Custis." Compiled Military Service Records, *National Archives* - Ancestry.com.

77. "John Bell." Compiled Military Service Records, *National Archives* - Ancestry.com.

78. "George Birch." Compiled Military Service Records, *National Archives* - Ancestry.com.

79. "Harris Lewis." Compiled Military Service Records, *National Archives* - Ancestry.com.

80. "Parker Williams." Compiled Military Service Records, *National Archives* - Ancestry.com.

81. "John Jines." Compiled Military Service Records, *National Archives* - Ancestry.com.

82. "James Grey." Compiled Military Service Records, *National Archives* - Ancestry.com.

83. "William Griffin." Compiled Military Service Records, *National Archives* - Ancestry.com.

84. "John Drummer." Compiled Military Service Records, *National Archives* - Ancestry.com.

85. "George Foskey." Compiled Military Service Records, *National Archives* - Ancestry.com.

86. "Alexander Anderson." Compiled Military Service Records, *National Archives* - Ancestry.com.

87. "The Election of 1864." *ushistory.org.* www.ushistory.org/us/34e.asp.

88. Basler, Roy P. et al. "Abraham Lincoln's Second Inaugural Address." *Abrahamlincolnonline.org.* www.abrahamlincolnonline.org/lincoln/speeches/inaug2.htm.

89. Lincoln, Abraham. "Second Inaugural Address." *(U.S. National Park Service.)* www.nps.gov/linc/learn/historyculture/lincoln-second-inaugural.htm.

90. "Abraham Lincoln's Second Inauguration." *Abrahamlincolnonline.org.* www.abrahamlincolnonline.org/lincoln/education/inaugural2.htm.

91. Gayley, Alice J. "45th Regiment U. S. Colored Troop." 11 Oct. 1996, *pa-roots.com.* pa-roots.com/pacw/usct/45thusct/45thusctorg.html.

92. "Natural Bridge." *American Battlefield Trust,* www.battlefields.org/learn/civil-war/battles/natural-bridge.

93. Jacobs, Adam. "The Command Advanced Gallantly: The Battle of Natural Bridge." John L. Nau III Center for Civil War History, 16 June 2020, naucenter.as.virginia.edu/blog-page/command-advanced-gallantly-battle-natural-bridge.

Chapter 11: More Virginia Soldier Stories
1. "Franklin Jasper." Compiled Military Service Records, *National Archives* - Ancestry.com.

2. "Peter White." Compiled Military Service Records, *National Archives* - Ancestry.com.

3. "John Parrish." Compiled Military Service Records, *National Archives* - Ancestry.com.

4. "Jorden Roberts." Compiled Military Service Records, *National Archives* - Ancestry.com.

5. "Adam Reynolds." Compiled Military Service Records, *National Archives* - Ancestry.com.

6. "Allen Reynolds." Compiled Military Service Records, *National Archives* - Ancestry.com.

7. "John H. Bogus." Compiled Military Service Records, *National Archives* - Ancestry.com.

8. "James Chafers." Compiled Military Service Records, *National Archives* - Ancestry.com.

9. "Joseph Lane." Compiled Military Service Records, *National Archives* - Ancestry.com.

10. "Charles Teeters." Compiled Military Service Records, *National Archives* - Ancestry.com.

11. "Jefferson Carpenter." Compiled Military Service Records, *National Archives* - Ancestry.com.

12. "John Anderson." Compiled Military Service Records, *National Archives* - Ancestry.com.

13. "Armistead Evans." Compiled Military Service Records, *National Archives* - Ancestry.com.

14. "William H. Johnson." Compiled Military Service Records, *National Archives* - Ancestry.com.

15. "Benjamin Nimo." Compiled Military Service Records, *National Archives* - Ancestry.com.

16. "Richard Page." Compiled Military Service Records, *National Archives* - Ancestry.com.

17. "Colonel Sprawles." Compiled Military Service Records, *National Archives* - Ancestry.com.

18. "Jackson Minnis." Compiled Military Service Records, *National Archives* - Ancestry.com.

19. "Albert Williams." Compiled Military Service Records, *National Archives* - Ancestry.com.

20. "Alembert G. Williams." Compiled Military Service Records, *National Archives* - Ancestry.com.

21. "Alexander Patterson." Compiled Military Service Records, *National Archives* - Ancestry.com.

22. Wert, Brynna, Plummer, Sarah, and Cummins, Cathie. "William Thompson." *Raising the Shade*, www.raisingtheshade.org/wthompson.

23. Steele, Rebecca, Plummer, Sarah, Cummins, Cathie, Wood, John, Bowers, Lauren, Rudd, Garreth, DiNardo, Payton, Frost, Alex, Nazliaka, Parmis, Fullman, Riley. "John Lynn." *Raising the Shade*, www.raisingtheshade.org/jlynn.

24. Smith, Toni, Adkins, Olivia, Venkatachalam, Ryan, Gahagan, Mary, Anspaugh, Bev. "Edward Arrington." *Raising the Shade*, www.raisingtheshade.org/earrington.

25. Helton, Brianna and Plummer, Sarah. "Jordan Hughes." *Raising the Shade*, www.raisingtheshade.org/jhughes.

26. Wert, Brynna, Plummer, Sarah and Cummins, Cathie. "Josiah Taitt." *Raising the Shade*, www.raisingtheshade.org/jtaitt.

27. Wert, Brynna, Plummer, Sarah and Cummins, Cathie. "Granville Taitt." *Raising the Shade*, www.raisingtheshade.org/gtaitt.

28. Cummins, Cathie, Messerschmidt, Lauren, Plummer, Sarah, Savage, Jesse, Sternitzke, Amanda, Scanlon, Liam, Deneke, Foster, Howard, Dyland and Krugh, Andrew. "Peter Hooks." *Raising the Shade*, www.raisingtheshade.org/phooks.

29. Helton, Brianna, Plummer, Sarah and Cummins, Cathie. "Andrew Jones." *Raising the Shade*, www.raisingtheshade.org/ajones.

30. Plummer, Sarah and Cummins, Cathie. "John Jones." *Raising the Shade*, www.raisingtheshade.org/jjones.

31. "William Noble." Compiled Military Service Records, *National Archives* - Ancestry.com.

32. "Austin Bronson." Compiled Military Service Records, *National Archives* - Ancestry.com.

33. "Levi Barer." Compiled Military Service Records, *National Archives* - Ancestry.com.

34. "David Freeman." Compiled Military Service Records, *National Archives* - Ancestry.com.

35. "Horace Lacy." Compiled Military Service Records, *National Archives* - Ancestry.com.

36. "Kelly Walker." Compiled Military Service Records, *National Archives* - Ancestry.com.

37. "Mark Addison." Compiled Military Service Records, *National Archives* - Ancestry.com.

38. "Edmund Fox." Compiled Military Service Records, *National Archives* - Ancestry.com.

39. "John Tyler." Compiled Military Service Records, *National Archives* - Ancestry.com.

40. "James Woolridge." Compiled Military Service Records, *National Archives* - Ancestry.com.

41. "Dick Drummond." Compiled Military Service Records, *National Archives* - Ancestry.com.

42. "Charles Lee." Compiled Military Service Records, *National Archives* - Ancestry.com.

43. "Oscar Irving." Compiled Military Service Records, *National Archives* - Ancestry.com.

44. "Keymore Wynn." Compiled Military Service Records, *National Archives* - Ancestry.com.

Chapter 12: Victory and Sorrow

1. Blackett, R. J. M. "Thomas Morris Chester, Black Civil War Correspondent." *Da Capo Press*, 1991. 226.

2. "The Campaign to Appomattox." *National Park Civil War Series*. npshistory.com/publications/civil_war_series/6/sec2.htm.

3. Schroeder, Patrick. "Appomattox Campaign." *Encyclopedia Virginia*, 18 Feb. 2025, encyclopediavirginia.org/entries/appomattox-campaign.

4. "The Campaign to Appomattox." *National Park Civil War Series*. npshistory.com/publications/civil_war_series/6/sec2.htm.

5.   "Surrender Documents - Appomattox Court House National Historical Park." *(U.S. National Park Service)*. www.nps.gov/apco/learn/historyculture/surrender-documents.htm.

6.   Ibid.

7.   Ibid.

8.   Mighty, Team. "What Does 'Damn the Torpedoes' Mean Anyway?" *We Are the Mighty*, 27 Apr. 2023, www.wearethemighty.com/history/damn-the-torpedoes-origin.

9.   "The Battle of Fort Blakeley - Spanish Fort, Alabama." *ExploreSouthernHistory.com*. exploresouthernhistory.com/blakeley4.html.

10.   Bunn, Mike. "Battle of Fort Blakeley." *Encyclopedia of Alabama*, July 2025, encyclopediaofalabama.org/article/battle-of-fort-blakeley.

11.   ushistory.org. "The Assassination of Abraham Lincoln." *U.S. History Online Textbook*. 2 Feb. 2026. www.ushistory.org/us/34f.asp.

12.   Rust, Randal. "Abraham Lincoln Assassination, Summary, Facts, Significance." *American History Central*, 15 Apr. 2025, www.americanhistorycentral.com/entries/abraham-lincoln-assassination.

13.   "The Assassin's Escape." *Ford's Theater National Historic Site. (U.S. National Park Service.)* www.nps.gov/foth/learn/historyculture/the-assassin-s-escape.htm.

14.   Stokes, Matt. "Last Days of the Confederacy: Jefferson Davis in Greensboro and Charlotte, April 1865." *NCpedia. State Library of NC.* 2007. https://www.ncpedia.org/jefferson-davis.

15.   Mark, Harrison W., and Mathew Brady. "Jefferson Davis: President of the Confederate States." *World History Encyclopedia*, Jan. 2026, www.worldhistory.org/Jefferson_Davis.

16.   Schaefer, Mathew. "Confederate Surrender at Bennett's Place (April 17 – 26, 1865)." *North Carolina History*, 25 Mar. 2025, northcarolinahistory.org/encyclopedia/confederate-surrender-at-bennetts-place-april-17-26-1865.

17.   Coffey, Walter. "Johnston Surrenders to Sherman a Second Time." *The Civil War Months*, 24 Apr. 2025, civilwarmonths.com/2025/04/26/johnston-surrenders-to-sherman-a-second-time.

18.   Carter, Jimmy. "Restoration of Citizenship Rights to Jefferson F. Davis Statement on Signing S. J. Res. 16 Into Law." *American*

Presidency Project.
www.presidency.ucsb.edu/documents/restoration-
citizenship-rights-jefferson-f-davis-statement-signing-s-j-res-
16-into-law.

19. "William Johnson." Compiled Military Service Records, *National Archives* - Ancestry.com.
20. Ibid.
21. Ibid.
22. "George Thompson." Compiled Military Service Records, *National Archives* - Ancestry.com.
23. Kautz, August Valentine. "Customs of Service for Non-commissioned Officers and Soldiers, as Derived from Law and Regulations." *J.P. Lippincott & Co.*, 1864.
24. "United States Colored Troops 2nd Regiment Cavalry." *Richmond National Battlefield Park (U.S. National Park Service).* www.nps.gov/rich/learn/historyculture/2nduscc.htm.
25. "George Thompson." Compiled Military Service Records, *National Archives* - Ancestry.com.
26. Wood, John, Wert, Brynna and Plummer, Sarah. "George Thompson." *Raising the Shade,* www.raisingtheshade.org/gthompson.
27. "Frank Butts." Compiled Military Service Records, *National Archives* - Ancestry.com.
28. "Wesley Wades." Compiled Military Service Records, *National Archives* - Ancestry.com.
29. "Palmito Ranch." *American Battlefield Trust,* www.battlefields.org/learn/articles/palmito-ranch.
30. Thompson, Jerry. *The Southwestern Historical Quarterly,* Volume 107, July 2003 - April, 2004. 337.
31. "Juneteenth: The Army's Role." *The Army Historical Foundation,* 19 June 2022, armyhistory.org/juneteenth-the-armys-role.
32. Ural, Susannah J. "News! The War on the Net." *HistoryNet,* 4 Oct. 2017, www.historynet.com/news-war-net-richard-baxter-forrester.

Chapter 13: Reconstruction

1. "Freedmen's Bureau Bill, 'An Act to Establish a Bureau for the Relief of Freedmen and Refugees' (1865)." *National Constitution Center – constitutioncenter.org,* constitutioncenter.org/the-constitution/historic-document-library/detail/freedmens-bureau-bill-an-act-to-establish-a-bureau-for-the-relief-of-freedmen-and-refugees-march-3-1865.
2. "The Freedmen's Bureau - Remaking Virginia: Transformation Through Emancipation. " *Library of Virginia Online Exhibitions.*

www.lva.virginia.gov/events/exhibitions/online/oe/exhibits /show/remaking-virginia/freedmens-bureau.

3. Blackett, R. J. M. "Thomas Morris Chester, Black Civil War Correspondent." *Da Capo Press*, 1991. 288.

4. "Andrew Johnson." Biography, 22 Apr. 2021, www.biography.com/political-figures/andrew-johnson.

5. "13th Amendment to the U.S. Constitution: Abolition of Slavery (1865)." *National Archives*, 10 May 2022, www.archives.gov/milestone-documents/13th-amendment.

6. "First Reconstruction Act of 1867." *Encyclopedia.com.* www.encyclopedia.com/history/encyclopedias-almanacs-transcripts-and-maps/first-reconstruction-act-1867.

7. "1870 Constitution of Virginia." *VirginiaPlaces.org.* 4 Nov. 2025, www.virginiaplaces.org/government/constitution1870.html.

8. "The Constitution: Amendments 11-27." *National Archives*, 20 Nov. 2025, www.archives.gov/founding-docs/amendments-11-27.

9. Ibid.

10. "Bruce, Blanche K." *Mississippi Encyclopedia*, 22 Sept. 2021, mississippiencyclopedia.org/entries/blanche-k-bruce.

11. "Revels, Hiram Rhodes." *Mississippi Encyclopedia*, 13 Oct. 2021, mississippiencyclopedia.org/entries/hiram-rhodes-revels.

12. "James Taylor." Compiled Military Service Records, *National Archives* - Ancestry.com.

13. Brooks, Christopher T. "James T. S. Taylor (1840–1918)." *Encyclopedia Virginia*, 3 May 2024, encyclopediavirginia.org/entries/taylor-james-t-s-1840-1918.

14. Plunkett, Michael. "Goodman Brown (1840–1929)." *Encyclopedia Virginia*, 22 Dec. 2021, encyclopediavirginia.org/entries/brown-goodman-1840-1929.

15. Tarter, Brent. "Robert Gilbert Griffin (March 1847–February 9, 1927)." *Encyclopedia Virginia*, 3 May 2024, encyclopediavirginia.org/entries/robert-gilbert-griffin-march-1847-february-9-1927.

16. Gunter, Donald W. "Peter Jacob Carter (1845–1886)." *Encyclopedia Virginia*, 16 Mar. 2023, encyclopediavirginia.org/entries/carter-peter-jacob-1845-1886.

17. Christenbury, Leila. "Littleton Owens (Ca. 1842–March 11, 1894)." *Encyclopedia Virginia*, 3 May 2024, encyclopediavirginia.org/entries/littleton-owens-ca-1842-march-11-1894.

18. Dinnella-Borrego, Luis-Alejandro. "John Mercer Langston (1829–1897)." *Encyclopedia Virginia*, 18 Feb. 2025,

encyclopediavirginia.org/entries/langston-john-mercer-1829-1897.

19.   "Reconstruction - Civil War End, Changes and Act of 1867." *HISTORY*, 2 Jan. 2026, www.history.com/articles/reconstruction.

20.   Mann, Harry C. "Black Members of the Grand Army of the Republic." *Encyclopedia Virginia*, 13 June 2023, encyclopediavirginia.org/garcrop.

21.   Heiby, David. "Discover the History of Alexandria National Cemetery: Resting Place of Civil War Soldiers and United States Colored Troops." *Gravestone Stories*, 28 Sept. 2023, gravestonestories.com/the-alexandria-national-cemetery.

22.   Murphy, Ric. "Our National Cemetery and Its Honored Dead: The African American History of Arlington." *Gilder Lehrman Institute of American History*. www.gilderlehrman.org/history-resources/essays/our-national-cemetery-and-its-honored-dead-african-american-history.

23.   Jordan, Elizabeth Ann. "Robert Gould Shaw and Massachusetts 54th Regiment Memorial." *(U.S. National Park Service)*. www.nps.gov/places/robert-gould-shaw-and-massachusetts-54th-regiment-memorial.htm.

24.   "African American West Point Monument at West Point Cemetery." *VisitNorfolk*, 6 June 2022, www.visitnorfolk.com/attraction/west-point-monument-at-west-point-cemetery.

25.   Wilkins, D.J., "Memorial to the 2nd Regiment Infantry, U.S. Colored Troops (Fort Myers, Florida)," *Contemporary Monuments to the Slave Past*, accessed February 3, 2026, https://slaverymonuments.org/items/show/1100.

26.   "African American Civil War Memorial Museum – Sharing Unknown Stories of African American Civil War History." *African American Civil War Museum*. afroamcivilwar.org.

27.   "Mississippi African American Memorial." *(U.S. National Park Service)*. www.nps.gov/places/mississippi-african-american-memorial.htm.

28.   "Chesapeake's UnKnown and Known Afro-Union Soldiers Memorial." *VisitChesapeake.com*. www.visitchesapeake.com/things-to-do/history/aaht/unknown-known-afro-union-civil-war-soldiers-memorial.

29.   "Simpsonville Massacre - Camp Nelson National Monument." *(U.S. National Park Service)*. www.nps.gov/cane/learn/historyculture/simpsonville-massacre.htm.

30. "Boundless – Cameron Art Museum." *Cameron Art Museum,* cameronartmuseum.org/boundless.

31. Visit St. Mary's MD. "United States Colored Troops Memorial Monument." *St. Marys County MD Tourism,* www.visitstmarysmd.com/directory/united-states-colored-troops-memorial-monument-african-american-heritage-sites.

32. Perry, Megan. "New Monument Honors African-American Soldiers Killed in the Civil War." *Northern Virginia Magazine,* 7 Dec. 2021, northernvirginiamag.com/news/2021/12/07/united-states-colored-troops-memorial.

33. "The Fuller Story &Amp; March to Freedom Statue." *Visit Franklin,* 22 July 2024, visitfranklin.com/history/the-fuller-story-project.

34. "Fort Defiance." *American Battlefield Trust,* www.battlefields.org/visit/heritage-sites/fort-defiance.

35. "United States Colored Troops (USCT)." *United States Colored Troops (USCT),* 10 June 2016, www.usct.org.

36. "Camp Nelson: In the Footsteps of Freedom." *(U.S. National Park Service).* www.nps.gov/cane/index.htm.

37. "New Market Heights Battlefield." *American Battlefield Trust,* www.battlefields.org/visit/battlefields/new-market-heights-battlefield?ms=home.

38. Beatty, Allyssa. "Monument Honoring Black Civil War Soldiers Unveiled in Rocky Mount." *WDBJ7.com,* 18 Jan. 2026, www.wdbj7.com/2026/01/18/monument-honoring-black-civil-war-soldiers-unveiled-rocky-mount.

Chapter 14: Glorious Work To Do

1. "Hannibal Cox" Compiled Military Service Records, *National Archives* - Ancestry.com.

2. Cox, Hannibal. "Poem, March 30, 1864." *Library of Congress - Abraham Lincoln Papers,* 1864. tile.loc.gov/storage-services/service/mss/mal/319/3195000/3195000.pdf.

3. "John Triplett." Compiled Military Service Records, *National Archives* - Ancestry.com.

4. "Virginia, Freedmen's Bureau Field Office Records, 1865-1967", *FamilySearch* (www.familysearch.org/ark:/61903/1:1:FP2N-PJ6: Tue Apr 29 15:07:00 UTC 2025), Entry for Daniel Pompey, 1 Oct 1868.

5. "Virginia, Freedmen's Bureau Field Office Records, 1865-1967", *FamilySearch* (www.familysearch.org/ark:/61903/1:1:FPLC-P2F: Thu Apr 18 14:41:18 UTC 2024), Entry for Stephen Blunt.

6. "Virginia, Freedmen's Bureau Field Office Records, 1865-1967", *FamilySearch* (www.familysearch.org/ark:/61903/1:1:FPKB-QNP: Tue Apr 29 15:04:32 UTC 2025), Entry for Elam Washington.

7. "Benjamin Whitfield." Compiled Military Service Records, *National Archives* - Ancestry.com.

8. "Virginia, Freedmen's Bureau Field Office Records, 1865-1967", *FamilySearch* (www.familysearch.org/ark:/61903/1:1:FP2S-R6N: Tue Apr 29 15:05:40 UTC 2025), Entry for Benj Whitfield.

9. "Virginia, Freedmen's Bureau Field Office Records, 1865-1967", *FamilySearch* (www.familysearch.org/ark:/61903/1:1:FP23-FJ4: Tue Apr 29 15:04:19 UTC 2025), Entry for James Gale.

10. "James Gail." Compiled Military Service Records, *National Archives* - Ancestry.com.

11. "Virginia, Freedmen's Bureau Field Office Records, 1865-1967", *FamilySearch* (www.familysearch.org/ark:/61903/1:1:FP23-G6J: Tue Apr 29 15:06:49 UTC 2025), Entry for Jerome Newman.

12. "Jerome Newman." Compiled Military Service Records, *National Archives* - Ancestry.com.

13. "Virginia, Freedmen's Bureau Field Office Records, 1865-1967", *FamilySearch* (www.familysearch.org/ark:/61903/1:1:FP2J-G46: Tue Apr 29 15:17:11 UTC 2025), Entry for Cleburn Hill, 1867.

14. "Cleburn Hill." Compiled Military Service Records, *National Archives* - Ancestry.com.

15. "George Pleasant." Compiled Military Service Records, *National Archives* - Ancestry.com.

16. "Virginia, Freedmen's Bureau Field Office Records, 1865-1967", *FamilySearch* (www.familysearch.org/ark:/61903/1:1:FPG5-F4C: Tue Apr 29 15:09:04 UTC 2025), Entry for George Pleasant.

17. "William H. Almstead." Compiled Military Service Records, *National Archives* - Ancestry.com.

18. "Virginia, Freedmen's Bureau Field Office Records, 1865-1967", *FamilySearch* (www.familysearch.org/ark:/61903/1:1:FPK9-4NL: Tue Apr 29 15:02:35 UTC 2025), Entry for Wm H Olmstead.

19. "Charles Dickenson." Compiled Military Service Records, *National Archives* - Ancestry.com.

20. "Virginia, Freedmen's Bureau Field Office Records, 1865-1967", *FamilySearch* (www.familysearch.org/ark:/61903/1:1:FPNF-JJ8: Sat Nov 22 01:55:05 UTC 2025), Entry for Charles Dickenson.

21. "Virginia, Freedmen's Bureau Field Office Records, 1865-1967", *FamilySearch* (www.familysearch.org/ark:/61903/1:1:FPLC-GTP: Tue Apr 29 15:12:16 UTC 2025), Entry for John King, 25 Jun 1869.
22. "John King." Compiled Military Service Records, *National Archives* - Ancestry.com.
23. "Virginia, Freedmen's Bureau Field Office Records, 1865-1967", *FamilySearch* (www.familysearch.org/ark:/61903/1:1:FPVV-GMP: Tue Apr 29 15:00:52 UTC 2025), Entry for Fleming Johnson, 17 May 1867.
24. "Fleming Johnson." Compiled Military Service Records, *National Archives* - Ancestry.com.
25. "Edwin Williams." Compiled Military Service Records, *National Archives* - Ancestry.com.
26. "Virginia, Freedmen's Bureau Field Office Records, 1865-1967", *FamilySearch* (www.familysearch.org/ark:/61903/1:1:FP2C-PNG: Tue Apr 29 15:06:35 UTC 2025), Entry for Edwin Williams.
27. "Henry Clay." Compiled Military Service Records, *National Archives* - Ancestry.com.
28. "Virginia, Freedmen's Bureau Field Office Records, 1865-1967", *FamilySearch* (www.familysearch.org/ark:/61903/1:1:FPF5-VYF: Tue Apr 29 14:53:06 UTC 2025), Entry for Henry Clay.
29. "John H. Bogus." Compiled Military Service Records, *National Archives* - Ancestry.com.
30. "Virginia, Freedmen's Bureau Field Office Records, 1865-1967", *FamilySearch* (www.familysearch.org/ark:/61903/1:1:FPGC-GJZ: Tue Apr 29 15:19:34 UTC 2025), Entry for John H Bogus, 4 Jul 1866.
31. "Thomas Monroe." Compiled Military Service Records, *National Archives* - Ancestry.com.
32. "Virginia, Freedmen's Bureau Field Office Records, 1865-1967", *FamilySearch* (www.familysearch.org/ark:/61903/1:1:FPJC-GNR: Tue Apr 29 15:16:20 UTC 2025), Entry for Thomas Monroe, 1 Jan 1866.
33. "Nelson Wallace." Compiled Military Service Records, *National Archives* - Ancestry.com.
34. "Virginia, Freedmen's Bureau Field Office Records, 1865-1967", *FamilySearch* (www.familysearch.org/ark:/61903/1:1:FPVP-CTP: Tue Apr 29 15:02:18 UTC 2025), Entry for Nelson Wallace, 10 Jan 1867.
35. "John Polat." Compiled Military Service Records, *National Archives* - Ancestry.com.

36. "Sonnie Brown." Compiled Military Service Records, *National Archives* - Ancestry.com.

37. "Jun 29, 1889, Page 10 - the Cincinnati Enquirer at Newspapers.comTM." *Newspapers.com*, www.newspapers.com/image/31327812/?match=1&clipping_id=new.

38. "Othello Fraction." Compiled Military Service Records, *National Archives* - Ancestry.com.

39. Foster, William G. "Thomas and Othello Fraction: From Slavery to Freedom." *Virginia Center for Civil War Studies | Virginia Tech,* civilwar.vt.edu/programs/drivingtour/africanamericanhistorydrivingtour/thomasandothellofraction.html.

40. "Sep 01, 1900, Page 3 - the Baltimore County Union, the Towson News at Newspapers.comTM." *Newspapers.com*, www.newspapers.com/image/890054817/?match=1&terms=%22Othello%20Fraction%22.

41. "Clayborn Bazell." Compiled Military Service Records, *National Archives* - Ancestry.com.

42. "United States, Census, 1880", *FamilySearch* (www.familysearch.org/ark:/61903/1:1:M8SM-B2J: Tue Jan 21 02:44:58 UTC 2025), Entry for Clayburne Bazil and George Subbledge, 1880.

43. "Thomas Woldridge." Compiled Military Service Records, *National Archives* - Ancestry.com.

44. "United States, Census, 1880", *FamilySearch* (www.familysearch.org/ark:/61903/1:1:M8MN-9B9: Thu Jan 16 23:18:51 UTC 2025), Entry for Joseph Valentine and Belle Valentine, 1880.

45. "Joseph Valentine." Compiled Military Service Records, *National Archives* - Ancestry.com.

46. "Edward Logan." Compiled Military Service Records, *National Archives* - Ancestry.com.

47. "Feb 15, 1892, Page 6 - the Cleveland Leader at Newspapers.comTM." *Newspapers.com*, www.newspapers.com/image/1077459054/?match=1&terms=%22Edward%20Calander%22.

48. "Edward Calander." Compiled Military Service Records, *National Archives* - Ancestry.com.

49. "May 29, 1892, Page 11 - the Tennessean at Newspapers.comTM." *Newspapers.com*, www.newspapers.com/image/603948127/?match=1&clipping_id=190558780.

50. "Henry Mozee." Compiled Military Service Records, *National Archives* - Ancestry.com.

51. "Walter Gilchrist." Civil War Pension Index: General Index to Pension Files, 1861-1934, *National Archives.*

52. "Walter Gilchrist." Compiled Military Service Records, *National Archives* - Ancestry.com.

53. "Edward Sorrell." Compiled Military Service Records, *National Archives* - Ancestry.com.

54. "Page 28 - US, Civil War &Quot;Widows' Pensions&Quot;, 1861-1910." *Fold3*, www.fold3.com/image/270854977/sorrell-edward-page-28-us-civil-war-widows-pensions-1861-1910.

55. "John Reed." Compiled Military Service Records, *National Archives* - Ancestry.com.

56. "Mark Addison." Compiled Military Service Records, *National Archives* - Ancestry.com.

57. "Abraham Williams." Compiled Military Service Records, *National Archives* - Ancestry.com.

58. "Abraham Williams." Civil War Pension Index: General Index to Pension Files, 1861-1934, *National Archives.*

59. "Julius Butler." Compiled Military Service Records, *National Archives* - Ancestry.com.

60. "Julius Butler." Civil War Pension Index: General Index to Pension Files, 1861-1934, *National Archives.*

61. "Charles Augustus." Civil War Pension Index: General Index to Pension Files, 1861-1934, *National Archives.*

62. "Jefferson Monroe." Civil War Pension Index: General Index to Pension Files, 1861-1934, *National Archives.*

63. "James Cannon." Civil War Sailor Records, *National Archives* - Ancestry.com.

64. "Page 2 - US, Navy Widows' Certificates, 1861-1910." *Fold3*, www.fold3.com/image/28392298/cannon-james-page-2-us-navy-widows-certificates-1861-1910.

65. "Nick Jones." Civil War Sailor Records, *National Archives* - Ancestry.com.

66. "Page 52 - US, Navy Widows' Certificates, 1861-1910." *Fold3*, www.fold3.com/image/30129978/jones-nick-page-52-us-navy-widows-certificates-1861-1910.

67. "Henry Burden." Compiled Military Service Records, *National Archives* - Ancestry.com.

68. Katz, William Loren. "The Black West." *Open Hand Pub LLC,* 1987.

69. "Oct 16, 1913, Page 2 - Dorchester Star at Newspapers.comTM." *Newspapers.com,* www.newspapers.com/image/672821163/?article=ff78fe54-

817d-41cb-8b8e-
fffe6c576987&terms=%22Henry%20Burden%22.

70. "John Ukkerd." Compiled Military Service Records, *National Archives* - Ancestry.com.

71. "May 02, 1876, Page 2 - Public Weekly Opinion at Newspapers.comTM." *Newspapers.com*, www.newspapers.com/image/552356550/?match=1&terms=%22John%20Ukkerd%22

72. Green, Hilary N. "Unforgettable Sacrifice: How Black Communities Remembered the Civil War." *Fordham University Press*. 2025. 94.

73. "Roots Tibbs." Compiled Military Service Records, *National Archives* - Ancestry.com.

74. "Jan 23, 1915, Page 3 - the Free Lance-Star at Newspapers.comTM." *Newspapers.com*, www.newspapers.com/image/867554863/?article=6fdb491b-6c0d-4c8a-8168-3d28ee837a67&terms=%22Roots%20Tibbs%22.

75. "Nathaniel Weaver." Compiled Military Service Records, *National Archives* - Ancestry.com.

76. "Apr 07, 1906, Page 1 - the Washington Post at Newspapers.comTM." *Newspapers.com*, www.newspapers.com/image/28887582/?match=1&terms=%22Nathaniel%20Weaver%22.

77. "Cheeseman Hughs." Compiled Military Service Records, *National Archives* - Ancestry.com.

78. "Cheeseman Hughs (Unknown-1915)." *Find a Grave*. www.findagrave.com/memorial/67542634/cheeseman-hughs.

79. "Beverly Harris." Compiled Military Service Records, *National Archives* - Ancestry.com.

80. "Beverly Harris (1838-1910)." *Find a Grave Memorial*. 1838, www.findagrave.com/memorial/71302478/beverly-harris.

81. "Henry Copeland." Compiled Military Service Records, National Archives - Ancestry.com.

82. "Mar 05, 1909, Page 7 - Virginian-Pilot at Newspapers.comTM." Newspapers.com, www.newspapers.com/image/844572423/?match=1&terms=%22Henry%20Copeland.

83. "James Copeland." Compiled Military Service Records, *National Archives* - Ancestry.com.

84. "Elijah Roberts." Compiled Military Service Records, *National Archives* - Ancestry.com.

85. "Dec 26, 1891, Page 4 - the Baltimore Sun at Newspapers.comTM." *Newspapers.com*,

www.newspapers.com/image/214515785/?match=1&terms=%22Elijah%20Roberts%22.

86. "Elijah Roberts (1842-1891)." *Find a Grave Memorial*. 1842, www.findagrave.com/memorial/2502882/elijah-roberts.

87. "Loyd Brickhouse." Compiled Military Service Records, *National Archives* - Ancestry.com.

88. "John Brickhouse." Compiled Military Service Records, *National Archives* - Ancestry.com.

89. "Nathan Brickhouse." Compiled Military Service Records, *National Archives* - Ancestry.com.

90. "Smyth Brickhouse." Compiled Military Service Records, *National Archives* - Ancestry.com.

91. "West Brickhouse." Compiled Military Service Records, *National Archives* - Ancestry.com.

92. "Pvt John Brickhouse (1840-1907)." *Find a Grave*. 1840, www.findagrave.com/memorial/114290948/john-brickhouse.

93. "Henry Bagby (1812-1878)." *Find a Grave*. 1812, www.findagrave.com/memorial/45865208/henry-bagby.

94. "Robert Bagby." Compiled Military Service Records, *National Archives* - Ancestry.com.

95. "Robert Bruce Bagby (1846-1903)." *Find a Grave*. 3 Sept. 1846, www.findagrave.com/memorial/45865212/robert-bruce-bagby.

96. "Edwin R. Bagby (1850-1901)." *Find a Grave*. 1850, www.findagrave.com/memorial/45865207/edwin-r-bagby.

97. "Benjamin D. Bagby (1852-1919)." *Find a Grave*. 1852, www.findagrave.com/memorial/45865203/benjamin_d-bagby.

98. "James Driff Bagby (1852-1888)." *Find a Grave*. 1852, www.findagrave.com/memorial/45865209/james_driff-bagby.

99. "Sawney Grimes." Compiled Military Service Records, *National Archives* - Ancestry.com.

100. "May 31, 1913, Page 2 - the Washington Post at Newspapers.comTM." *Newspapers.com*, www.newspapers.com/image/29007137/?match=1&terms=%22Sawney%20Grimes%22

101. "Elijah Hines." Compiled Military Service Records, *National Archives* - Ancestry.com.

102. "Elijah Hines (1848-1925)." *Find a Grave*. 1848, www.findagrave.com/memorial/14743496/elijah-hines.

103. "Ellis Kile." Compiled Military Service Records, *National Archives* - Ancestry.com.

104. "Ellis Kile (1842-1936)." *Find a Grave.* 9 Aug. 1842, www.findagrave.com/memorial/129199462/ellis-kile.
105. "Silas Lightfoot." Compiled Military Service Records, *National Archives* - Ancestry.com.
106. "Silas Lightfoot (1844-1884)." *Find a Grave.* 25 Dec. 1844, www.findagrave.com/memorial/31102138/silas-lightfoot.
107. "Stanley Ward." Compiled Military Service Records, *National Archives* - Ancestry.com.
108. "Stanley Ward (1847-1931)." *Find a Grave.* 1 Jan. 1847, www.findagrave.com/memorial/63186307/stanley-ward.
109. "Charles Dillard." Compiled Military Service Records, *National Archives* - Ancestry.com.
110. "Pvt Charles D Dillard (1845-1891)." *Find a Grave.* 1845, www.findagrave.com/memorial/11587876/charles-d-dillard.
111. "Harrison Shipe." Compiled Military Service Records, *National Archives* - Ancestry.com.
112. "Feb 26, 1913, Page 2 - the Franklin Repository at Newspapers.comTM." *Newspapers.com,* www.newspapers.com/image/842059785/?article=ff3b21c6-a4f3-4ba0-b365-6cac9e4cb664&terms=%22Harrison%20Shipe%22.
113. "Isaiah Fassett." Compiled Military Service Records, *National Archives* - Ancestry.com.
114. "Jul 09, 1946, Page 16 - the News Journal at Newspapers.comTM." *Newspapers.com,* www.newspapers.com/image/154314791/?match=1&terms=%22Isaiah%20Fassett%22.
115. "Feb 17, 1880, Page 2 - St. Louis Globe-Democrat at Newspapers.comTM." Newspapers.com, www.newspapers.com/image/571033926.

Cover Photo Image: Library of Congress
"Jackson Ridgeway." Compiled Military Service Records, National Archives - Ancestry.com.

INDEX

350

Please visit my website at johnlwoodii.com

9 798995 045205